Marketing to Moviegoers

A Handbook of Strategies Used by Major Studios and Independents

Robert Marich

AMSTERDAM • BOSTON • HEIDELBERG • LONDON
NEW YORK • OXFORD • PARIS • SAN DIEGO
SAN FRANCISCO • SINGAPORE • SYDNEY • TOKYO

Focal Press is an imprint of Elsevier

ELSEVIER

Focal Press

Focal Press is an imprint of Elsevier
30 Corporate Drive, Suite 400, Burlington, MA 01803, USA
Linacre House, Jordan Hill, Oxford OX2 8DP, UK

Library of Congress Cataloging-in-Publication Data
Marich, Robert.
    Marketing to moviegoers : a handbook of strategies used by major studios and independents / Robert Marich.
        p. cm.
    Includes bibliographical references and index.
    ISBN 0-240-80687-5 (alk. paper)
    1. Motion pictures–Marketing.   2. Motion pictures–Distribution. I. Title.

PN1995.9.M29M37 2005
791.43′068′8–dc22

                                                                    2004065952

British Library Cataloguing-in-Publication Data
A catalogue record for this book is available from the British Library.

ISBN: 0-240-80687-5
For information on all Focal Press publications
visit our website at www.books.elsevier.com

05 06 07 08 09 10 9 8 7 6 5 4 3 2 1

Printed in the United States of America

Contents

Preface

When I was a cub reporter in the early 1980s, I broke into business covering Hollywood as an epochal shift engulfed movie marketing. The incumbent film executives had spent their entire careers in publicity with an emphasis on newspapers for both advertising and publicity efforts. In the late 1970s, shifts in the core movie business gradually made television advertising the centerpiece of marketing.

The major studios began importing marketing executives from the packaged-goods business, literally plucking them off of Madison Avenue. The very insular old-timers were suddenly working shoulder-to-shoulder with younger and more worldly newcomers who alone seemed to hold the key to the magic of the television medium. Yet, the old-timers were not supplanted and, in fact, managed the transition until they retired.

There are two pearls of wisdom I still remember from this previous generation of movie marketing executives. The first is to always "sell the sizzle and not the steak." If one is marketing a monster movie, the trailer and advertising should show terrified people, but not the monster. Leave the moviegoers intrigued enough to want to buy a ticket to see that. Interestingly, the opposite philosophy prevails today, because film marketing is an era of the "tell-all trailer."

The other pearl, from the early 1980s, is that film marketing is a puppet show and, as I frequently was told when I tried to extract information for my film marketing stories, "why should we tell you how we pull the strings?" The old-timers that I encountered referred to their careers in entertainment as "working in the trenches"—which reflected camaraderie—and anybody outside the movie business was a "civilian." In another quirk of the era, their job titles often included the word "exploitation," which is a long lost bit of jargon.

By the early 1990s, sophisticated marketing techniques such as advertising testing and product placement in films became firmly rooted in the business, but still the inclination to secrecy prevailed. Anita Busch, who was the first reporter to cover entertainment marketing on a daily basis for the Hollywood trade papers, recalls the chilly reception she received when she started on the beat. "It was a brand new area for coverage but nobody was willing to talk to me," she said.

Busch particularly remembers the response when she called one of the old guard of marketing executives at a major studio. "He said to me, 'You cover marketing? Well, we don't talk about marketing here.' And with that, he hung up on me. I immediately called back and asked why he so rudely cut me off. He said, 'I didn't hang up on you. I was just finished talking with you.'" Those crusty old-timers reveled in being gruff and aloof.

Marketing to Moviegoers: A Handbook of Strategies Used by Major Studios and Independents draws on my personal resources of information and contacts from covering the movie and television business for a quarter century. I knew this book was a great idea when every fifth person that I talked to in Hollywood while gathering information said he or she wanted to write a book like this too.

Many people were helpful in the preparation of this book. I'd like to acknowledge the valuable assistance of Tim Baskerville, cofounder of an eponymous-named publishing company where I worked from 1997–2003. Tim provided expert advice that helped me navigate the complexities of book publishing deals, and even came up with the title *Marketing to Moviegoers*.

I also acknowledge the following film industry executives and journalists: Richard Abramowitz, Brian Ackerman, Rob Aft, Meredith Amdur, Christian Anthony, Steve Apkon, Louis Balaguer, Michael Barker, Martin Brochstein, Brad Brown, Vincent Bruzzese, Anita Busch, Scott Carman, Geoff Cottrill, Jay Craven, Dave Davis, Anna Marie de la Fuente, Richard del Belso, Carl Di Orio, Jeff Dowd, Nancy Gerstman, Jeff Godsick, Kevin Goetz, Karen Gold, Mitch Goldman, Shannon Treusch Goss, Rafi Gordon, Scott Hettrick, Doug Hirsch, Devery Holmes, Lee Isgur, Jason Klein, Paul Lenburg, Mitch Levine, Pamela Levine, Burt Levy, Marvin Levy, Doug Lowell, Marie Silverman Marich, Rick Markovitz, Dan Marks, Ira Mayer, Vera Mijojlic, Andy Mooney, Susan Nunziata, Steve Ochs, Tom Ortenberg, David Riley, Vincent Roberti, Janice Rowland, Nikki Ruschell, Emily Russo, Roger Schaffner, Henry Shapiro, Tom Sherak, Tony Seiniger, Joanne

Smith, David Stern, and Shelley Zalis. There are a half dozen other film executives who were extremely helpful, but they asked not to be identified.

From Focal Press, I'd like to thank Elinor Actipis and Christine Tridente, the production team of Brandy Lilly and Phil Bugeau, as well as the following Focal associates: Amit Das, John Cones, Louis Levison, Sharon Badal, and Jay Mower.

The *Variety* website is an invaluable resource, especially for most of the box-office figures in *Marketing to Moviegoers*. The library of the Academy of Motion Pictures Arts and Sciences in Beverly Hills was another wonderful resource, as was its staff.

And with those thoughts and acknowledgement, I sign off. Now I can catch up on movies that I missed while assembling this book.

Robert Marich
November, 2004

Introduction

You can fool all of the people all of the time—if the advertising is right and the budget is big enough.

Joseph E. Levine

Hollywood still lives by those words, uttered decades ago, which play off a famous Abraham Lincoln quote. Joseph E. Levine, who passed away in 1987, was the film impresario whose eclectic credits range from the Oscar-winning period drama *The Lion in Winter* to *Santa Claus Conquers the Martians.* Levine pioneered the coupling of heavy spending on-spot television advertising with saturation theater bookings in a city to make box office hits out of unlikely films such as *Hercules,* an Italian import released in 1959.

The major studios today are not above likewise stooping to "buy" an audience for a film release. For the opening weekend, clever ads can bring hefty box office to mediocre films, after which word of mouth buzz takes over. The majors routinely mount preopening ad campaigns ranging from $15 to $35 million, with huge national theatrical bookings of more than 3000 theaters with over 6000 screens in the United States and Canada. Movies tend to open in the two countries simultaneously, making them a single territory—the domestic market—for theatrical distribution.

Marketing to Moviegoers: A Handbook of Strategies Used by Major Studios and Independents demystifies theatrical marketing, which is booking films in cinemas and coaxing audiences to see those films. Theatrical marketing requires a combination of science, art, and good old-fashioned showmanship.

The domestic market is the most important in the world for the movie business. The United States and Canada account for just 5% of the world's population but 50% of global box office, according to London-based researcher Informa Media. Box office is the revenue at the consumer-spend level from ticket sales. Further, new marketing trends and techniques surface first in the domestic market, so movie executives from around the world observe, take notes, and imitate.

Some pundits call Hollywood's emphasis on big movie marketing campaigns an exercise in madness. But the major studios are not fools. Box office is increasingly front loaded as 45–50% of a film's gross now comes from the opening week versus 20% in 1990, according to investment house Merrill Lynch. This is a good thing from the perspective of film distributors because they collect a higher percentage of box office in the first weeks of a film's release. Also, heavy spending in theatrical marketing drives box office higher, which is a springboard for collecting more money out of pay television and video. Thus, there is a method to the madness of outsized theatrical campaigns.

Still, escalating spending on marketing troubles the major studio and independent film distributors, which is a *raison d'être* for *Marketing to Moviegoers*. The Motion Picture Association of America (MPAA), which is the trade group of Hollywood's seven major studios, said that the average advertising expense per film spiked 28% in 2003 to $34.84 million. The MPAA's figure includes the costs of publicity and creative materials, in addition to advertising buys. Looking at a slightly different landscape, Nielsen Media Research measured a 7.6% rise in 2003 ad spending by both majors and indies for television spots and print ads, which amounted to $3.4 billion. Although the Nielsen figure points to a lesser increase, it's still steep given the figure is triple the inflation rate. The Nielsen figures include independent distributors and only look at buying advertising, thus excluding publicity and other collateral expenses counted by the MPAA.

The culprit in booming ad spending on movies is network television advertising, which film distributors must use in order for a big film to open well. To support a Friday premiere, movie marketers pile into NBC Television's pricey sitcom bloc on Thursday, where 30-second commercials in the top comedy cost $325,000–$600,000 in the 2003-2004 season.

It's tempting to say that everything is getting more expensive, but actually just the opposite is true, because we are in the grips of The Cheap Revolution. Just look around. Computer prices are falling. Automobiles, clothing, air travel, and telephone service cost less when inflation is factored in.

Hollywood production is caught up in The Cheap Revolution too. Digital technology—essentially computers—replaces the analog film equipment of yesteryear in editing, storage, and special effects. Enterprising filmmakers made scuba diving thriller *Open Water* for $130,000 using high-definition digital cameras that Lions Gate films is said to have acquired for $2 million.

But the word cheap is seldom used in movie marketing, where the industry's predicament runs deeper than just spiraling advertising costs. Consumer research for film marketing is in crisis on several fronts as its veil of secrecy is being pierced. Research results circulate so widely within the movie business that theater operators now know which films are doing poorly in prerelease test screenings and audience tracking surveys. Theaters use that information to negotiate lower payments and book fewer playdates for struggling films.

In addition, moviegoers who view movies in private prerelease test screenings are posting commentaries on Internet sites. This leakage undermines carefully orchestrated theatrical release marketing and can disparage a film for faults that are fixed by the time the film goes into commercial release. Before the Internet era, test audiences had no outlet to broadcast their opinions.

However, the Internet also represents an enormous opportunity for film marketing. Web sites are eager for entertainment content, so they post film clips, complete movie trailers, and other promotional material, which can be viewed as good-quality video by the growing number of United States households with high-speed Internet connections.

While the deep-pocket major studios are kings of the expensive advertising campaign, the film industry's independent distributors—indies—are feasting on the Internet. By marketing via the Internet, film marketers reach geographically scattered, special interest audiences on a low-cost basis. They send e-mails to targeted audiences, place film footage on Web sites, mount contests, and surreptitiously seed cyberspace with marketing materials that promote films.

The niche orientation of indie films is ideal for promotion via the Internet. The mock documentary *The Blair Witch Project*, a low-budget film, generated a blockbuster $140.5 million in box office, based largely on a buzz generated via the Internet. No other film has since milked an Internet-centric ad campaign to such riches, but indies still keep trying.

Movie marketing used to be an insular and backwater function in the movie business. However, with film advertising expenses soaring and competition for moviegoers on the rise—just look at how young males are consumed by video games—marketing is now top of mind in the film business. Film producers, film creative executives, and movie financiers want to understand how films will be launched and at what price.

Movie marketing directly impacts other industries. Consumer goods companies—such as fast food restaurants, automakers, and soft drink companies—mount massive tie-in promotions with films. The companies that make movie-themed products, from simple caps to expensive jewelry, are joined at the hip with movie marketing. At schools that teach film, marketing is—or should be—part of the curriculum. All eyes are on the theatrical release, because this is where a film's marquee value is established and will be carried over to video and television.

Theatrical release is increasingly being compressed to 6–8 weeks, which is a short window into the consumer market. Film marketers have just one chance to get it right, because few films in all of history have ever recovered from a poor opening weekend. Each film in theatrical release is a new product that needs to be explained, positioned, and promoted to consumers on its way to that short and fragile shelf life.

A marketing campaign for a single film pulls together a range of basic disciplines covered in this book's first eight chapters. Because the handbook format segments what are interconnected disciplines, there is some unavoidable repetition of famous anecdotes and data. Cutting a germane point because it is cited in another chapter would result in making some chapters incomplete. Also, there is some minimal repetition in the "History of" sections at the end of most chapters, which is unavoidable given these are summaries. Duplication has been kept to a minimum and where it exists, unique details and context are presented that are not found elsewhere.

1   Creative Strategy

Prepared for the first almost-free parliamentary elections in Poland in 1989, the (political) poster shows Gary Cooper as the lonely sheriff in the American Western High Noon. *Under the headline "At High Noon" runs the red Solidarity banner and the date—June 4, 1989—of the poll. . . . Cowboys in Western clothes had become a powerful symbol for Poles. Cowboys fight for justice, fight against evil, and fight for freedom. . . . Solidarity trounced the Communists in that election.*

Lech Walesa, President of Poland, 1990–1995

Movie ads can be powerful. Poland's insular communist party mocked the Solidarity poster of 1989 by portraying cowboys as reckless and an unwanted foreign intrusion, not understanding that the country's population had a completely different interpretation.

In an ideal world, movie advertising should simply be an extension of the films themselves. But this is often not the case. Despite all the purported sophistication of Hollywood, even today marketing executives privately express dismay at some of the films that occasionally land in their lap. "How does the boss expect me to sell this?" is the refrain.

Salability isn't always a top consideration in picking film projects for production. Filmmakers and actors may be passionate about a story concept or script, but that doesn't mean the moviegoers will embrace the resulting movie. In other instances, film companies make what they perceive as mainstream, crowd-pleasing commercial films, yet some of them fail because moviegoers feel that the films are formulaic. Although films are made for a lot of reasons, advertising is always supposed to drive a big audience to the films' opening weekends (Fig. 1.1).

For all the gripes from film marketing executives about poor choices their bosses make in picking movie scripts for production, the movie business is constantly full of surprises. A film about a mentally retarded man who is rejected by his lifelong love may not sound too promising on paper. Yet, *Forrest Gump*—the $55 million budgeted Paramount release—was an Oscar-winning hit in 1994, with $330 million in domestic (United States and Canada) box office. There was little suspense about the ending of *Titanic*, yet it became the top grossing film domestically, with a staggering $601 million after its 1997 release by Paramount Pictures (Twentieth Century Fox separately handled international territories).

Figure 1.1 Top Weekend Openings 1982–June 2004

Rank	Title	Weekend Box Office ($ mil.)	Distributor	Date	Total Box Office ($ mil.)
1	*Spider-Man 2*	$115.8	Sony/Columbia	Jun. 2004	$373.4
2	*Spider-Man*	$114.8	Sony/Columbia	May 2002	$403.7
3	*Shrek 2*	$108.0	DreamWorks	May 2003	$418.5
4	*Harry Potter and the Prisoner of Azkaban*	$93.7	Warner Bros.	Jun. 2004	$232.8
5	*The Matrix Reloaded*	$91.8	Warner Bros.	May 2003	$281.5
6	*Harry Potter and the Sorcerer's Stone*	$90.3	Warner Bros.	Nov. 2001	$317.6
7	*Lost World: Jurassic Park*	$90.2	Universal	May 1997	$229.1
8	*Harry Potter and the Chamber of Secrets*	$88.3	Warner Bros.	Nov. 2002	$262.0
9	*The Day After Tomorrow*	$85.8	Fox	May 2004	$182.1
10	*Bruce Almighty*	$85.7	Universal	May 2003	$242.7
11	*X2: X-Men United*	$85.5	Fox	May 2003	$214.9
12	*The Passion of the Christ*	$83.8	Newmarket	Feb. 2004	$370.2

Note: Box office figures cover United States and Canada
Source: Nielsen EDI

Overview

The most important concept to keep in mind when creating movie ads is that most film releases are analogous to "new product" launches. Certainly, consumers are predisposed to various elements of familiarity in a movie, such as well-known actors or films based on preexisting properties such as popular novels. Tom Hanks and Harrison Ford are somewhat brand names as heroic good guys, and the *Harry Potter* books have legions of fans. Yet, films with popular stars and films based on popular books bomb all the time.

Thus, familiar elements simply represent marketing hooks because the movie itself is a freestanding consumer product—its own brand. New brands must be positioned and promoted in the consumer marketplace, which is a costly and difficult process. For example, Coca-Cola—an acknowledged master at consumer marketing—stumbled with the seemingly can't-miss introduction of the New Coke brand in 1985. New Coke had beaten old Coke in taste tests, yet New Coke flopped in the marketplace and the original formula was brought back.

A few types of films are prebranded prior to theatrical release. There's the occasional film sequel (which is a brand extension of sorts) or the rare theatrical re-release of an old film. The Disney name alone draws a sizable family audience. A few filmmakers have a somewhat branded image because of consistency in their films. Spanish director Pedro Almodovar makes witty and stylish comedies aimed at sophisticated tastes, so his films have a built-in demand from a relatively small but loyal core audience.

Key copy lines—the short slogan that presents a movie to consumers—exemplify the fact that a film is a new product by giving it a unique positioning. Humanity's uneasy interaction with technology is evident for the Warner/DreamWorks 2001 release of *A. I. Artificial Intelligence* with the advertising text, "His love is real. He is not." The dog-eat-dog world of business practically shouts, "Show me the money!" in the 1996 release of Sony/TriStar's romantic drama *Jerry Maguire*. The terror of *Alien*, the Twentieth Century Fox thriller from 1979, was conveyed with, "In space, no one can hear you scream." Miramax/Dimension's 2003 black comedy *Bad Santa* is positioned directly opposite a popular icon with the key copy line, "He doesn't care if you're naughty or nice." "Love means never having to say you're sorry" propelled Paramount's 1970 weeper *Love Story* to blockbuster results; that film was adapted from a best-selling novel.

For the majority of films that are released with national ratings, the Advertising Administration—a separate but related group to the national rating organization—reviews advertising and promotional materials to ensure they are consistent with the film's classification. Ad materials must display prominently a film's audience classification to help audiences judge a film's suitability.

The Advertising Administration checks trailers, television commercials, print ads, and certain promotional materials, such as in-theater lobby stands. Child abuse, sex, violence, nudity, drug use, cruelty, depictions of death, mentions of bodily functions, crude language/behavior, and denigration of ethnic/minority groups in marketing materials elicit close scrutiny. Film trailers, the first wave of marketing materials to appear in public, often run before a film is classified and are obligated to indicate the film is not yet rated.

Besides Advertising Administration evaluation, ad materials are subject to review by media outlets such as broadcast television networks, which make sure the materials contain no objectionable elements. Localized media such as newspapers can apply standards that are peculiar to their region, requiring costly modifications. For example, some visual media outlets don't allow ads that picture guns pointed at the audience.

The job of creative advertising is to give a face to a film—the new product—and make it appealing (Fig. 1.2). Through the first week of theater release, films are largely defined by their creative message in ads because most moviegoers have not seen the films and can't judge for themselves. Once films have been in theaters for a week, advertising can

Figure 1.2 A – The black humor of anti-Iraqi war documentary *Fahrenheit 9/11* **shines through in print ads for the 2004 joint release by Lions Gate Releasing and IFC Films. B – Twentieth Century Fox positions** *Dodgeball: A True Underdog Story* **as a comedy with a snapshot of a wipeout on the playing floor. The comedy was a sleeper blockbuster in summer 2004. (***Dodgeball: A True Underdog Story,* **Copyright 2004 Twentieth Century Fox. All rights reserved.) C – Walt Disney's Buena Vista Distribution emphasizes mystery in the 2004 drama** *The Village* **with ad copy: "Let the bad color not be seen. It attracts them/Never enter the woods. That is where they wait/Heed the warning bell. For they are coming". (Copyright Touchstone Pictures, All Rights Reserved.) D – Twentieth Century Fox emphasizes the spectacle of natural disasters in the 2004 summer blockbuster** *The Day After Tomorrow.* **(***The Day After Tomorrow,* **Copyright 2004 Twentieth Century Fox. All rights reserved.)**

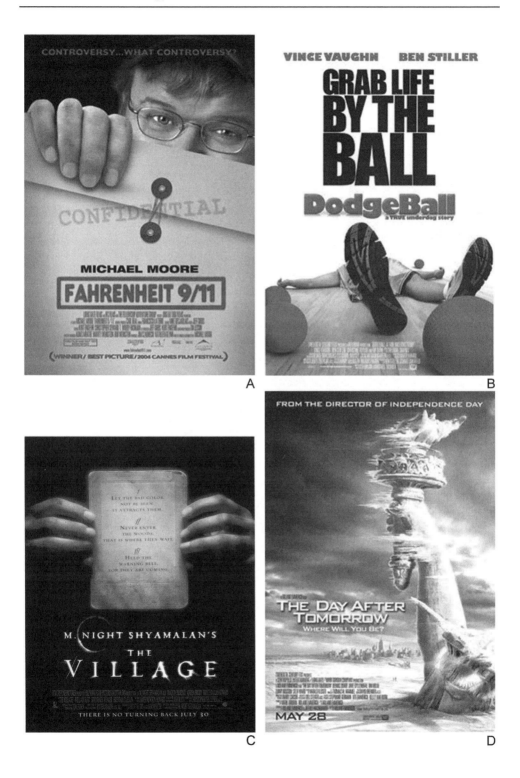

Figure 1.2 *Continued* E – Walt Disney Pictures and Pixar Animation Studios highlighted the colorful underseas world and occasional jeopardy—such as Bruce the Shark—in the family animated blockbuster *Finding Nemo* from 2003. Copyright 2004 Disney Enterprises, Inc./Pixar Animation Studios.

E

Figure 1.2 *Continued* **F – Zeitgeist Films trumpets that its German import *Nowhere In Africa* won the Oscar for best foreign film in 2003 and swept Germany's Golden Lola Awards. Images in the same ad highlight both the relationship of a husband and wife and their daughter's affection for the family's African servant (Source: Zeitgeist Films).**

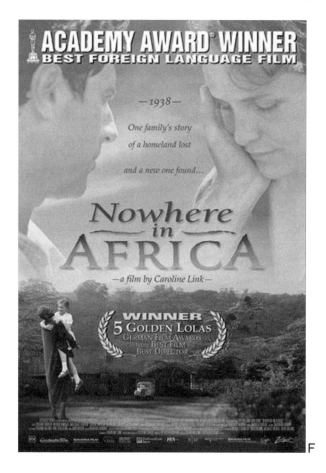

Figure 1.2 *Continued* G – **The trailer for German import** *Nowhere In Africa* **presents a story trajectory that starts with fleeing Nazi Germany to a new life in Africa (Source: Zeitgeist Films).**

do little to alter the public's impression because word of mouth takes over as moviegoers spread their opinions about movies to peers.

In creating advertising material, the top priorities are television commercials and trailers. Hollywood film marketers view them as the most crucial advertising materials, believing they are the most persuasive in convincing moviegoers to buy cinema tickets. They reason that film itself is an audio–visual medium, so the audio and visual qualities of television and the cinema trailer best convey flavor and nuances. Radio lacks visuals. Print advertising such as posters and outdoor billboards lack audio, so they are limited to still photo visuals.

The creative process is the most elaborate at the major studio level because of the large amounts of money at stake. A major studio film typically opens with a $15–$35 million launch campaign with paid ads placed via television, newspaper, magazine, radio, and outdoor billboards. The studios don't want ineffectual ads to undercut the weight of the media buy, so they try out a dozen or more concepts, tossing out most and using just a few in the final campaign.

Outside Agencies

To get fresh ideas, the studios usually hire two to four outside creative boutiques—ad agencies that develop advertising materials—to develop a trailer. Two to five outside shops are hired to create television advertising. For key art, which is the central design of print ads, one to three boutiques usually are hired. These boutiques are mainly located in Los Angeles, with staffs ranging from 5 to 50 employees.

Two to five outside vendors may be working simultaneously on the same portion of the campaign, with output from only one vendor actually used in the main advertising effort. Often, a new agency is added if the first wave of submissions are deemed off the mark. The materials from vendors not making the cut for the main campaign may just be tossed. Passed-over materials that have strong appeal to narrow audience segments are used for cable television commercials or are placed on Internet sites that are a good fit for their particular creative thrust. For example, a commercial with strong appeal to women—but deemed not so effective for men—will be used on cable and Internet platforms tilting to women.

Rates for a trailer or television commercial campaign run from $25,000 (for independents) to $250,000 (for studio films). Key art—which is the signature graphic presentation for print ads—can cost $5,000–$200,000. Again, the wide range is mostly the gulf between the deep-pocket seven major studios—such as Universal Pictures and Warner Bros.—and the smaller independent distributors, which tend to spend at the low end of the scale.

The more costly boutiques earn their money by employing accomplished creative talent, using the latest equipment for high technical quality, and operating virtually 24 hours a day for fast turnaround. The total cost to conceive of and polish creative materials into a finished advertising campaign for a big Hollywood film ranges from $1–$3 million, depending on how many outside ad shops are involved. Independents spend drastically less, often using one shop to create both the trailer and television commercial. Independents also may opt for less expensive shops, not the top Hollywood boutiques hired by the major studios.

Outside boutiques argue that their prices are not out of line. A rule of thumb in the advertising business is that the creative costs should be about 5% of the media buy. The major studios routinely spend $30 million to buy television, print, and other media advertising for their big films. Using the 5% rule, this correlates to paying $1.5 million to create the ads.

From the 1970s to the 1990s, the top creative boutiques serving major studios tended to have reputations for specializing in specific types of films, although they sometimes downplayed this for fear of becoming too pigeonholed. Powerful Hollywood producers, directors, and actors would twist the arms of the distributors to hire their favorite creative shops for their films. For instance, Clint Eastwood has used the same poster designer for his films for three decades.

These days, creative shops work hard at handling all genres because being specialized is a liability if a shop's main genre runs dry. Film producers have become less interested in directing distributors to hire specific creative boutiques, in part because producers' emphasis has shifted away from creative materials to monitoring the weight of ad spending in television and print media. Also, when creative advertising concepts from many shops are tested for the same ad campaign, a producer's favorite shop sometimes does not produce the ad campaign that scores the best in the ad creation process.

For their part, the boutiques increasingly solicit creative assignments outside their core Hollywood work today as a cushion for down time in the feast-or-famine movie business. The boutiques seek assignments for video release campaigns, self-promotion image campaigns by television channels, casino advertising, and other leisure industries.

In an attempt to reign in costs, major studios occasionally have tried to bring creative work in-house, rather than using outside boutiques. At the moment, Universal Pictures—at the behest of new controlling owner

General Electric, which has a reputation for stringent management procedures—and Walt Disney operate the biggest in-house creative departments of the major studios. Under previous management, Paramount Pictures made a big in-house push in the early 1990s. The in-house drives fizzled in the past because of pressures to tap high-profile outside creative shops for big films for which the stakes are highest. The result is that only the smaller films were available for in-house studio work.

Talent Presentation

Hollywood is something of an anomaly in the business world because the people who create the product—the filmmakers—often exert extraordinary influence on the marketing. Contracts of top film talent may specify a minimum type size for their names in ads. They also may have other stipulations about their presentation in film credits. Some contracts include approval rights for all images of an actor used in ads, which creative executives say sets limitations for advertising materials.

Labor unions for top Hollywood talent—actors, directors, and writers—mandate parameters in industrywide contracts, which inject a degree of consistency in presenting names in advertising. For example, the basic agreement of the Directors Guild of America (DGA) stipulates that signatory companies—the major studios and others—list the director's name no less than "15% of the size of type used for the title of the motion picture, but in no event less than the size and style of type for any credit accorded any persons other than actors."

Marketplace sensibility figures into various labor guild rules. Given that actors are the biggest audience magnets, they are permitted to be the only persons listed in ads under certain conditions. For example, looking again at the DGA's basic agreement, a director's name can be dropped from big outdoor billboards if the advertisements are simple and list only actors. The DGA's basic agreement states: "The employer need not accord credit to the director on an outdoor-type advertisement, provided the advertisement contains no more than the title of the motion picture, key art (which may include likenesses or photographs of no more than two starring actors), logos, the motion picture's rating and copyright notice and copy of no more than 25 words, which may not include reviews or the name of any person, whether or not connected with the production."

If the outdoor billboard doesn't meet those criteria, then the director's name must be included at no less than 35% of the size of the film's title or biggest name (such as an actor). "If the name of the writer or producer appears in a Presentation Credit in addition to his or her other credit, the director's credit must be boxed," the DGA's basic agreement continues. "If the advertisement contains five or more personal credits (or mentions), the director's credit shall be boxed. If the advertisement contains six or more personal credits (or mentions), the director shall also be accorded an additional credit above the title in the form A Film By, which shall be not smaller in size of type than the Directed By credit."

In addition to the labor guild requirements, individuals may negotiate further rights in advertising billing. For example, a lead actor's contract may specify that no other actor's name be listed in larger type. Besides creative persons in labor unions, independent film companies and nonunion producers also angle for prominent billings.

Contract language may specify that one of several independent film companies that worked on a film is entitled to billing "no smaller than any other possessory credit on a separate line." A possessory credit is an extra citation for a filmmaker stating A Film By or some similar phrasing that designates a creative signature on a film, which often appears above the title in ads that contain full billing. Directors, producers, and writers often battle for such possessory credits.

A contract for a cinematographer, who is in the second tier of creative talent, may specify that the cinematographer be listed in type size equal to the director and writer, but only in full-page ads in general newspapers in Los Angeles and New York, and in ads in specified trade newspapers. Because Hollywood executives read those media, cinematographers and others angle for inclusion in hometown outlets, figuring this will enhance their career standing.

Talent contracts often specify that no other person in the same class gets superior placement or a larger type size. When two top stars vie for top billing, the solution can be to place both names in identical type and side by side. Because the left-hand position is considered better, the name on the right might be elevated slightly to achieve parity. The jockeying isn't just egotistical, because billing can determine salary and standing on future films.

Top talent often has a contractual right to be consulted about advertising. In this case, the studio must present marketing materials to actors, directors, and producers, who are entitled to review advertising and trailers prior to placement. Studios often go to great lengths to appease talent concerns about advertising, hoping to cement a relationship so that talent will be inclined to make other films for the studio. In some cases, top talent has a right to veto ad materials and not merely be consulted.

In approving ads, it is not just the talent that is knocking on the marketing department's door. Other constituencies within a major studio (or independent film distributor) also may need to be included in the consultation process for approvals of creative materials. A film company's top executives, the distribution department that books films at theaters, and the development/production department often are involved to various degrees.

Figuring out which constituency should review what material and at what point in the ad creation process puts movie marketing executives on a constant treadmill of simply soliciting input and approvals. As a result, one of the arts in marketing is employing deft people skills for dealing with objections from creative talent and executive constituencies.

A common challenge is having to defend a decision to leave out a powerful participant's favorite scene from trailers and television commercials. Often, film companies battling with talent in disagreements over advertising are least inclined to compromise on television commercials, because this is the most costly medium for ad buys. As a compromise, talent might be allowed to get its way with changes to print ads.

"Some advertising executives excel at presentation," wrote author Fred Goldberg in *Motion Picture Marketing and Distribution: Getting Movies in a Theatre Near You* (Focal Press, 1991). "They establish the proper setting and atmosphere, deliver a slick introduction, and present each layout separately. . . . The best layouts are generally the last [to be presented]. The layouts are passed around the room to give everyone a chance to comment."

Conceptual Approaches

Selecting and developing a marketing approach is the meshing of art and science, and the process starts before the movie is even made. Top executives and the marketing department at a film distributor make an early estimation of the film's prime demographic audience, with input from filmmakers. This prime target will be the emphasis in the early stages of developing advertising materials but may be modified along the way as the film takes final form and as marketing research samples audiences.

Identifying the primary audience is crucial because this audience is most easily motivated and is expected to be the first wave of ticket buyers. The risk in not making a strong pitch to the prime audience is that it won't show up in force on opening day. Making advertising overly broad can result in no audience segment being influenced.

Developing concepts for creating advertising is a commercial art that does not easily lend itself to systematic description. David Stern, senior vice president at Los Angeles-based Intralink Film and Graphic Design, said,

"You want to hit an emotional chord. Can you get someone to feel something?"

Intuition, imagination, and experience play a role. The following points typically are considered in the creative process:

- Are there well-known stars—actors and a director, for example—and do they have an audience that will show up opening weekend? The latter point—whether the audience will really follow—is crucial because some actors may be familiar faces but are not necessarily audience magnets.
- Is the story intriguing and unusual, which can be a key selling point?
- Will the film be dependent on opinions of film critics, and are the critics' reviews expected to be positive? The art film audience is driven by reviews, while the youth audience is not.
- Does the title communicate what the film is about? If so, ads can build up other aspects of the film. If not, the ad message will have to position the film in its genre so that the audience is given a starting point of reference.
- Will the audience take a rooting interest in a sympathetic character? Is this character experiencing a crisis that should be presented in ads?
- Are there subplots that can be highlighted to attract a broader audience? Advertising for *Rocky* in 1976 emphasized the romantic travails of the Sylvester Stallone character and his rags-to-riches personal story in what was a male action film set in the boxing world.
- Does the film transport the audience to some magical place that could be a selling point?
- Is the music memorable and a selling point that can be used in trailers and television advertising?

A corollary to zeroing in on a prime audience is settling on what kind of movie is being marketed, which in some instances may be somewhat different from the film being made. The assignment to create ads comes before a film is finished and, in some cases, before principal photography starts. Creative talent may film an epic love story in turbulent times, while top studio brass believes it commissioned an action adventure film with a little bit of romance.

"Completed motion pictures sometimes do not exactly conform with the type of film the studio believed it was making when it originally green lit [approved] the project," MGM vice chairman and chief operating officer Chris McGurk told a United States Senate hearing in 2000 on film marketing practices. "In addition, completed pictures often appeal to an audience different from the one that they were originally supposed to reach." McGurk added that MGM tightened internal monitoring to avoid the potential for diverting from original plans.

In one famous example, Universal Pictures executives were surprised to find that the 1998 sequel *Babe: Pig in the City* was darker than its warm predecessor in 1995. The sequel's audience classification initially was PG, although it was re-edited for a G, which was the rating of the original.

Another reason for poor positioning is that well-known actors go against their type. For instance, a new film with the world's top martial arts star would be expected to have plenty of action and appeal to male teens and young adults, yet the 2004 remake of *Around the World in 80 Days* starring Jackie Chan was a family film. *Around the World in 80 Days* did not connect with audiences, grossing around $24 million domestically via distribution by Walt Disney in June 2004 (independent producer Walden Media reportedly spent $120 million to make the film). In another example, when comedy star Jim Carrey took a dark and serious turn in *The Cable Guy* for Columbia Pictures in 1996, the domestic box office was an underwhelming $60.2 million.

Advertising and trailers need to convey an overall point of view to make an impression on moviegoers. It's not enough to simply elicit emotional responses or pique interest with intriguing scenes if they are disconnected. Moviegoers want a sense of story, so communicating a central theme is crucial.

Early concepts for television commercials and trailers are mapped out on story boards, which are still photos or drawings in sequence. The creative boutique presents story boards to the film distributor to get feedback, after which the concept is advanced to a rough cut, is modified before being developed further, or is dropped to start over. Trailer makers often skip story boards, going from text script directly to a rough cut.

Teaser Campaigns

The main blast of advertising hits the consumer market just days before a film is released, but sometimes it is preceded by a teaser campaign, which starts weeks or months in advance. Perhaps the most memorable teaser of modern times was the early campaign for *Ghostbusters*, the 1984 comedy blockbuster from Columbia Pictures that grossed $239 million in domestic box office. Columbia placed the comical signature art—a white ghost pictured within a red-colored cross-out—in small ads in an assortment of media, including media slots not normally associated with movie ads. Those early ads did not always clearly explain that the ad was for a movie, but they created a mystique and established the key art in the minds of consumers.

The objective of teaser campaigns is to create awareness, convey a sense of genre to position a film in the minds of moviegoers, and pique interest so that audiences will want more information later. The teaser arrives too early to attempt a hard sell, because a film needs to be introduced first as a new product. Besides, if moviegoers are convinced to see a film by the teaser campaign, the effort is simply wasted because the film is many weeks or a few months from playing in theaters.

Teaser trailers usually are short—typically 90–120 seconds—because the more compact the teaser trailers are, the more likely theaters will screen them. The regular trailers placed in theaters just a few weeks before release usually run 120–150 seconds. Another reason teaser trailers are short is the lack of available footage from the film, so there's not much to show at this early stage. If early footage is available, it's usually not so complete as to be able to present a film's entire story. Thus, a typical ploy is to present quick cuts as a montage for teaser trailers, or what is called a scenic trailer.

In such trailers, voiceover narration and music provide the sense of unity. "You have to start from dailies because the time frames for making movies are getting shorter," said Intralink's David Stern. "You generally want a teaser campaign at Christmas for a summer movie and a teaser in summer for a Christmas movie. It's very tricky working with dailies because you haven't yet seen a cut of the movie and you don't fully have the director's point of view for the film." The main television ad campaign also can be preceded by a teaser television commercial, sometimes just 15 seconds long to create awareness, which is less expensive to place than the conventional 30-second spot.

The most significant teaser is a commercial on the Super Bowl—the professional football championship game in early February—which has a huge average audience of 83–90 million viewers. A 30-second Super Bowl commercial costs about $2.3 million, so teaser ads tend to be highly polished and contain film footage. They also make a harder sell than most other teaser commercials, which appear in less costly time slots. "It has to look like a large, expensive, and important motion picture if it's in the Super Bowl," said creative ad executive Tony Seiniger. "It's what I call an 'event' spot." Seiniger is president of Seiniger Marketing Group, an ad boutique in Santa Monica, California and one of the oldest independent film creative shops.

If a teaser trailer is not part of the marketing plan, then the first main advertising produced is the print campaign.

Trailers

Movie trailers usually are free samples of a movie that are packaged to communicate a sense of story. The obvious goal is to convince the audience to come back for more when the film opens in theaters. Although the tendency is to pack trailers with thrills and chills, there's pressure to keep trailers to two minutes' running time, because theaters usually will play shorter trailers over long trailers.

Although much of the early marketing planning focuses on specific prime target demographics, trailers must be crafted to play to a broader audience. The trailer will be screened before assorted types of films—comedies, dramas, or adventure films—so the audience will be diverse. No film marketer wants to let slip away the chance to rope in a secondary audience demographic.

The trailer shops receive film footage immediately once a film starts principal photography or—if the distributor acquires a movie from an outside party—when a film is acquired. "When we buy a picture, we start working on the trailer the next day," said Michael Barker, co-president of Sony Pictures Classics, the specialty film arm of major studio Sony/Columbia. It's a bit overwhelming for trailer shops to receive footage in dribs and drabs as a film is being produced. When the footage arrives, the trailer makers do not know what will and won't be used in the final movie.

Teaser campaigns usually start well before a film has received its audience rating, so the industry's Advertising Administration approves trailers to ensure they are suitable for all audiences. No scenes that would garner a PG or more restrictive rating are allowed.

To make compelling trailers, special footage often is filmed during principal photography solely for use in a proposed trailer. Rapid planning is required because talent is available in costume and on location for only a limited time. Such special shooting is done for about half the major studio films and is on the rise because of demands to generate extra content. The extra content is given to Internet Web sites to promote theatrical release, incorporated into making-of minidocumentaries geared toward telecast on cable television networks, and included as bonus material in the DVD version of a film (see Chapter 6).

Another source of extra material for use in trailers and television commercials is special effects, which can be created all or in part by computers. Perhaps the most famous special effects scene made for marketing materials was a snippet giving moviegoers the visual perspective of an arrow shot from a bow in *Robin Hood: Prince of Thieves*. The scene of the flying arrow splitting another arrow was so arresting that it was later edited into the film, a 1991 Warner Bros. release starring Kevin Costner. For the 1979 release of the Universal comedy *The Jerk*, one trailer offered no footage. Instead, it featured the star Steve Martin giving what is allegedly a private, closed-circuit message to theater operators telling them the movie is boring in the middle, which he said would be good for popcorn sales.

For major studio films that use several outside creative boutiques, the studio typically lets each boutique see the trailers of their competitors once trailers are submitted. This creates what is called a trailer derby. After evaluating the work of rivals, each boutique refines its version in another round of creative work. The studio typically chooses just one or two trailers as its main trailers.

Major studios evaluate the first round of trailers, seeing rough versions of several trailers from each shop. The studios can ask for revisions after further consultations or deem them ready to be tested by research outfits (see Chapter 2) once the trailers are technically more polished. With feedback from studio brass and test audiences, trailer shops may revise their trailers again. In some cases, one creative shop may be dropped from the trailer derby to simplify the next round of evaluation if the shop's initial work is deemed to be far off the mark. When all submitted trailers are deemed ineffective, the film distributor may opt to splice together bits from different shops out of desperation.

One trend in the movie creative advertising field today is not to be shy about being derivative. A trailer that reminds moviegoers of hit films from the past is considered effective in selling the new film, and a new trailer may imitate the style of an old trailer. Another movement in trailer making is to be comprehensive in telling the story in a film, especially giving a clear sense of the ending climax. In the past, trailers were not always so inclusive. In fact, they intentionally were not explicit about a film's ending. The trailers with the comprehensive approach tend to score better in audience testing, which is one reason this technique is popular these days for hard-to-sell films that struggle in consumer research evaluations.

Wall Street Journal film critic Joe Morgenstern labored to write a review that didn't reveal a crucial plot twist in Paramount Classics' release of the French import drama *Intimate Stranger*, not wanting to ruin the film for readers. In a July 2004 review column, he wrote that he then came across "eye-catching [television] spots in which an announcer reveals, in voice-over, that *Intimate Strangers* is 'the story of a woman who bares her soul to an accountant when she mistakes him for a therapist.' So much for keeping secrets in the age of tell-all trailers."

Sometimes moviegoers gripe that all the best scenes were in the trailer, so the film itself was something of a letdown. Creative executives say that it's their job to make the trailer as engaging as possible, which means shoehorning in all the good parts of a film.

As stated earlier, teaser trailers—which screen months before films' premieres and ahead of main trailers—often use footage from the film itself only sparingly or in a general montage. The regular trailers that later run in theaters tend to emphasize scenes from the film. The regular trailers—which build on a general awareness moviegoers already should have with the film—tend to hold nothing back, making a complete and compelling pitch for audiences to see the film. Because the film is about to open, a soft-sell approach with subtleties is avoided at this stage.

"We want a dramatic trajectory for a trailer," said Nancy Gerstman, co-president of Zeitgeist Films, the United States distributor of *Nowhere in Africa,* which won the Best Foreign Film Oscar for 2002. "Even if it doesn't tell the whole story, it should tell some of the story. And trailers should have good flow."

Television Commercials

One view of television commercials is that they are minitrailers, which are themselves minimovies. Each creative boutique assigned to a film will make 3–10 commercials called rough television spots, which are commercials made for internal review but not so polished as to be suitable for telecast. The inspiration for the creative approach comes from direction provided by the film distributor and from the creative shop's own evaluation of film materials.

After rounds of consultations, the distributor picks somewhere between 4 and 10 commercials at a time for audience testing. The best commercial with the broadest appeal typically is designated for broadcast network television. Others with narrower appeal—such as commercials that tests found were effective in reaching teenagers or young adult women—can be used on cable television networks that are demographically focused. Television commercials often are the object of the most frenzied revisions because they can be run on short notice, unlike an ad in a monthly magazine. In contrast, trailers in theaters play to layers of small audiences over months.

For television commercials, marketers can draw from a movie's subplots to try to entice a secondary audience. Advertising might pump up a small romantic interlude in an action adventure film to court the female audience for a film with strong male appeal. For example, Disney gave prominence to the character portrayed by the comely Keira Knightley in the 2004 action period drama *King Arthur*.

Television outlets have their own standards for acceptable content in advertising, which often vary according to the part of day a commercial is telecast. "The best scenes in the movie cannot be used on television," DreamWorks marketing executive Terry Press said in a panel discussion at a theater owners' convention in 2003, "so you are dependent on other people telling people what's good about the movie."

Creative/Print Ads

Outside creative boutiques usually are hired to create the key art, which is the poster and print media materials. When ads are created in-house, the procedures are much the same. Studio brass still reviews and approves the work.

After receiving direction from film distributors and possibly creative talent, the outside shops devise sketches of proposed concepts—the roughs, so called because they are unfinished but drawn to actual size. The roughs are presented to the film distributor for evaluation, after which a more polished version is created. A concept can be modified or abandoned along the way. As a concept is developed further, it eventually takes the form of a comp, or comprehensive layout, which is polished but still subject to discussion and modification.

"Print is much more difficult than television spots and trailers because you have to pretty much focus on a single image," said creative maven Tony Seiniger. "You don't see many montages in print today, thank goodness. They don't reduce down in newspapers very well and they look busy. So you try to come up with what I call the single image. By its very nature, you're having to make a choice to appeal more to one segment of the audience than others."

A mainstay of print is the endorsement ad using quotes from film critics. Sentences or phrases from reviews praising the film are incorporated in the advertising, along with the name and media outlet of the critic. Even films with uneven reception in the marketplace invariably have critics from small media outlets with upbeat reviews whose praise can be plucked for reproduction in ads.

For films voluntarily submitting to the national ratings service, their marketing materials are subject to review as well by the Advertising

Administration, which ensures that promotional material is consistent with the classification. There are occasional disputes, for example, the tiff involving the controversial documentary *Fahrenheit 9/11*. The distributors Lions Gate and IFC Films appealed a decision preventing ads for the film from including a quote from Chicago-based critic Richard Roeper saying, "Everyone in the country should see this film."

The original decision was upheld because it is inappropriate for an advertising message to exhort all to see an R-rated film, which requires children under age 17 to be accompanied by a parent or adult guardian. According to the Motion Picture Association of America (MPAA) Advertising Handbook: "Phrases such as, 'for the whole family,' 'family entertainment,' or 'a movie for everyone' cannot be used in any advertising unless the film has received a G or PG rating."

Taking the quote chase to an extreme, in 2001 Sony Pictures was caught manufacturing quotes that were attributed to a fictitious critic. The films receiving praise included *A Knight's Tale* and *Hollow Man*. Sony Pictures reportedly agreed to pay $1.5 million to settle the case in September 2004. Such extreme abuses in movie advertising are rare.

Besides reviews from critics, another form of endorsement is the touting of strong opening box office, which presents the opportunity to advertise the film as a crowd pleaser. A film that ranks number one in national box office one week can be presented as "America's most popular movie" for the next seven days. If a comedy ranks third behind two dramas in the closely watched weekend box office, then it can be advertised as "American's number one comedy!"

Film distributors sometimes accuse one another of inflating box office to gain promotional advantage. Freewheeling independents, with fewer corporate constraints, often are singled out. In 1997, Miramax issued a press release acknowledging that a previously announced opening box office figure for its horror film *Scream 2*—which became a genuine hit—was a sizable $6 million too high. With the downsizing, *Scream 2* lost its claim on the record for biggest nonsummer opening. It's believed Miramax was forced by parent company Disney to make a correction so that Disney shareholders wouldn't claim later they were misled.

A July 2004 report by the Federal Trade Commission (FTC) on movie industry marketing practices knocked some print ads for not providing clearly legible explanations behind audience classifications. These are elaborations in short text phrases on why films received PG-13 or R ratings to help parents determine suitability for children. The ads nominally complied with film industry self-regulation practices, yet rating explanations were sometimes "so small or obscured that they were very difficult to decipher," the FTC report stated. In some cases, shading and overlays muddled the elaboration text.

Titles

An evocative title can be the most effective single element of creative material in a broad marketing program, because a film's name is relentlessly pushed into the marketplace with giant billboards, television ads, and print ads.

There's not much room to maneuver for films based on books or preexisting properties, of course. However, for the majority of films, the slate is effectively clear, because a title is a malleable item. Scriptwriters may affix titles to their screenplays, but these titles are subject to change. Once a film is cast and about to start production, it's advisable to have settled upon a name because at this point the film starts to generate significant publicity.

The major studios' trade group—the MPAA—operates a title registry that is an industry clearinghouse and which is also used by independents that are not MPAA members. Film companies currently have claims on 120,000 different film names in the MPAA's Title Registry Bureau. The MPAA's seven major studio members are obligated to use the bureau. Usually, a film company has done a full copyright search before attempting to register a name with the bureau.

The independents work the hardest at serving up catchy titles. These include Miramax-distributed *Sex, Lies and Videotape*, Lions Gate-distributed *House of 1,000 Corpses*, Nu Image's *Diary of a Sex Addict,* and Vestron/Lions Gate's *Dirty Dancing*, which actually wasn't all that risqué.

There's a trend toward punchy one-word titles, such as New Line Cinema's *Elf*, DreamWorks's *Gladiator,* and Universal's *Seabiscuit* (based on a book). The solo word title rips a page out of the playbook from the magazine industry, which also embraces catchy one-word titles, such as *People* and *Newsweek*. Two-word movie titles, such as *Finding Nemo* and *Love Actually*, also are trendy.

Mainstream films undergo titles changes, which often amount to fine tuning. DreamWorks's animated film *Shark Tale* started as *Sharkslayer*. Lucasfilm is very fond of tweaks. The movie outfit owned by filmmaker George Lucas unveiled the name *Star Wars: Episode III: Revenge of the Sith* for its scheduled May 2005 release to 6,500 cheering diehards at a comic book enthusiast convention held in San Diego in July 2004. In

1983, Lucasfilm felt an initial title *Revenge of the Jedi* was not copasetic with the chivalry-minded The Force, so the title was later revised to *Star Wars: Episode VI: Return of the Jedi*. Universal's low-budget cheerleader saga *Bring It On* in 2000 originally was titled *Cheer Fever*, which was dropped because research indicated the title had no appeal to boys.

Changing the title of a TriStar Pictures release from *Cop Gives Waitress a $1 Million Tip*, which left nothing about the plot to the imagination, could not save the retitled *It Could Happen to You* from being a box office bomb in 1994. *It Could Happen to You* was used at least three times in the past by other films.

After an MPAA arbitration, Disney adopted the name *The Village* for M. Night Shyamalan's thriller after MGM's United Artists unit pressed a claim to the original title, *The Woods,* for one of its films. *The Village* opened to a dazzling $50.7 million over a three-day weekend in August 2004, although the film faded quickly.

Columbia/Revolution had to give up *Skipping Christmas* (since retitled *Christmas with the Kranks*) after the MPAA agreed with a DreamWorks complaint that the title sounded too similar to *Surviving Christmas*. *Skipping Christmas* was based on a John Grisham bestselling book, but *Surviving Christmas* staked out the movie title first. Universal's retelling of the famous horror saga *Van Helsing* used a title drawn from the name of a vampire's nemesis found in Bram Stoker's 1897 book *Dracula*. The title attempted to create a separation from the various movies that have used the word Dracula over the years.

Hollywood is not shy about playing off of corporate names and brands for movie titles. Examples are New Line Cinema's raunchy comedy *Harold and Kumar Go to White Castle* in 2004 (White Castle is a regional restaurant chain famous for its small square hamburgers), Metro-Goldwyn-Mayer's *Harley Davidson and the Marlboro Man* in 1991, Twentieth Century Fox's *The Adventures of Ford Fairlane* in 1991, Orion Pictures's *Cadillac Man* in 1990, and *The Coca-Cola Kid* in 1985. In a 1989 case, MGM turned aside a lawsuit clearing the way to distribute *Ginger & Fred* after dancer–actress Ginger Rogers objected to the title.

History of Creative Advertising

Until the 1960s, creating movie advertisements was an uncomplicated business. The major studios operated big poster departments that churned out graphic ads that were hand drawn because they were easier to reproduce in color than photographs.

By the 1970s, the landscape for the modern movie creative advertising business started to take form. There was a shift to using photos in posters because advances in graphic arts technology made photo printing feasible. A drawback to hand-drawn graphics was that the whole graphic had to be redrawn from scratch if changes were made.

In addition, the major studios were under siege as television siphoned audiences and the independents pioneered innovative television advertising campaigns for movies. The majors plunged into television advertising as the 1970s progressed, diversifying from print media such as newspapers and magazines and following the lead of independents. Because of the demands of multimedia ad campaigns, the majors began contracting with outside boutique agencies to create marketing materials on an assignment basis. Powerful filmmakers accelerated the shift by insisting important creative work on their films be done by outside boutiques instead of the studios' in-house staff. The filmmakers wanted to use the outside shops given their reputations for excellence and because filmmakers had often worked with them in the past on films at other studios.

The late Saul Bass, who started in movie advertising in 1954 and later created renowned title sequences to start films, was on the vanguard of the movement to independent creative shops. Working with filmmakers such as Alfred Hitchcock, Otto Preminger, and Martin Scorsese, Bass was most famous for creating opening sequences whose look and images often carried over into advertising. He was in the first of a wave of independent creative shops that proliferated in Hollywood advertising by the 1980s.

Other pioneers of the modern era include Tony Seiniger, whose work spans *Jaws* in 1974 to *Terminator 3: Rise of the Machines* in 2003, and Steve Frankfurt, who created the advertising campaign for Paramount's *Rosemary's Baby* in 1968.

In the late 1980s and the early 1990s, mainstream advertising agencies began buying film creative shops to get a foothold in the Hollywood ad business. However, the trend fizzled because of economic travails in the mainstream ad agency business. Both Frankfurt and Seiniger sold their agencies. Frankfurt worked at his shop, which was owned by Bozell Kenyon & Eckhardt from 1974 to 1989, and then left. Seiniger bought back his shop from J. Walter Thompson in 1995 to go independent again.

The digital revolution is marching into the creative ad business. Print ads increasingly are made on computer screens, eliminating the need for handwork. Although the process is quicker, some lament that computers make for a more sterile, less personal type of advertising.

2 Market Research

I don't want any yes-men around me. I want everybody to tell me the truth, even if it costs them their jobs.

Samuel Goldwyn

Movies experience a charmed life early in their existence because layers of cheerleaders surround them. The senior company executives who made the decision to produce a film (or acquire a finished movie for distribution) feel vested with a sense of ownership. The creative talent that sold the project to the movie company and then made the film itself becomes more certain that they are sitting on top of a blockbuster with each hurdle that they clear. The publicity and distribution departments are presented the film by the top brass—their bosses who approved the film in the first place—and the enthusiastic creative talent.

Then, reality sets in. The task of getting the first opinions from outside this small adoring circle of admirers falls to the research department. It exposes the film to a small slice of the outside world—the test audiences. In the best case, the audience reaction is what the inside admirers expected. In other instances, the public's reaction is mixed but not disastrous. Then there's the worst-case scenario, which would make even the legendary producer Samuel Goldwyn wish he hadn't insisted on the unvarnished truth.

Of all the components of the theatrical distribution process, research is the least understood and the most misunderstood. The dichotomy exists because research is the most secretive part of the marketing process, and its impact is supposed to never be seen or heard by the outside world.

"Research serves the straightforward purpose of providing more information," said Henry Shapiro, vice president and general manager of entertainment research company MarketCast. "It's a tool for risk management and resource allocation, and a relatively inexpensive source of insurance that introduces accountability and objectivity into the marketing process. But it's certainly not a replacement for the gut instincts of creative executives."

Boiled to its essence, consumer research is the science of polling a small, defined sample of people. Done correctly, consumer research provides information that is representative of a larger population. In Hollywood, the main role of research is to help identify target audiences for films and to determine which advertising and promotions have the most impact.

"The moviegoers today have so many more choices for entertainment than just a few years ago and more choices to learn about movies," said Shelley Zalis, CEO of OTX Research. "There's the general media buzz, e-mail, phone text messaging, the Internet, and other emerging ways of communicating. Moviegoers aren't waiting to hear about movies, they are actively searching for information."

Seven distinct types of research can be done in the movie business. All types elicit responses from groups recruited from the general public:

1. *Concept testing*—which is rare—evaluates reactions to film ideas and casting for proposed films in development. In a related activity, alternative titles for a film are evaluated at an early stage to settle on one by the time a film is in production.
2. *Positioning studies* analyze a finished script to evaluate strengths and weaknesses of the prospective movie. The goal is to shed light at a very early stage on what to emphasize in subsequent marketing.
3. *Focus group tests* are conducted with small groups, typically fewer than 10 people, in a closed room to probe their opinions of a film or its advertising material prior to theatrical release. The group is shown movie materials via a television screen or on a cinema screen either during or before the focus group.
4. *Test screenings* of finished and nearly finished films often are conducted prior to theatrical release. Such screenings sometimes are referred to as *preview screenings*.
5. *Tracking surveys* gauge the public's awareness of an array of movies on a weekly basis prior to theatrical release. An outgrowth

of tracking is a forecast of opening weekend box office just before a film opens.

6. *Advertising testing* evaluates response to marketing materials, usually trailers and television advertising.

7. When films are in commercial release in movie theaters, *exit surveys* of moviegoers who are intercepted immediately after they view a film are conducted to elicit the moviegoers' reaction.

Except for concept testing, research comes into play in Hollywood after a film gets a green light to go into production. Research is mostly designed to prepare a marketing strategy. The only significant way research shapes the final film is via test screenings of finished films before a recruited audience. If the test audience is dissatisfied or confused about parts of films that can be tweaked, filmmakers may try to reshape a film by recutting, adding, or enhancing narration or by inserting newly filmed footage. Like in any big industry, Hollywood companies can order up custom research on any topic, and this does not fall into any specific research category.

Quirks of Hollywood

A common presentation of findings divides the audience into four big groups, called quads, for quadrants. The grouping structure divides the audience into male and female and then again into ages over 25 and ages under 25. This type of data presentation is found in virtually all types of movie research. Film industry executives are particularly attuned to results in the two quads for ages under 25 because the youth demographic dominates the cinema-going audience.

Another aspect of movie research is that findings often become embroiled in studio politics. Results can be used as a club by warring parties when studio executives and creative filmmakers lock horns over a film as it is being prepared for release. "The combat has been underway for a while and suddenly we walk on to the battlefield," notes one research executive. That sets up research findings as something of an unofficial tiebreaker for disputes surrounding a film, which puts research executives in an uncomfortable position. Research executives say the solution is to listen to both sides and to ensure their key issues are designed into questionnaires in order to get an audience response. Then, let the chips fall where they may when the verdicts of test audiences are tabulated.

A friction point that is very specific to Hollywood is some senior studio executives' dismissive attitude toward modern research techniques. The executives usually are from the old school; they prefer to rely on their personal experience and intuition—their gut—instead of data collected from test audiences. Hollywood only started seriously using research in the late 1970s, so senior film executives who are dismissive remember a time when decisions were made without the benefit of today's sophisticated research. Hollywood research executives agree that experience and intuition are very important, and today's sophisticated research is just another tool to use in a broad decision-making process.

Although Hollywood may view movie research's function as an exotic or sort of black art, in reality research is the same statistical science that is practiced in every other corner of the consumer-marketing world. The methods may be universal, but some aspects separate Hollywood from the other businesses. For example, the creators of the product are exalted film directors, actors, and producers who have more clout in the marketing process than the engineers or designers who create new cars or toasters.

Also, films tend to have shorter shelf lives, typically just six weeks, than most other consumer products, so there's virtually no chance for a resurrection if there's an initial stumble. That perishable quality—the fact that a film is unlikely to ever return once it is out of the theaters—makes movie research all the more important because there's really just one shot to get the sales pitch right. Most film research attempts simply to gauge consumer attitudes toward movies, which is sufficient for Hollywood's purposes. Big consumer goods companies also research consumer behavior, which is another strand of research not pursued by Hollywood.

Of course, not all films and their ad campaigns get research treatment. Independent distributors with modest advertising campaigns for low-budget films often dispense with research completely or use it only sparingly. Independent films whose maximum theatrical circulation is not expected to surpass around 600–800 theaters at any time during their theatrical run typically don't receive formal testing because the ad campaigns involved are modest. The closest thing to test screenings for most independent films are showings at film festivals, at which filmmakers informally witness audience reactions that can be used as guides for making changes, such as cutting scenes to reduce running time.

Distributors of foreign language films aimed at the art-house crowd typically don't conduct significant research. As a class, these films don't hit 600–800 theaters. Also, their distributors in the United States often can do little else but shorten these imported films because the distributors don't have access to original elements residing overseas that are necessary for extensive recutting.

Overview

Film distributors—and consumer goods marketers generally—are secretive about their consumer research activities on which they spend tens of millions of dollars per year. In lifting the veil, think of the scene in *The Wizard of Oz* when professor Marvel, who is also Oz and is sequestered in a curtained control room, bellows into his loudspeaker: "Pay no attention to that man behind the curtain!"

Research is mainly the province of Hollywood's major studios as a component of their costly marketing campaigns. The majors distribute mainstream films, so it's crucial to understand a film's strengths and weaknesses in the seemingly amorphous consumer market. To make sense of the whole consumer market, researchers generally divide the market into demographic groups according to age, income, frequent/infrequent moviegoer, etc. After putting each section under a microscope, researchers reassemble the pieces to make a mosaic that attempts to outline the prime audience for each film. The same mosaic identifies audience segments not interested in a given film to curb waste in marketing efforts.

Film distributors typically hire outside vendors to conduct research. The major studios each tend to have a handful of full-time research executives as part of the larger domestic theatrical marketing staff. These in-house studio research executives supervise outside research companies. In a preparatory phase, the small research departments at the major studios collect information internally about marketing goals that filmmakers and top studio brass want explored in research. Studio research executives also solicit input from others in the marketing unit, such as creative advertising, publicity, and distribution sales (the latter licenses films to theaters).

Hollywood has three main specialist movie research outfits. The oldest is National Research Group, which is part of media conglomerate VNU, whose other businesses include Nielsen Media Research that provides television ratings. Another player is MarketCast, which is owned by media giant Reed Elsevier (a separate division of Reed Elsevier owns Focal Press, the publisher of this book). OTX Research (Online Testing Exchange), founded in 2000, is the newest. It is owned by ZelnickMedia, whose chairman is ex-major studio executive Strauss Zelnick.

Although film companies rely on outside vendors, they are sticklers about keeping results confidential to avoid seepage of test results at an interim stage. A leak would undermine the paid advertising and publicity campaigns that come later.

Some directors, producers, and actors are dismissive of conducting research on their films for varying reasons. They can be suspicious because research is a science that they don't understand and can't control, unlike most other parts of the filmmaking process. Further, filmmakers who view themselves as artists argue that research pushes films to the safe middle ground and waters down breakthrough movies.

From time to time, allegations are made that research findings are manipulated or even faked, although this doesn't seem plausible. Film distributors aren't inclined to pay for made-up data, and research has a good track record in identifying audience attitudes that later prove to be correct. One reason for allegations of fabrication may be misconstruing what is simply a hurried pace that is normal for processing raw audience data. A film that is completed 1 or 2 months before its release date requires rapid evaluation with consumer research to make demanding deadlines of film companies.

Another knock is that film companies simply use research as a shield. If a film opens badly, marketing executives point to test results indicating they produced the best release campaign possible. If not a shield, perhaps movie research can be viewed as a comforter in the film business where job security for executives is fleeting, audience tastes fickle, and the pace is rapid fire because of a succession of film releases.

Filmmakers also worry that poorly testing films will be abandoned by distributors. For their part, distributors might be inclined to open a film that tests poorly as wide as possible in theaters, because poor word of mouth can be expected to deter audiences in subsequent weeks. This move points to distributors spending heavily before the release date but not after. Another gripe is that film distributors sometimes inflate the positives in test results shown to talent simply to persuade talent to stop tinkering with a film that the distributor is already satisfied with.

In answering critics, research executives counter that their contribution is simply one piece of input, and film companies have multiple sources of information. Research findings are supposed to be a tool, not a crutch or a bludgeon. Finally, a common retort is: Doesn't it make sense to find out from the audience what it thinks at the earliest stage possible?

Current Crisis

Research practitioners talk of a crisis in the movie field today on at least two fronts: (1) it's increasingly difficult to recruit test audiences that are representative of the entire population, and (2) movie research increasingly leaks out.

Regarding the first point—it's getting harder to assemble audience samples that match the real world—this is a problem for consumer research in every industry. Ten years ago, simply phoning up households to randomly solicit participation in a telephone survey or to extend an invitation to a test screening reached a fairly wide audience spectrum. However, today's households increasingly opt for unlisted telephone numbers and use call blocking.

In a related recruitment headache, on-the-go consumers, who are particularly crucial given that movie attendance is an out-of-home activity, may not use their home phones these days as much as they use their cell phones. It is not always clear where cell phone users actually live, making it difficult to categorize a respondent by geography.

Also related, the time-honored process of soliciting persons at shopping malls for tests is being undermined by shifts in consumer behavior. Some segments of the population now do most of their shopping at big discount stores, such as Wal-Mart, which are not part of diversified malls. It's tougher for audience recruiters to gain access to single-store shopping locations because of the lack of general public areas.

"[Shopping] mall intercepts and phone surveys may be getting a little outdated," said Pamela Levine, co-president of domestic theatrical marketing at Twentieth Century Fox. "But they still provide you with reasonably good, broad stroke information on whether you have a hit or you are in trouble."

The second crisis is specific to the movie industry. Movie research increasingly is circulated widely within the film industry, which is a problem (see Test Screening Travails and Tracking Surveys later in this chapter).

Film distributors may add a third crisis point: the cost of research (although higher expenses are mostly a function of demanding more types of information). A thorough research effort for an important major studio film runs $500,000–$1.5 million. Despite all the knocks, Hollywood seems addicted to using research. It is only common sense to check consumer reaction to a film's positioning and its advertising materials before unleashing preopening advertising campaigns of $15–$35 million for major studio films.

Besides simply confirming that an approach works, research often turns up the unexpected. The female audience may find an action film has surprising appeal because of the likeability of the film's star, so it would be a mistake to downplay marketing efforts aimed at the female demographic. Another unexpected discovery might be that audiences find a subplot in a film riveting, which means marketing efforts can push the sidelight as well as the main story line.

In 2000, the Federal Trade Commission (FTC) issued a stinging report of movie industry practices. The FTC report was critical of audience recruitment in research, which the industry promised to remedy. Of 44 films examined by the FTC that ultimately received R ratings, test screenings and ad tests for 33 were conducted in an audience sample with children as young as age 10.

Concept Testing

In a chronological context, getting consumer feedback on film projects in development is the earliest type of movie research. However, such concept testing is used only sparingly and is not as significant to the distribution or the marketing process as the other types of research.

Concept testing is controversial because creative talent often is suspicious that its use is the reason their promising movie ideas are rejected. Obviously, the phrasing in presenting movie concepts is key. A film about a dying person can be described as a classic tragedy or a poignant relationship drama.

Movie titles also are evaluated in this early stage of testing because the title is used in all marketing efforts and can be a tool for establishing the branding of a film. "You need to get this settled early because you don't want the cast and crew walking around in silk jackets that have a discarded title emblazoned on the back," says one filmmaker.

A given film might have 2–10 titles under consideration. Most title tests focus on around four alternatives. One goal of the title is to impart the correct genre to the main target audience. With a slapstick comedy, the youth market that embraces physical humor needs to be able to grasp the genre from the title alone.

For movie names, questionnaires often are set up as monadic tests, in which no respondent is presented with more than one title under consideration. Presenting a range of choices to the same respondent—the competitive method—yields poor results.

Film companies can commission custom research for movie ideas as the subjects of one-time research. "Custom brand studies are useful for properties being considered for adaptation from other media, such as comic books or TV shows, or for older movies that are being re-done, or for sequels," said MarketCast's Shapiro. "Marketers want to know what type of awareness the property already has and what type of brand associations, whether positive or negative. Among people that are fans of the original, what are their thoughts about an adaptation? For those with no built-in awareness, familiarity, or fondness, can enthusiasm be stimulated out of nothing?"

Positioning Studies

When distributors want to get a big head start on designing a marketing campaign, they order positioning studies. These studies analyze the strengths and weaknesses of a film's marketing assets prior to production, when there are no visuals but there's a final script and talent already committed. In a search for hooks to sell a film to consumers, this type of research elicits consumer reactions to an assortment of components from the film's story, talent, and other marketing assets in various combinations.

Respondents are probed on a single aspect of a film, such as one character. This is a monadic test, in which respondents are exposed only to one combination of elements. Respondents are not presented with alternative choices being considered from the same category. The objective of positioning studies is to identify the best elements to promote, which immediately gives a focus to advertising and promotional efforts for a movie.

Researchers use regression models, which make predictions for one variable using other fixed values, to obtain results that can be projected to a larger population. "With a sample of 800 and compact scenarios developed with the studio, we can make very early recommendations about the best way to market and position a movie," says MarketCast's Shapiro. Researchers say there's a financial benefit to using positioning studies because the studies eliminate the need to make a wide range of creative materials and the extensive testing of those items. "The positioning study finds blind alleys that would otherwise only be identified through repeated trailer testing," Shapiro said.

Focus Groups

There's an old business saying that "what you don't know can kill you," and it very much applies to movie research. Filmmakers, top brass at a film company, and the marketing department may think they know who the audience will be for a film and how the audience will react to the various components of a film. However, the conclusions are the product of "group think" from insular executives, even if they have considerable experience in predicting consumer responses.

The focus group often is the starting point to test preconceived ideas of film executives about the consumer market and, even more importantly, to discover unanticipated issues. The focus group brings together 5–10 moviegoers to discuss a film or its promotional materials in a closed room for 90–120 minutes under the direction of a moderator. Sessions often are videotaped, and executives observe the sessions behind one-way glass mirrors. Focus groups provide qualitative information—subjective responses that defy simple statistical interpretation—so executives can benefit by simply watching nuances of participants. Conducting a focus group for a film can cost up to $10,000, given expenses in preparing questions, renting a facility, recruiting participants, and analyzing the discussion.

In the consumer goods world, some focus groups are conducted by telephone or, in a new technique, via the Internet, but these methods often are impractical for films because of the difficulty in presenting film clips and the need to explain unfamiliar concepts to participants. Telephone focus groups are useful when addressing sensitive subject matter because participants can't see each other and thus may speak more freely. Leakage is more likely with telephone and Internet focus groups, in comparison to sessions held at a central site where materials are always under the control of researchers.

Because of its purpose to confirm theories about consumers and to uncover the unexpected, the focus group study often is conducted before test screenings of a film. Findings from a focus group help identify topics to be explored in later, larger tests. Focus group results are not projectable to large populations because the sample is too small.

"Consider the focus groups only to be a thermometer that allows you to test the 'temperature' of consumers' reactions to your research topic," according to *The Focus Group Research Handbook* by Holly Edmunds (NTC Business Books, 1999). "Focus groups should never be utilized to make a final decision."

The focus group discussion might uncover secondary actors in a film who are well liked and thus should be highlighted in marketing. Conversely, focus groups' discussions might reveal that a famous actor in a film doesn't elicit a favorable response. This finding would prompt the researcher to put more emphasis on evaluating other elements of a film later in mass preview screenings to find alternative hooks for the marketing campaign. Typically, a minimum of two focus group sessions is recommended because experience has shown relying on only one can be misleading.

Large groups tend to be unwieldy. Limiting the number of participants to 10 is necessary so that each person has a chance to speak. Also, the larger the focus group, the greater the group discussion. In this setting, some participants may refrain from expressing independent ideas.

Recruiting a desired demographic makeup for a focus group is a science. Two weeks before the focus group is held, recruiters search for prospective participants, who fill out short questionnaires for demographic information. Once the actual participants are selected from the recruitment roll, they are invited to the focus group and typically promised $20–$100 as an incentive to show up as promised.

Whereas recruiting is a science, the art lies in the interpersonal skills of the moderator, whose foremost requisite trait is the ability to appear neutral and unbiased. The moderator also must put the participants at ease, keep any one person from dominating the discussion, steer participants away from bickering with each other, and coax shy participants to speak. The moderator's job is to move the discussion from point to point while encouraging spontaneity within a framework. Some focus groups have two moderators because their interactions can put participants at ease. In addition, each participant may not relate well to a given moderator, so having two moderators increases the likelihood that at least one moderator will be sympathetic.

Test Screenings

When films are finished or nearly finished, such as a rough cut without final music or some special effects, test screenings (also called preview screenings) are conducted. These screenings usually are outside of Hollywood at a rented commercial cinema. Audiences are recruited in advance and then sent follow-up confirmations (Fig. 2.1). The location often is a Los Angeles suburb, although a minority of preview screens are held in distant cities.

Test screenings have two general objectives. One is to evaluate the playability of the film itself; the other is to obtain insights useful for marketing, that is, to find out which elements will hook a target audience and which won't. Sometimes a film has separate production and marketing screenings, although often issues from both types are addressed to some degree at each preview screening.

Figure 2.1 Sample Invitation Confirmation to Test Screening

Film Industry Research Company
153 Third Avenue
Los Angeles CA 90001
(323) 123 4567

November 2004

Dear Moviegoer,

Thank you for accepting our invitation for a private screening of chilling suspense thriller *Far Away Voices*. This movie has been rated R and is not yet in release.

Admission is for you and only one guest. We ask that your guest be either approximately your age or within the 18-49 age group. No one under 18 will be admitted, due to the R classification of this film.

This invitation is nontransferable and is intended only for moviegoers ages 18-49 who are not associated with the entertainment industry. Anyone who presents an invitation that is not in this age group or is associated with the entertainment industry will not be admitted.

While the screening starts at 8 p.m., it is recommended that you arrive at the theater door by 7:30 p.m. Seating is on a first come, first serve basis. Seating is not guaranteed regardless of when you arrive.

SCREENING DATE

INSERT SCREENING TIME

SCREENING LOCATION

PARKING INFORMATION

We look forward to seeing you! Thank you for your cooperation.

After seeing the film, moviegoers fill out questionnaires to determine which characters they liked and disliked, and whether they will recommend the film to their friends. The cost of conducting such a screening typically runs $7,000–$15,000 for an audience of 200–400 persons. The cost covers theater rental, a projectionist, audience recruitment, and data analysis, including a final written report. Major studios tend to conduct from one to five test screenings per film, but three is a common number. An outside research vendor usually is hired to run the test screening.

Much of the data drawn from test screenings are quantitative information suitable for statistical analysis and projectable to a larger population. The test audiences are polled for their opinion of films on a five-point scale of Excellent, Very Good, Good, Fair, and Poor (Fig. 2.2). When executives say a film tested with a 73% for "the top two boxes," 73% of the target audience chose Excellent or Very Good on the five-point scale. Scores falling below the 55–65% range for the top two boxes are a cause for worry.

After seeing a film, audiences are asked for their opinions via a two-sided, single-sheet questionnaire. Audiences are quizzed about what they liked and didn't like, including characters, scenes, and the film's pace. A focus group with a small, preselected group of moviegoers usually is conducted immediately following the screening. "Often what's not mentioned is as important as what is mentioned," said Kevin Goetz, managing director/executive vice president of entertainment research at OTX and who also heads up the screening division. "If a particular scene or character is not mentioned either in the audience questionnaire comment cards or during the focus group, it could indicate that no problem or issue exists, or it could mean that a specific scene or character that the filmmaker or studio thought would be a big audience pleaser or integral to the film's playability simply is not."

Filmmakers and studio brass may find that a particular scene they thought would really work with audiences elicited less of a reaction than they wanted. Also, the sample might single out one or more scenes that initially were thought not to be significant. Evocative scenes are prime candidates for inclusion in television commercials and trailers. Test findings also might point to making changes either to the movie itself to improve its playability or to the marketing strategy. Results from test screening may lead marketers to conclude that a horror film without excessive blood but lots of suspense plays surprisingly well to females, who often are written off as not interested in the genre.

The starting point for test screenings is examining results from the total audience, and the customary five-point scale is used for answers. As is always the case in the science of consumer research, audience members provide demographic information about themselves individually, so their opinions can also be grouped by various population categories. By culling

Figure 2.2 Sample Test Screening Summary Report

Movie Title: PG-13 Romantic Drama

Screening Date: Dec. 15, 2004
Total Cards Tabulated: 403
Walk Outs & Spoiled Cards: 7

Overall audience	Totals		Males				Females			
			Under age 25		Over age 25		Under age 25		Over age 25	
	Persons	%	Persons	%	Persons	%	Persons	%	Persons	%
Totals	403	100%	109	100%	85	100%	88	100%	121	100%
Excellent	143	35%	31	28%	24	28%	39	44%	49	40%
Very Good	135	33%	40	37%	29	34%	27	31%	39	32%
(subtotal-Top 2 Boxes)	278	68%	71	65%	53	62%	66	75%	88	72%
Good	84	21%	21	19%	23	27%	17	19%	23	19%
Fair	35	9%	15	14%	9	11%	4	5%	7	6%
Poor	6	1%	2	2%	0	0%	1	1%	3	2%
Definitely recommend	231	57%	54	50%	43	51%	62	70%	72	60%

Source: *Marketing to Moviegoers*

answers only from respondents in a certain demographic group, researchers project an average score that a film gets on the five-point scale, for example, from males ages 17–29.

The film's director is granted creative rights that impact test screenings, according to the basic labor agreement of the Directors Guild of America (DGA). The DGA labor contract gives the director the right to deliver the first version of a film, and the producer must conduct at least one screening of this director's film cut before a general public audience if the director requests. This is among several creative rights reserved for directors.

There are many stories about films that were re-edited because of reactions from test screenings, although film companies often deny changes were made because of research findings. Whatever the motivation, an estimated 80% of major studio films undergo significant reshoots after principal photography to create new scenes, although not all are as drastic as changing endings. Such extra filming was less frequent decades ago but was still done on occasion. Endings were changed occasionally, even in Hollywood's Golden Era of the 1930s, as with *Wuthering Heights* in 1939. The original opening prologue of the 1950 classic *Sunset Blvd.*, which was set in a morgue, was replaced because audiences found the prologue too dark.

These days, filmmakers and studios are loath to admit that unfavorable test screenings are largely responsible for a reshoot decision because doing so makes them seem slaves of research. Often, the truth is muddy. Filmmakers and distribution executives frequently go into previews thinking a film needs fixing, so research mostly confirms a preexisting suspicion and helps isolate specific areas.

Famously, one ending of the 1987 thriller *Fatal Attraction* had the Glenn Close stalker character survive the climax, but test audiences reportedly found that ending unsatisfying. So the character was killed off in the final version of the Paramount Pictures release. A serious ending was inserted in Metro-Goldwyn-Mayer's comedy *Legally Blonde* after test audiences found the original comedic ending unsatisfying.

According to a 2001 article in *The Wall Street Journal*, a character that audiences disliked was cut completely from *American Pie 2*, and new scenes were shot to give more screen time to another character. Director Steven Spielberg said that he shot two endings in principal photography before getting any feedback for *The Terminal*, his whimsical airport yarn from summer 2004 that starred Tom Hanks. On the other hand, New Line Cinema's *Lord of the Rings* films reportedly were not previewed, which didn't deter them from achieving blockbuster status.

Test Screening Travails

The previewing screening process is experiencing its own crisis these days. One problem is that results tend to leak out within the movie industry. Film distributors worry that simply screening a flawed film will trigger a bad buzz, even if the film is easily fixable. Now film executives start retooling films before the first test screening rather than waiting for the first wave of audience research, for fear poor feedback will haunt the film.

Another problem is that, with the Internet, test audiences aren't as isolated as they used to be. Enterprising participants in test screenings can post unauthorized reviews that become widely circulated. In July 2004, the popular movie Web site *AintItCool.com* served up evaluations supposedly from members of a test audience who claimed to have previewed Twentieth Century Fox's *Alien vs. Predator*, but those missives apparently came from pranksters. The commentaries were removed from the site when they were learned to be not genuine, according to *Variety*.

For decades, apocryphal stories circulated in Hollywood about filmmakers supposedly packing a preview audience with friends in order to get good scores out of test screenings. In past decades, test screenings were less structured and almost always in the Los Angeles area, so slipping in a few friends and family may have been possible in theory. However, these days the audience recruitment process is rigorous, and dissemination of questionnaires to the preselected audience is carefully controlled.

About three quarters of test screenings are conducted in and around Los Angeles or New York City so that film company executives and talent can be present to get a "feel" for the audiences and their reactions. For the minority of preview screenings conducted out of town, cities near Los Angeles usually are chosen so executives and talent can make round trips in the same day. Popular cities for out-of-town screenings are Sacramento, San Jose, and Phoenix/Scottsdale. More distant cities that sometimes are used include Austin, Minneapolis, and Milwaukee because they have sophisticated movie audiences.

Test screenings figure into business-to-business transactions in which the producer of a finished independent film seeks a domestic distributor to handle its release. In such cases, acquisition executives from distributors view films in private industry screenings to determine if they wish to make a bid for distribution rights. A distributor might be interested in a screened film but is not ready to make a firm financial offer based on just a viewing by its own executives. The distribution company then asks the producers to allow it to conduct a test screen with a general audience to gauge consumer response.

Such a conditional offer puts the producers of the independent film in a dilemma. First, if the test screenings go badly and the distributor decides not to acquire the film, that information tends to become known within the industry and the film in question becomes an even tougher sell elsewhere. Furthermore, the distributor conducting the test screening typically will not let the film's producers get involved or give them access to results.

Testing Advertising and Trailers

The most important promotional materials to be tested are television commercials and trailers because they have proved to be the most effective in selling movies to consumers. Given that dozens of versions of trailers and television commercials are commissioned by major studios for big films, a lot of advertising concepts are being tested.

Several hundred moviegoers typically participate in ad tests. This is a sample size necessary to be projectable to a larger population. The cost of testing a cluster of 3–10 commercials runs somewhere between $12,000–$14,000.

A full campaign boils down dozens of trailers and television commercials made in rough form to a final three trailers and 6–10 television commercials. For films scheduled for release in off-peak periods, the marketing department may weed out some television commercials and test only what it feels are best. Usually all trailers are tested.

Ad tests often are structured as monadic tests, in which each respondent sees only one advertisement and is probed extensively for a response. "You may find the romantic angle works better for women and the comedy angle plays better to men in the same film," notes MarketCast's Shapiro. "It's an exercise in comparisons."

The Internet is the new wrinkle in the past two years as a vehicle to test promotional material. Respondents who were recruited and evaluated in advance can self-administer tests at home on their computers. The test materials go to just a select audience and have antipiracy encoding so that they cannot be easily copied. The test materials lack rewind capability and never reside on the hard drive of a respondent's computer.

In theory, respondents could try to capture images from in-home movie tests from their computer screen, but fortunately image quality suffers from such unauthorized copying. One advantage of using the Internet is that results can easily be tabulated at a central data center and sorted for near-instant analysis.

This area is experiencing considerable upheaval in terms of where testing is conducted. For years, respondents would be enlisted at movie theater lobbies or shopping malls, where they immediately view materials on site or are recruited for mass screenings in private auditoriums at a later date. These are termed nonrandom intercepts because the recruiter picks respondents out of a crowd.

In analyzing results, movie marketers want to learn which ads play well with which audience segments. This is particularly important for television commercials destined for cable television, because most cable networks are demographic specific. For example, MTV draws the youth audience, ESPN pulls men, and Lifetime corrals women.

Marketers are looking for television commercials that they initially thought would play well only to a narrow audience, for example, just male teenagers, but in fact have impact across a broader audience. Commercials with broad audience appeal are necessary for broadcast network television. Even though commercials are placed on broadcast network television to reach a specific demographic (for example, men ages 18–34), there's always considerable audience spillover to other demographics, so broadcast ads need to play to a broad audience.

The process of testing promotional material has some quirks. First, trailers always tend to get higher approvals from audiences than do television spots. Trailers run from 90–150 seconds, longer than the 30-second television spot, so they are more satisfying.

These days, the trend is for trailers to provide a complete summary of a film, meaning they tell the whole story. Some pundits complain this is a poor strategy because there's nothing left to the imagination, as was the case with trailers in past eras. Testing may be the catalyst for telling the whole story because such trailers tend to get higher marks from test audiences than versions that are more nuanced. "So if your movie or movie trailer is testing poorly, simply re-cut the trailer to tell more of the story, and your scores will go up," said a marketing executive.

Tracking Surveys

The weekly surveys quantifying consumer awareness of films are perhaps the most ubiquitous single strand of research in Hollywood. A given film appears in tracking surveys about six weeks before theatrical release. At that point, the film is locked into a premiere date that can't be changed. Each of the three main movie research outfits conducts its own tracking surveys, so three different sets of data are always floating around Hollywood.

Research vendors survey consumers several times a week or even daily, and results are summarized weekly. These data are sold to multiple film companies and are the only type of movie research that is consistently shared because each Hollywood film distributor can't afford to bankroll its own private tracking study. Major studios typically pay around $250,000 per year for weekly tracking surveys, whereas independent distributors tend to buy on an *a la carte* basis just for their wide-release films. Research companies tend to customize reports. Film companies get great depth of data for their own films in tracking studies, whereas research companies tend to provide more sketchy information on films from rival distributors.

Starting six weeks before a film's premiere, trailers begin to saturate theaters, big waves of publicity hit, and teaser advertising appears in the marketplace. After each wave of advertising and publicity washes over the consumer market, film marketing executives expect the awareness levels to rise. The outside research firms compare the tracking results for a new film hurtling toward theatrical opening against benchmarks of past similar movies. This is called checking against norms, that is, normative historical data.

If a film is tracking poorly compared to norms, there's an immediate panic at the film distributor, after which the advertising creative may be tweaked or advertising spending levels changed. The scramble to make last-minute changes usually is designed to ratchet up a given film's norms for the next week. Of course, a distributor could decide that a film's box office prospects are so poor based on tracking results and its own evaluation that it gives up on the film.

In tracking surveys, consumers are presented all the significant films in a release period because one objective of the surveys is to compare films, especially those opening at or around the same time. Typically, 1,000–2,000 consumers are polled each week (Fig. 2.3). Usually, 30–35 films are included in a normal report. The most widely cited tracking data are for the general audience, but various demographic segments can be isolated as well, as is the case with any research polling a large sample.

Tracking surveys typically are not useful for films going into narrow release—fewer than 600–800 theaters—because these types of films lack the marketing campaign that registers with the broad consumer market.

The most significant finding is desirability of a film on a five-point scale expressed in percentages. The top response is that respondents are Definitely Interested in seeing a given film. Other choices are Probably Interested, Might/Might Not Be Interested, Probably Not Interested, and

Figure 2.3 Tracking Survey Format for Results Summary

Distributor	Release Date	Title	Unaided Awareness	Total Awareness	Definite Interest	Possible Interest	Might/Might Not be Interested	Probably Not Interested	Definitely Not Interested	First Choice	Have Seen
Studio X	Nov 05 04	Offbeat animated drama	20	87	25	18	17	18	22	17	21
Indie Distribution	Nov 12 04	Quality adult drama	5	54	27	35	6	2	30	8	5
Major Releasing	Nov 12 04	Popular studio comedy	24	95	38	23	19	12	8	24	17
Distributor Z	Nov 17 04	Glossy adventure film	17	84	29	21	25	7	18	9	13
Constant Films	Nov 19 04	Female comedy	12	81	31	25	10	9	23	9	0
Studio X	Nov 19 04	Youth comedy	14	90	28	32	14	11	15	7	0

Note: Distributor names and movie titles are made up for this demonstration. A normal tracking survey typically lists 30–35 films.
Source: Marketing to Moviegoers

Definitely Not Interested. A final category often is Have Seen for films already in theaters.

A related component of tracking surveys answers this question: Which three movies currently in theaters are the first choices of filmgoers? The tracking survey also asks respondents which film titles they have heard about without giving them any choices or prompts. This question measures unaided awareness. "While the new measures we have added to tracking help us gain a more detailed understanding of moviegoing behavior, unaided awareness and first choice in theaters are still the most important measures at predicting box office," said Vincent Bruzzese, vice president for entertainment research at OTX Research.

An outgrowth of tracking is a prediction of opening weekend box office revenue, which is issued just before each film premieres. The margin of error in predicting 3-day opening weekend box office is between 15% and 20%. Thus, when a 20% accuracy range is used and a $10 million weekend is forecast, the survey is deemed accurate if actual box office falls anywhere between $8 and 12 million. The bigger the forecast, the wider the accuracy range stated in absolute dollars. If a $50 million opening is forecast, the accurate range is a rather wide $40 to 60 million at 20%.

The industry follows tracking surveys very closely because they usually are correct, thus providing valuable marketing intelligence. However, the various tracking surveys have been off the mark from time to time. For example, some tracking reportedly forecast *The Passion of the Christ* would open at $15–30 million in February 2004, which was far short of its $83.8 million opening 3-day weekend. Later in the year, another tracking survey predicted an opening in the low 30s for Universal's *The Bourne Supremacy*, which came in higher at $52.5 million.

Looking back further in history, Twentieth Century Fox's animation film *Ice Age* did poorly in prerelease tracking but proved to be a blockbuster in 2002, rolling up $176.4 million in domestic box office. Perhaps the most famous miss came in June 2000. Tracking indicated that Columbia's colonial era war drama *The Patriot* would beat Warner Bros. disaster drama *The Perfect Storm* on opening weekend. However, *The Perfect Storm* won the 3-day opening battle with $41.3 million in box office, versus $22.4 million for *The Patriot* (both films proved to be hits). Again, the forecasts that did not come true are in a small minority.

The new twist is the wide circulation of tracking surveys in the film business. What used to be seen by only a few major studio executives is now in the hands of exhibitors. Research firms say they only sell to film distributors, who apparently leak findings to exhibitors who are not subscribers.

The fallout is that if a tracking survey shows a film is lagging—performing below the norms—movie theaters may give up on the movie before it even opens. "It changed the way the business is done," said Tom Sherak, partner at Revolution Studios, which supplies films to Sony Pictures. "Movie tracking helped the marketing departments at the studios sell their movies, but it has been turned into a sales tool that has an effect on the [financial] terms the studio gets for its movie. The studios still use tracking surveys because they are useful."

Tracking surveys are often telephone surveys. To make sure unlisted numbers are included, survey takers dial numbers randomly. To exclude jaded film industry people, surveys tend to exclude Beverly Hills, Hollywood, and other areas with a high concentration of film industry workers. However, call waiting, call blocking, and Internet dial-ups that block telephone lines for long periods tend to put a large chunk of the high-income population out of reach, which has made getting a representative sample increasingly difficult.

Exit Surveys

When films are in theaters, there's an opportunity to elicit information from an important target audience—the people who actually bought tickets for movies. Exit surveys are conducted at theater locations by survey takers who intercept moviegoers moments after they have seen a film.

One key finding is the demographic profile of respondents because the result reveals the makeup of a film's true audience and is not simply an estimate. Another key finding is whether the respondent will recommend the film to peers, which can impact how heavy or light future waves of ad support will be.

Exit surveys also represent a method to check the accuracy of earlier research prior to theatrical release. Film marketing researchers want to know if audience profile matches expectations and, if not, how it was different. Respondents also are queried about which advertising or promotional materials triggered their decision to attend the film and which creative materials were not persuasive or memorable (Fig. 2.4). The response to this question also can quantify the impact of critic reviews, talk show appearances of talent, and contest promotions.

When television commercials are found to be ineffective, the ads may be changed if time permits. Typically, there's not enough time to start

Figure 2.4 Sample Questionnaire for Exit Survey

List ALL ways you have already heard about this movie.

Note: check as many as apply
- In theater trailer
- In theater lobby poster
- Television commercials
- Television reviews
- Television talk shows
- Radio reviews
- Radio news/talk shows
- Newspaper ads
- Newspaper reviews
- Magazine reviews
- Magazine articles
- Internet banner ads
- Internet articles/features
- Internet official website
- Entertainment websites
- Outdoor billboards
- Comments from friends/relatives
- In store promotion
- Official movie contest

Before coming to the theater today, which were key to choosing to see this film?

Note: check all that apply
- Lead actor #1
- Lead actor #2
- Lead actor #3
- Lead actor #4
- The story
- Comedy genre
- Action genre
- Reviews
- Music
- In-theater trailer
- Television ads
- My child wanted to come
- Recommendation of a friend

Figure 2.4 *Continued*

How long ago did you make your choice for this movie?

Note: pick only one
- Today
- Prior two days
- Over prior week
- Over prior month
- More than one month

Did you choose to come today or did someone else choose?

Note: pick only one
- I chose it
- Someone else chose it
- I chose together with someone else

Who did you come with today?

Note: check all that apply
- Alone
- Spouse or date
- Friends
- My children
- My children and other children
- My parents or other non-spouse family

Gender
- Male
- Female

Age
- Under 12
- 12-17
- 18-24
- 25-34
- 35-49
- 50-65
- Over 65

Figure 2.4 *Continued*

Including today, how often did you go to the movies in the past two months?

Note: pick only one
- 1 time
- 2 times
- 3 times
- 4 times
- 5 times
- 6 times or more

Your favorite types of movies are?

Note: check all that apply
- Children
- All family
- Action adventure
- Suspense thriller
- Serious drama
- Physical/visual comedy
- Dialog-driven comedy
- Documentary
- Foreign language

Before coming today, how did you select this theater and showtime?

Note: check all that apply
- Looked at all movies listed in newspaper before deciding
- Looked at all movies listed in a magazine before deciding
- Looked at all movies on an Internet site before deciding
- Looked at other media not listed above before deciding
- Used newspaper only to select theater and start time
- Used magazine only to select theater and start time
- Used Internet only to select theater and start time
- Others in my party identified theater and start time

Figure 2.4 *Continued*

After seeing the movie, how would you rate the film?

Note: pick only one
- Excellent
- Very Good
- Good
- Fair
- Poor

After seeing the movie, how likely are you to see it again in a theater?

Note: pick only one
- Definitely
- Probably
- Might/might not
- Probably not
- Definitely not

After seeing the movie, would you recommend others see it at a theater?

Note: pick only one
- Definitely
- Probably
- Might/might not
- Probably not
- Definitely not

After seeing the movie, would you recommend others see it on video or pay TV?

Note: pick only one
- Definitely
- Probably
- Probably not
- Definitely not

After seeing the movie, did it meet your expectations?

Note: pick only one
- Better than expected
- About what I expected
- Not as good as I expected

Figure 2.4 *Continued*

After seeing the movie, what will you talk about to friends regarding the movie in a positive light?

Note: check all that apply
- Lead actor #1
- Lead actor #2
- Lead actor #3
- Lead actor #4
- The story
- Comedy genre
- Action genre
- Sub plots
- Clever dialog
- Music
- The ending

After seeing the movie, how interested are you in renting it on video?

Note: pick only one
- Definitely
- Probably
- Might/might not
- Probably not
- Definitely not

After seeing the movie, how interested are you in buying it on video?

Note: pick only one
- Definitely
- Probably
- Might/might not
- Probably not
- Definitely not

Source: Marketing to Moviegoers

from scratch, so all that's possible is dusting off and tweaking commercials that previously were passed over. Newspaper and radio ads can be changed on fairly short notice too, although these ad forms are thought to be less persuasive than television commercials.

Finally, audiences can be quizzed regarding which parts of the films they liked or didn't like and anything they found confusing. The well-liked parts can be played up in future advertising. All the findings end up with the distributor's home video department, which has up to four months to shape its own marketing for video release for the same film.

Although research findings used to be very hush-hush in past years, snippets of results now make their way into the press. For example, in June 2004 a *Variety* story on sleeper summer comedy hit *Dodgeball: A True Underdog Story* said that "Fox exit surveys found 38% of the aud was males under 25 years old. Overall, the aud was 57% male."

History of Research

Test screenings of Hollywood films go back to the golden era of the 1930s when audience recruitment, measurement, and sampling techniques were less sophisticated. The television era was a catalyst for more systematic and scientific methods as broadcasters measured audience reactions to programs and advertisers tested their commercials.

In the 1950s, an engineer working for Columbia Pictures developed a research technology that utilized handheld dials to provide instantaneous reactions from audience members during theatrical film screenings. Jack and Harry Cohn, the legendary heads of Columbia at the time, supported and funded the technology, and they used it on a limited basis.

By the early 1960s, an advertising and marketing executive at Screen Gems, a unit of Columbia, asked permission to develop the technology for television program and advertising research. Using the Directors Guild theater on Sunset Boulevard, early experiments were successful. The studio created a research business called Audience Studies Inc. (ASI), and its own facility, Preview House, was built on Sunset Boulevard. Audiences were recruited by both telephone and intercept interviews in high-traffic areas within 30 miles of the facility. Participants provided reactions by turning a handheld instantaneous response dial and filling out written questionnaires. Broadcast networks, advertisers, advertising agencies, and film studios used ASI.

By the late 1960s, ASI and NBC Television experimented with cable television as an in-home testing methodology. Early in the 1970s, NBC decided to utilize this system, and ASI set up operations in many cable systems across the United States. Cable testing faded as the economies of central telephone facilities enabled researchers to discontinue costly local interviewing sites.

Through the 1960s and 1970s, ASI was the leading theatrical film research supplier until its entertainment and advertising divisions were sold off separately. In 1978, National Research Group (NRG), founded by Joe Farrell, entered the market and became the most influential player in the modern era of film research. NRG became the research vendor to all Hollywood studios, which dramatically increased their spending and reliance on audience testing. Today, three film research companies dominate the landscape: NRG, MarketCast, and OTX Research.

Farrell became a godfatherlike counselor to Hollywood majors with NRG's tracking studies. They are weekly surveys of filmgoers' perceptions of films approaching and in release. A big part of Farrell's appeal was his database and historical knowledge, giving him the ability to draw on marketing data from past films to apply to new releases. Media giant VNU acquired NRG in 1997 from advertising agency Saatchi & Saatchi, which had purchased the movie research outfit in 1988. Farrell left NRG in 2002 to become a film producer based at Walt Disney Studios.

By the 1980s, the major studios had collected enough accurate historical data to apply sophisticated modeling techniques and to forecast potential ticket sales and box office receipts. The major studios, wanting to keep closer tabs on their audience, also have ramped up their research activities since the 1970s by hiring executives from Madison Avenue with experience in the sophisticated packaged goods world.

Over the past decade, movie research experienced crises, and the Internet influenced the business. One dilemma is that the tracking studies evaluating audience perceptions of films circulate ever more widely, and movie theater operators increasingly see data. Film distributors worry that theaters will give up on films tracking poorly before the films open in cinemas.

Another headache is increased leaks from test screenings. Participants now can post minireviews on Internet sites devoted to movies, giving wide exposure to what in past years usually had remained confidential. Internet leaks are a problem because commentaries are unsophisticated, films often undergo subsequent revision, and unauthorized write-ups from leaks tend to undercut studio-generated publicity later. Finally, people attending test screenings may attempt to record the film and later send it over the Internet or transfer the film to DVD.

Film research is also helped by the Internet because it is a platform to conduct research. Respondents recruited by research companies can view movie commercials, trailers, and other materials on their computer screens at home. Participants take self-administered tests, and the results are compiled almost immediately because responses are recorded electronically.

3 Paid Media Advertising

I know that half of my advertising budget is being wasted, I just don't know which half.

John Wanamaker

A famous retailing mogul uttered the preceding pithy statement more than a century ago, and the statement still has relevance to the movie business today. Film distributors sense they are overspending but can't quite figure out where, which makes them reluctant to institute cuts.

Spurred by competitive pressures and a buoyant business climate, movie marketing expenses skyrocketed a startling 28% per film for Hollywood's major studios in 2003, according to the trade group the Motion Picture Association of America (MPAA). That percentage encompasses buying ads, costs of creating ads, publicity, promotion, and making film trailers for screening in theaters.

The main culprit is broadcast network advertising, where audience shares get smaller because cable channels fragment television viewing, yet network ad rates increase. The ad expenditure escalation has transformed the media buying function from a dull backwater into the front lines in the war on rising film marketing costs. Buying advertising used to be a robotic exercise of simply soliciting television channels, radio outlets, and print media to obtain a price for advertising that would achieve a requested audience delivery. What was once a boring science is today where a lot of innovation—the art—is found in movie marketing, with cutting edge Internet ads and demographically focused cable television buys.

Hollywood is a big spender. Nielsen Media Research estimates the movie sector is the fifth largest category for paid advertising on a national basis, sandwiched between department stores and fast food restaurants (factory automotive is the top ad category). In 2003, movie marketers spent $3.4 billion to buy advertising in the United States (Fig. 3.1), according to Nielsen Monitor-Plus. In 2004, ad rates spiraled upward because of the once-every-four-year effect of the convergence of the summer Olympics and presidential election, which generate one-time surges in ad spending. The economy also rebounded from the 2000 dot-com bust.

The stakes are high to launch films right. With just a few exceptions in history, films don't recover from failed openings in theatrical distribution. Mounting an advertising barrage is the most certain method of rousing moviegoers to buy tickets for a movie opening. Film distributors control the exact message delivered, pick the timing when the message is sent, and know in advance how large an audience will see the message, because independent measurement companies estimate audience size of electronic and print media.

The case is frequently made that the size of an advertising launch does not directly correlate with box office. Big films with big marketing campaigns bomb all the time. On the other hand, *My Big Fat Greek Wedding,*

Figure 3.1 Movie Advertising Spending by Media 2003

Media	$ Mil.	%
Network television	$1,253	36%
Cable television	$ 625	18%
Spot television	$ 617	18%
Syndicated television	$ 124	4%
Hispanic network television	$ 70	2%
Local newspaper	$ 546	16%
National newspaper	$ 121	3%
National Sunday supplement	$ 1	n/a
National magazine	$ 28	1%
Local magazine	$ 1	n/a
Outdoor	$ 37	1%
Spot radio	$ 43	1%
Network radio	$ 4	n/a
Total	**$3,472**	**100%**

Note: Figures cover the United States only.
Source: Nielsen Monitor-Plus

which cost just $5 million to make, achieved blockbuster box office of $241.4 million with a relatively modest $30 million in ad spending over its long theater run. The rub is that a good film with weak advertising support will underperform in box office.

Crisis in Media Buying

The opportunity to reach the mass market inexpensively is fast vanishing as a consequence of media fragmentation. Cable television networks cut into broadcast television audiences. Lower printing costs have opened the door for more specialized magazines and newspapers, which nip at the heels of longstanding print giants.

Network television audiences fell by 41% from 1977 to 2003 while network revenues soared nearly fivefold, according to *Business Week* magazine. This fragmentation trend, which forces film marketers to buy specialized media with high unit costs, is expected to continue for the balance of the decade. Wall Street research house Sanford C. Bernstein & Co. forecasts that revenue at the new wave of narrowcast media will grow a hefty 13.5% annually to 2010, while established mass media will increase just 3.5% annually, trailing the growth rate of the general economy.

Media is becoming more niche oriented, which is an advantage to films with narrow appeal because more options are available for advertising to demographically concentrated audiences. However, mainstream films aimed at large audiences are experiencing soaring costs for mass media ad vehicles, whose clout is diminishing amid fragmentation. Each year, mass market films require more ads simply to maintain constant audience delivery levels. Thus, eroding mass advertising platforms must be augmented by advertising in less efficient narrowcast media. "We are pushing for new ways to break through to audiences beyond the 30-second television spot," said Pamela Levine, co-president of domestic theatrical marketing at Twentieth Century Fox.

Another knock to efficiency is the personal video recorder (PVR), sometimes called a digital video recorder. PVRs are easy-to-use television recording devices with large storage capacity via hard drives and an ability to skip through advertising. PVR penetration stood at about 4% of United States television households at mid-2004 but is expected to jump to 30% in 3 to 4 years. Although it's a worry that viewers will skip commercials using PVRs, a small offsetting benefit is that early adopters of PVRs watch 20–30% more television. However, it's not clear if the trend to higher overall viewing will be sustained.

Besides fragmenting media, the population is increasingly more diverse because of immigration and uneven birth rates between ethnic populations. The greater diversity steps up the pressure on film marketers to buy more ads to reach diverse pools of moviegoers.

Overview

Ad campaigns usually are framed in terms of prerelease launch, which is the 3-week period leading into and through opening weekend. For major studio films, this generally involves $15–$35 million in advertising, of which 80% is allocated to television (broadcast, cable, and television syndication).

A mainstream major studio release in 2003 averaged $34.84 million in total spending for consumer marketing in the United States, according to the MPAA. Marketing costs at major studios have experienced sharp increases, as evidenced by the comparable figure of $24 million in 2000, $12.13 million in 1993, and just $4.18 million in 1983 (Fig. 3.2). These expenditures are made directly by film distributors and do not include tie-in advertising from promotional partners, such as restaurant chains, soft drink companies, and other consumer goods outfits (see Chapter 4). In a separate but related expense, the cost of release prints also is rising as the major studios tilt to increasingly wide release patterns for theaters.

The advertising spending for major studio-owned independent subsidiaries, such as Fox Searchlight and Disney's Miramax, also is up sharply.

Figure 3.2 Major Studio Spending on Prints and Advertising 1983–2003

Year	Prints	Advertising	Total P&A
2003	$4.21	$34.84	$39.05
2002	$3.31	$27.31	$30.62
2001	$3.73	$27.28	$31.01
2000	$3.30	$24.00	$27.30
1999	$3.13	$21.40	$24.53
1993	$1.94	$12.13	$14.07
1983	$1.02	$ 4.18	$ 5.20

Note: All figures in millions. Figures cover United States only. Prints are release prints used by theaters. Advertising category also includes costs of publicity, movie trailers, and creating marketing materials.
Source: Motion Picture Association of America

Studio-affiliated independent (indie) distributors averaged $12.8 million in consumer marketing ad spending per film in 2003, a 31% increase from $9.76 million in 2002. In 1999, the comparable figure was just $5.74 million (Fig. 3.3). These indie style affiliates are adding more substantial major-studio-caliber films to their slates, which probably is responsible for some of the increase in consumer advertising expense.

For independent films, the range for prerelease campaigns runs from tens of thousands of dollars to $15 million but typically is in the low single-digit millions for mainstream indie films. The longer an ad campaign runs, the more its media spend will tilt toward newspapers and weeklies because of the need to place ads containing specific theater playdates.

Film distributors tend to hire outside media buying advertising agencies to handle purchases of advertising. These agencies follow a budget that originates from the distributor. Because the advertising placement process is highly complex, it is best suited for specialist media buying agencies (Fig. 3.4). They have the clout to negotiate the lowest prices from electronic and print media, given the high volume of their ad spending from handling numerous clients. In the broader advertising business, mainstream ad agencies—battered by clients grinding down prices for most of their services—find that their media buying units are their most profitable businesses.

Media buying agencies are highly compartmentalized. Media planning executives draw up a detailed outline. Media buying executives—segmented by radio, newspapers, cable television, magazines, etc.—negotiate with their category of media outlets to price advertising.

Figure 3.3 Major Studio–Affiliated Indies' Spending on Prints & Advertising 1999–2003

Year	Prints	Advertising	Total P&A
2003	$1.87	$12.80	$14.67
2002	$1.42	$ 9.76	$11.18
2001	$1.21	$ 8.29	$ 9.50
2000	$0.75	$ 8.96	$ 9.71
1999	$0.78	$ 5.74	$ 6.52

Notes: All figures in millions. These are independent film units owned by major studios such as New Line Cinema, Miramax, Sony Pictures Classics, etc. Figures cover United States. Prints are release prints used by theaters. Advertising category also includes costs of publicity, movie trailers, and creating marketing materials
Source: Motion Picture Association of America

Figure 3.4 Media Buying Agencies For Top Film Distributors

Media Buying Agency	Film Distributor Clients
BBDO	MGM
EDB/Needham	Universal Pictures
Grey Advertising	Warner Bros.
GSD&M/Austin	DreamWorks
Mediaedge: CIA/WPP Group	Paramount Pictures
MindShare	Twentieth Century Fox*
StarCom	Disney
Palisades Media	Miramax, Lions Gate, Fox Searchlight, Paramount Classics
Universal/McCann	Sony/Columbia

*Fox does some media buying in-house
Source: Marketing to Moviegoers

At the major studios, the marketing departments have executives dedicated to overseeing media planning and ad buying by outside agencies.

The media objectives come out of the broad marketing plan set by the film distributor, based on its knowledge of which demographics are the most promising for a given film. Because each film is a new product launch (except sequels and the rare re-issue), the pressure is on to quickly assemble the media buys that fulfill the plan.

"There's no client that's as demanding as a movie account," said Roger Schaffner, president of Palisades Media Group, which is a media buyer in Santa Monica, California, whose clients include film distributors. "Every day, you are looking at the tracking research. You could learn that, hey, men are buying into this romantic comedy movie, so you've got to start advertising to men. This means that we need advertising creative that will appeal to men. So we ask, when will this be ready so we can start buying advertising targeting men? That's just one example of what could happen."

Another quirk of the business is that producers of independent films who license films to distributors often require that distributors promise to spend a minimum amount of advertising in theatrical release. Producers seek this contractual obligation so distributors can't later decide to bury the film with a truncated release. At major studios, the same objective is pursued differently. Film producers compare the ad spending for their films versus others. Producers of films that will be released by majors and independents often bring in their own marketing consultants to keep an eye on marketing executives on staff at the film distributor.

Hollywood media buying practices got a black eye in a Federal Trade Commission (FTC) report in 2000, which documented examples of advertising for films with restrictive ratings aimed at inappropriately young audiences. In the aftermath, the major studios adopted a voluntary code of conduct, organized through their trade group the MPAA (see Chapter 7). A fourth follow-up FTC report in July 2004 indicated film industry practices "continue to improve," but the FTC still identified some breaches.

The original report in 2000 was highly critical and prompted the industry to enact reforms. "Clearly there were times during the period discussed in the FTC report where we allowed competitive zeal to overwhelm sound judgment and appropriate standards in the marketing of some of our R-rated films," Robert Iger, president and chief operating officer of the Walt Disney Co., testified before a United States Senate hearing in 2000. The R rating restricts children under age 17 unless they are accompanied by a parent or adult guardian.

Alan Horn, Warner Bros. Entertainment president and chief operating officer, added: "We will step up our vigilance in our media buys and our marketing using the [Federal Communications Commission] definition of what constitutes a substantial portion of the audience. That is 35% of the measurable audience. In other words, we will not advertise our R-rated movies in venues in which over 35% of the audience is under the age of 17."

In the original 2000 report, the FTC found that of 44 R-rated films analyzed, media plans for 28 films "contained express statements that the film's target audience included children under 17." Another seven films bought ads in media that were heavy with an under-17 audience, without specifically stating that youngsters were a target. The original FTC report did praise the movie industry's Advertising Administration, which approves advertising materials, such as commercials, for enforcing standards effectively.

The issue may never quite die, because any advertising medium with a large audience is never completely homogenous, and children inevitably will be a small part of programming that attracts mostly adults. Also, because children are allowed to see R-rated films when accompanied by a parent or adult guardian, it's not automatic that such films are inappropriate.

"No matter how carefully we target our advertising, some people under 17 will inevitably see ads for R-rated movies in specific media with broad demographic reach," Stacey Snider, Universal Pictures chair, testified in 2000. "*Monday Night Football* (on ABC Television) is a classic example of that and also a good place to advertise movies. Here we may market to men and young adults, but some younger football fans, whose parents let them watch, will also see our ads. By the way, they also might see ads for other products that their parents might not want them to consume."

Strategies

The first fork in the road when mapping out a plan for media buying is whether to emphasize reach or frequency. Reach refers to the percentage of households or population in a target that see an advertisement at least once in a measurement period. Each household or person is counted only once, no matter how many times they see the same advertisement. Therefore, reach is a measure of the breadth of an advertising campaign.

Frequency is a percentage that expresses the number of times households or persons in a target audience are exposed, on average, to advertisement in a measurement period. In frequency, there is double and triple counting of the same household or person. Therefore, frequency is a measure of depth.

Reach is a metric that is valuable when evaluating multiple media buys that overlap. The media planner attempts to determine unduplicated audience delivery to minimize the size of the target audience that won't see the advertisement.

The major studios tend to emphasize reach because their goal is to cast a wide net to snare moviegoers, given their big advertising budgets and the mainstream nature of their films. Independent distributors lean to frequency because their films tend to be niche oriented, so they want to saturate the small core audience for a given film. Also, indie film ad budgets are smaller than those of major studios, so indie campaigns make an impact only when they are concentrated on a small audience target.

Another important metric that cuts across all media buys is cost per thousand (CPM), which is the expense per 1,000 households or persons in the audience. CPM is a measure of efficiency. A network that charges $250,000 for a 30-second commercial in a program delivering an audience of 12.5 million viewers in the target demographic is charging a CPM of $20.00 (or $20.00 cost per 1000 persons). The CPM metric can be used to compare relative cost for programs with different audience deliveries and different ad prices stated in dollars.

Ad campaigns are always a mix of media such as newspapers, national cable television commercials, local radio, outdoor billboards, and other media. Media tend to be grouped into two categories for speed in delivering audiences. *Fast load media,* such as network television, reach millions of moviegoers in an instant (Fig. 3.5). Therefore, broadcast media deliver audiences quickly. Slow load media, such as outdoor bill-

Figure 3.5 Comparative Media Attributes

Media	Audience Accumulation Speed	Buying Lead Time	Geography	Reach	Demographic Concentration
Network television	Fast	Long	National	Wide	Moderate
Spot television	Fast	Short	Local	Wide	Moderate
National cable	Fast	Moderate	Patchy national	Moderate	High
Spot cable	Fast	Short	Patchy local	Moderate	High
National radio	Fast	Short	National	Moderate	High
Spot radio	Fast	Short	Local	Moderate	High
Newspapers	Moderate	Moderate	Local	Moderate	Moderate
National magazines	Slow	Long	National	Moderate	Moderate
Outdoor billboards	Slow	Long	Local	Wide	Low

Source: Marketing to Moviegoers

boards, reach large numbers of moviegoers only in a trickle. This group of media requires days, weeks, or even months to achieve delivery of large audiences. Magazines, given that they often are passed around and sold by newsstands over a period of time, are a slow load outlet.

Television is the major component of advertising spending at the major studios, according to data from the MPAA. In 2003, the majors allocated 23.2% of the $34.84 million average marketing expense per film to network television (Fig. 3.6). Spot broadcast television—local ads bought by national advertisers—was the second biggest single category at 15.7%. These two categories together were 39% of ad spending. The majors bought cable television and television syndication advertising as well, but these figures were not broken down by the MPAA.

The indie film arms affiliated with major studios also emphasize network television but not spot broadcast television. In 2003, network television was 20.9% of the studio affiliate ad spending of $12.8 million, with newspaper at 18.6% and spot television at 7.3% (Fig. 3.7). As a rule, the longer a given film lingers in theaters, the more the newspaper category grows as a percentage because of the need to support theater playdates with daily directory advertising.

When determining the size of the advertising launch, film distributors take into account their estimate of a film's likely box office and whether the film faces heavy or light competition from other films when their film premieres. A media buying plan for a given film will be measured against the anticipated ad campaigns of other films being released at or near the same time, particularly those films vying for a similar audience demographic.

When evaluating benefits of ad budgets, distributors often estimate the impact each additional dollar spent on theatrical advertising will have

Figure 3.6 Allocation of Marketing Spend by Major Studios

Year	Newspaper	Network Television	Spot Television	Internet/ Online	Trailers	Other Media*	Other Non-Media**
2003	13.9%	23.2%	15.7%	1.3%	4.4%	21.9%	19.5%
2002	13.5%	23.0%	17.6%	0.9%	4.5%	21.4%	19.1%
2001	13.1%	25.4%	16.9%	1.3%	5.1%	20.2%	17.9%
2000	15.6%	23.8%	18.3%	0.7%	6.4%	18.8%	16.3%
1999	17.6%	23.5%	19.8%	0.5%	7.8%	15.4%	15.5%

*Other Media encompasses cable, network radio, spot radio, magazines, and billboards.
**Other Non-Media encompasses production/creative services, exhibitor services, promotion, publicity, and market research.
Source: Motion Picture Association of America

Figure 3.7 Allocation of Marketing Spend for MPAA-Owned Indies

Year	News-paper	Network Television	Spot Television	Internet/ Online	Trailers	Other Media*	Other Non-Media**
2003	18.6%	20.9%	7.3%	1.6%	4.7%	28.0%	19.0%
2002	22.0%	25.7%	5.6%	0.9%	6.1%	21.1%	18.6%
2001	18.6%	42.8%	3.2%	0.4%	5.2%	9.9%	19.9%
2000	20.5%	36.4%	6.1%	0.5%	5.5%	13.8%	17.3%
1999	23.8%	35.4%	6.8%	0.3%	4.1%	10.5%	19.1%

Note: MPAA indies include Fox Searchlight, New Line, Miramax, and other indie-style film distributors owned by major studios.
*Other Media encompasses cable, network radio, spot radio, magazines, and billboards.
**Other Non-Media encompasses production/creative services, exhibitor services, promotion, publicity, and market research.
Source: Motion Picture Association of America

on revenue that the film returns. Obviously, when the combined forecasted return of film rental revenue from cinema, video, and television is less than the cost of incremental theatrical ad spending, the theatrical campaign has reached the point of diminishing returns. The exercise to calculate return on advertising investment depends on accurate forecasts of box office, video, and television revenue for a given film.

In advertising buys, the top two metropolitan areas—New York City and Los Angeles—tend to get extra weight because the film community resides in those cities. Filmmakers watch how their movies are promoted and judge the weight of the media buy in comparison to other films. Newspapers ads often are larger in these two cities than elsewhere in an effort to impress the film community.

Consumer usage of most media is seasonal. Television viewing rises during the winter in Northern climates (ad rates also go up) because audiences tend to remain indoors due to inclement weather. During the summer in the same Northern climates, people head outside. Out-of-home media such as outdoor billboard advertising becomes more valuable, and television viewership declines.

In the Eastern United States, advertising at mass transit platforms, such as bus shelters and commuter train stations, reach a large audience. Mass transit is less of a factor in the West, where there is an automobile culture. The college campus market also is very seasonal because schools are out during summer vacation and holidays. The availability of the children's audience is impacted by school calendars.

On media pricing, it's important to understand that rates for broadcast media function like an auction. Television and radio outlets have fairly fixed inventory, which means slots for commercials. Any ad slot that is unsold close to airdate usually is discounted to ensure its sale. If the slot remains unsold at broadcast time, the broadcaster gets no revenue whatsoever. Conversely, when buying demand is brisk and few ad slots are vacant, broadcasters jack up ad rates for their scarce unsold commercial inventory.

Given that movie marketers require precise timing—a film premieres on a Friday and the film's opening weekend box office largely determines its ability to hold playdates—they don't have the leeway to shop for discounted commercial slots over a broad time range. Concentrating ads immediately before release is imperative so that films open strongly.

For print media, advertising inventory is very adjustable, so pricing is not as variable as in broadcasting. Print publications simply increase or decrease the page count in a given edition to match the scale of advertising volume. All media usually have extra fees for a premium position, such as being the first in a crowded pod of television commercials. In magazine media, a back page and the page opposite a main feature story are among prized positions.

Conventional wisdom holds that youth-oriented movies such as lowbrow comedies and action films can't be resuscitated after poor opening, so there's reluctance to spend heavily to save this category of struggling film. The youth audience tends to come early or not at all. For more sophisticated movies appealing to adults, mediocre attendance may be shored up with a fresh advertising approach or greater ad spending if a good movie opens poorly. The adult audience is influenced by good reviews and word of mouth, and it tends to be slow to jump on films, unlike the youth demographic.

Buying Mechanics

A formal media plan outlines the cost of ads by medium on a day-by-day basis. Spending by medium usually is presented in weekly subtotals. This spending also is segmented by media—radio, newspaper, magazines, and outdoor are separated. The segments are subdivided into individual media outlets, such as specific television channels.

With most ad dollars in television advertising for mainstream films, the heaviest spending is seven days before premiere and in the first weekend. After a film opens, television spending falls, but ads continue in daily and weekly publications that provide local theater playdate information.

Separate from the calculation of ad spending measuring in dollars, media buyers construct a parallel chronological grid to quantify impressions on audience. Dollar spending across media is comparable, but audience impressions are not. For example, a television commercial is considered more valuable than a newspaper advertisement, which lacks audio and moving video.

An important strategy to increase media weight in selected geographic areas is spot television and radio, which is local advertising purchased by national marketers such as movie companies. For example, if a mainstream movie has special appeal in Texas, a film marketer could opt to increase film bookings in the Lone Star State and support the heavier theater bookings with spot advertising in Dallas, Houston, and other Texas cities. Also, spot buys are made in geographic areas where it is felt national advertising does not effectively reach the target audience, resulting in underdelivery.

Television

Television is the most popular medium with film marketers because television commercials deliver both video and audio, although marketers gripe that the medium is too expensive. Television is broadly divided into network, syndication, and cable.

Television media buys focus on a target audience defined by population age, such as men ages 18–34. With over-the-air broadcasting, spillover into other age groups is considerable because broadcast audiences are diverse. Cable television networks tend to be niche oriented, so their audiences are more demographically concentrated, such as sports-minded viewers for ESPN or women for Lifetime.

Each rating point is 1% of a given population. For example, there are 109 million television households in the United States, so a 1 rating in national households translates to delivery of 1.09 million homes. When a media buy specifies 200 rating points against a specific audience, say women ages 18–34, that means the advertising blitz on average will be seen twice by each woman in the target age. Of course, some women in the target audiences will actually see the commercial three times and others just once, but the average is two impressions per capita.

For broadcast spot television, the United States is divided into 210 markets, or urban areas. Some attractive programs are available only in local ad buys, such as local television news and games of hometown sports teams televised on local television stations.

Spot cable television—usually local slots within national cable networks that individual cable systems get to sell—is more geographically specific than is spot broadcast. Spot cable commercials can be as localized as a single cable system's franchise area, although cable systems typically band together to offer interconnects to give media buyers wider coverage with a single ad buy.

Another alternative for national coverage is syndicated shows on broadcast television stations. These are non-network programs on an *ad hoc* lineup of broadcast channels that have national ads. Syndicated shows selling national ads are televised on broadcast television stations that reach anywhere from 75% to 99% of all television households in the United States. Network programs routinely attain national clearances in the high 90s.

Syndicated programs are the lowest-cost vehicles for national coverage via broadcast television, as measured by CPMs, because syndicated programs price their ad inventories at lower rates than network television. The drawback to syndicated programs is that they pull in small audiences compared to network programs, especially as television stations have cut back on time periods allocated to syndication shows. A notable exception is the women-oriented weekday talk show *The Oprah Winfrey Show,* which averaged 8.7 million viewers in the 2003–2004 season, according to Nielsen Media Research. A 30-second spot on *Oprah* or *Entertainment Tonight,* another highly viewed syndicated program, is $80,000 for a non-repeat episode.

The cheapest national broadcast television buy on a CPM basis is to purchase syndicated television shows, and the lowest rated programs on the Fox and UPN networks.

When placing movie ads, R-rated films are advertised only after 9 p.m. so as not to be seen by significant children's audiences. Late-night talk shows are ideal for R films. For example, CBS's late-night talk show hosted by David Letterman averages 4.4 million viewers. A 30-second commercial on the Letterman show costs about $60,000. On NBC's rival *The Tonight Show with Jay Leno,* an ad is $75,000. Other popular programs for movie ads outside of prime time on broadcast networks are NBC's *Saturday Night Live* at $130,000, *Late Night with Conan O'Brien* at $25,000, and ABC Television's *Jimmy Kimmel Live* at $15,000. These prices are for 30-second commercials in original programs, not repeat episodes.

Although network television commercials are pricey, they deliver big audiences at low CPMs. A 30-second commercial in prime time on a top-rated network costs $150,000 or more. "No matter what we've tried to do as an industry—using the Internet, radio, magazines, and trailers—most people still find out about their movies from television," said Tom Sherak, a partner at Revolution Studios, which is a film supplier to Sony Pictures. National television commercials—encompassing broadcast, cable, and syndication—are the most costly component of movie ad campaigns (Fig. 3.8).

Looking at high-profile events, a 30-second commercial costs on average $200,000–$350,000 for *Monday Night Football,* $1.5 million for the Academy Awards Oscar telecast, and $2.3 million for the pro football championship Super Bowl. The Super Bowl averages a staggering 83–90 million viewers each year. During the 2004 Summer Olympics, NBC sold 30-second commercials for $700,000–$760,000.

Nine pricey movie ads were telecast during the 2004 Super Bowl. The ads were for *The Alamo, Hidalgo, Ladykillers,* and *Miracle* from Disney; *50 First Dates* and *Secret Window* from Sony Pictures; *Van Helsing* from Universal; and *Starsky & Hutch* and *Troy* from Warner Bros.

The movie industry's most prized placement, which is costly, is NBC Television's Thursday night comedy bloc. The sit-coms draw a huge young adult audience (ages 18–34), which is a good fit for movies. Even more useful is that these programs are telecast the night before Friday film premieres. NBC Television extracts top dollar from movie advertisers, partly because the network knows that Thursday night ads are crucial to launch films.

NBC's top Thursday show in the 2003–2004 season—the comedy *Friends*—commanded prices ranging from $325,000–$600,000 for each 30-second spot. In 2003, film distributors spent $51.9 million advertising theatricals on NBC's *Friends,* which averaged 20.5 million viewers according to Nielsen Media Research. Elsewhere, movie ad spending was $38.0 million on Fox's *American Idol,* $28.6 million on NBC's *Today,* $27.2 million on NBC's *Will & Grace,* $26.0 million on CBS's *The Late Show with David Letterman,* $26.0 million on CBS's 2003 Super Bowl, and $25.8 million on NBC's *The Tonight Show with Jay Leno.*

The anchor of NBC's Thursday schedule, *Friends,* went off the air in early 2004, but the network still has a potent lineup. Hospital drama *ER* returned in 2004 after 10 straight seasons as network television's top-rated drama among adults ages 18–49.

"Men are the hardest to find on television," said Palisades Media's Roger Schaffner. "Women generally watch more television, and they are available in daytime and early morning." In the quest for male television viewers, media buyers also have to decide whether to go for low unit price—the cheapest CPM—or larger audiences with a higher CPM. A male audience is cheaper on The History Channel cable network on a

Figure 3.8 Ad Spending Breakdown from Diverse Films, 2003–2004

Movie	Total Spent	Network Television	Television	Spot Radio	Newspapers	National	Outdoor
50 First Dates	$30,123,991	$20,392,342	$4,442,652	$187,822	$4,893,319	$203,981	$3,875
Cold Mountain	$39,989,228	$23,460,251	$7,728,728	$1,053,954	$7,626,701	$119,594	$0
The Day After Tomorrow	$31,570,907	$23,923,360	$3,530,032	$180,483	$3,929,272	$7,760	$0
Dodgeball: A True Underdog Story	$18,231,881	$12,949,020	$3,207,217	$4,577	$2,071,067	$0	$0
Elf	$30,641,792	$21,652,648	$1,038,617	$64,420	$7,872,588	$13,519	$0
Garfield: The Movie	$19,672,381	$14,985,181	$1,568,281	$259,663	$2,744,993	$114,263	$0
Jeepers Creepers 2	$11,000,426	$4,876,608	$3,614,696	$793,427	$1,709,908	$5,787	$0
Kill Bill Vol. 1	$23,429,204	$16,527,158	$3,150,779	$0	$3,748,672	$2,595	$0
Kill Bill Vol. 2	$16,474,373	$9,960,303	$2,785,724	$477,114	$3,144,176	$107,056	$0
Man on Fire	$27,107,587	$19,351,596	$4,105,386	$150,611	$3,492,282	$7,712	$0
Mystic River	$46,476,939	$17,242,438	$9,460,880	$994,899	$18,370,104	$408,618	$0
The Notebook	$19,889,656	$16,024,886	$1,463,878	$9,418	$2,381,303	$10,171	$0
The Passion of the Christ	$24,623,441	$14,389,000	$390,312	$0	$9,776,356	$67,523	$250

Movie						
Pirates of the Caribbean: Curse of the Black Pearl	$32,535,528	$17,171,984	$7,548,735	$138,050	$7,556,014	$120,745	$0
Punisher	$18,802,777	$11,917,742	$4,547,258	$413,577	$1,753,795	$170,405	$0
Scary Movie 3	$22,607,375	$15,318,091	$2,780,985	$720,596	$3,702,178	$85,525	$0
Scooby-Doo 2: Monsters Unleashed	$26,726,310	$16,995,614	$3,674,737	$368,314	$4,621,085	$1,066,560	$0
Seabiscuit	$31,093,822	$17,074,546	$3,692,451	$1,697,772	$7,860,169	$761,584	$7,300
Shrek 2	$34,600,449	$23,329,140	$3,475,216	$0	$7,673,993	$122,100	$0
Spider-Man 2	$28,387,316	$24,059,952	$2,735,261	$0	$1,556,233	$4,345	$31,525
Super Size Me	$760,472	$37,436	$14,100	$0	$669,524	$39,412	$0
Texas Chainsaw Massacre	$16,446,739	$11,487,656	$1,600,972	$366,863	$2,983,337	$7,911	$0
You Got Served	$13,093,234	$7,959,876	$3,155,550	$288,677	$1,675,920	$9,336	$3,875

*Network Television includes broadcast, cable, syndicated, and Spanish-language.

Note: Ad spend figures from June 1, 2003–June 30, 2004; movies are listed alphabetically.

Source: Nielsen Monitor-Plus

CPM basis than on ESPN, but the latter sports channel has bigger total audiences. In another travail in chasing male viewers, network television suffered an abrupt 8% loss of the young adult male audience in early 2003, which some interpreted as reflecting a drain to Internet surfing and video game playing.

Men are more costly to reach than women in terms of efficiency of advertising spending. According to Media Dynamics, the average CPM for men ages 18+ was $22.55 on network television in 2003 and $18.10 for women ages 18+. The average CPM in spot broadcast television was $30.80 for men ages 18+ in 2003 and $24.31 for women 18+. Because most of box office comes from the top 15 metropolitan areas in the United States, film marketers tend to use spot buys in those cities, which range from New York City down to Cleveland–Akron.

Broadcast network advertising is sold on a long-lead basis during May–July in the upfront market, which is a selling period before the television season starts in mid to late September. Once the season is under way, ad selling continues in what is referred to as the scatter market. About 60% of broadcast network advertising is purchased in the upfront market and 35% in the scatter market. A small slice of television advertising—less than 5%—is heavily discounted if it remains unsold days before airdate; purchasing of such commercials is called opportunistic buying. These commercials are sold in such a hurry they typically can't be included in an advertiser's formal media plan.

Commercials bought in the scatter market usually are 10–15% more expensive than similar ads bought in the upfront market. Unfortunately, movie marketers often are forced into the higher price scatter market because premiere dates of films are uncertain or subject to change.

The broadcast networks promise minimum levels of target audience delivery for ads purchased in the long-lead upfront market, which are called guarantees, but not for ads in the scatter market. Cable networks and syndicated programs make audience guarantees for most of their commercials. Nielsen Media Research conducts independent measurement of television audiences and thus provides data on actual audience delivered. Television outlets make up any shortfall with make-good ads, which are additional commercials. Media buying agencies compile post-buy analysis reports to measure whether audience target goals were met and to determine if broadcasters should provide free ads when a guaranteed audience level was not delivered.

For movie marketers, cable television networks are attractive because their thematic focus delivers demographically concentrated audiences. For example, Nickelodeon attracts kids, sports channels corral males, and news channels are a magnet for high-income and literate adults. However, cable networks have patchy coverage; cable television penetration in the United States is about 68% of all television households. Multichannel, which adds in burgeoning satellite television, lifts the penetration rate to about 84%. Multichannel is television delivered by any means outside of regular broadcasting, thus encompassing cable, satellite, wireless microwave, and high-speed connections.

Cable channels are not carried by all multichannel platforms, or they may be on extra-charge tiers not taken by all subscribers. At the high end, the Discovery channel is seen in 82% of all United States television households and ESPN in 81.5%. In the middle, Bravo has 70% coverage and Hallmark 54%. At the lower end of the scale, The Outdoor Channel is in 24% of television households and VH1 Country is in 13%.

Radio

The United States has about 10,000 radio stations, of which two thirds are part of some radio network, meaning advertisers can buy both national network and local-focused national spot commercials. Radio stations have highly targeted programming, such as album-oriented rock or talk shows, so their audiences tend to be highly concentrated in specific demographics.

To be effective in pitching movies, radio is a platform that needs commercials designed specifically for the medium and not simply audio tracks lifted from television commercials. Radio does have a unique attribute in that on-air talent sometimes reads commercials, which marketers say is impactful because of implied endorsement from the reader. For example, controversial shock jock Howard Stern will do such "live reads" for films that he likes.

Radio is a depressed medium in which pricing is weakening, which is good news for ad buyers. Radio is coming out of a boom time, during which it increased amounts of airtime devoted to commercials. Radio averages 15 minutes of commercials each hour, with up to 22 minutes in peak listening drive time, versus a 12.5-minute ad load per hour for television. Radio's creeping advertising clutter irked advertisers, and the 2000 dot-com recession dried up ad spending.

Media Buys/Newspapers

Daily newspapers are mostly local in geographic coverage and thus are the prime platform for listing theater playdates and showtimes for specific films, in what is called directory advertising. Two dailies are national: *USA Today* and *The Wall Street Journal.*

A newspaper ad campaign often starts the Sunday before a given film's Friday theatrical opening. In some cases, an upcoming movie is advertised on two consecutive Sundays before the film's release. Sunday entertainment sections are the largest of the week and often are kept for reference by readers until the following Sunday. Prestige films appealing to sophisticated adult audiences are the best prospects for prerelease Sunday ads because the literate adult audience is an avid reader of newspapers.

Daily newspapers in Los Angeles and, to a lesser extent, New York City are lavished with movie spending. The reason is that film distributors try to impress the filmmakers who made their movies and the hometown film industry in general with the extent of their advertising. In an example of mass advertising targeting a business community, Disney and Walden Media placed a two-page, four-color ad in a March 2004 edition of *The Wall Street Journal* to announce their collaboration on *Chronicles of Narnia: The Lion, the Witch and the Wardrobe,* which is a family film scheduled for theatrical release 20 months later.

Many film distributors badmouth newspaper advertising, dismissing it as simply a directory medium that is useful only for providing information about theaters and screening times. In their line of thinking, by the time a moviegoer thumbs through a newspaper to get playdate information, the moviegoer has already decided which film to see, having been influenced by television advertising and trailers.

Not surprisingly, newspapers disagree, saying their entertainment sections are vital to persuading moviegoers because advertising runs next to lots of movie editorial matter. That's not the case for movie ads in most other media. "No studio has ever called us and told us to stop writing about movies because newspapers are not important," said Burt Levy, director of major accounts and motion picture advertising for the *Chicago Sun-Times.* "When it comes to writing and promoting movies, we're the most important medium." The lead film critic at the *Sun-Times* is the nation's most well-known, Roger Ebert, who is the only journalist to have won the Pulitzer Prize for film commentary.

Still, by all accounts film distributors are trimming newspaper advertising. There are fewer or smaller preopening Sunday advertisements and day-before-opening ads on Thursdays (for Friday premieres). Also, film distributors have cut newspaper advertising in smaller cities from the 125th metro area and lower, leaving the purchase of directory ads to local theaters. Most newspaper advertising in big cities is co-op (cooperative), with film distributors paying most of the cost and theaters chipping in. The trend is for film distributors to reduce their co-op obligations.

In other ways, film distributors are maintaining advertising in newspapers. Prestige films still get splashy quote ads when film critics heap praise. Distributors run unusual, eye-catching ads in newspapers more now than in the past. An example is characters from the same movie facing each other from different ads on the same page spread. "We're seeing some unique positioning and more creative use of newspapers," said Scott Carman, senior vice president of MovieMarketPlace, a consultant in movie newspaper advertising. "That will continue to be a boon to newspapers because they are a strong target marketing vehicle when used that way."

In general, newspapers are battling to hold their place in the media world as their aggregate penetration is steadily shrinking, falling to 55% of United States households in 2002. Newspapers face competition for directory advertising from Internet Web sites, which in the past few years have presented localized movie playdate information. However, newspapers are making gains with big new multiplex theaters that advertise to build a profile. "With individual exhibitors, there is a demand for branding," said Joanne Smith, major accounts/entertainment at *St. Paul Pioneer Press* in Minnesota.

Newspapers are the front line in the occasional battles over racy film advertising. Children can potentially read every page of a newspaper. In contrast, broadcast media doesn't have that problem because it can segregate films with restrictive audience classifications to late-night television.

Films with restricted ratings or with no rating at all want newspaper ads to promote local playdates, and this desire sometimes results in friction. For example, in 2001, newspapers balked at suggestive ads for the unrated *The Center of the World,* distributed by Artisan Entertainment, which now is part of Lions Gate Entertainment. The ad pictured a naked woman with a lollipop in her open mouth and just one leg crossed over her crotch. The copy line was "Warning. Sex. Come closer. Enter." Some newspapers let the text run without graphics, while others rejected the text but let more subdued art run, according to *Variety*.

The newspaper sector is more than just the high-profile dailies in city-center metropolitan areas. Cities have suburban dailies and weeklies that saturate portions of a metropolitan area. An assortment of weekly newspapers focus on entertainment, and the alternative press typically cover the arts, society, and politics. Other weeklies target specialized audiences, such as ethnic and religious groups. Ad rates for pages range from hundreds of dollars to $500,000 for the national daily *USA Today.*

At standard rates, a black-and-white full-page ad costs $132,678 in the *New York Times,* whose weekday circulation is 1.13 million, and a Sunday black-and-white page is $148,680 with 1.68 million Sunday circulation. Elsewhere in New York, the *Daily News* charges $51,730 for a daily black-and-white page, with weekday circulation of 747,051, and $64,321 for a Sunday page, with 802,103 circulation. At the *Los Angeles Daily News,* a suburban newspaper, the rate is $64,638 for a black-and-white daily page, with weekday circulation of 522,077. In other examples of a standard black-and-white daily page rate, the *Houston Chronicle* charges $83,286 (549,299 circulation), the *Atlanta Journal-Constitution* $64,060 (447,067 circulation), and the *St. Louis Post-Dispatch* $62,548 (281,198 circulation). These figures are from SRDS Newspaper Advertising Source® in August 2004.

Finally, looking at the cost per black-and-white column inch for Sunday, the *New York Times* is $1,180 (1.68 million Sunday circulation), the *Los Angeles Times* $1,050 (1.39 million circulation), the *Houston Chronicle* $778 (740,005 circulation), the *St. Louis Post-Dispatch* $685.47 (454,998 circulation), and the *Atlanta Journal-Constitution* $649.15 (629,505 circulation). The column inch is a metric for small ads used by independents and for films in narrow release. All the figures come from SRDS Newspaper Advertising Source® in August 2004.

One peculiarity of the movie business is that regional advertising agencies handle newspaper advertising for multiple film distributors. This results from overlap between film distributors and theaters, which makes centralization imperative in larger cities with numerous theaters. A multiplex theater books films from multiple distributors.

The two biggest ad placement agencies handling the biggest cities are Allied Advertising of Boston, Massachusetts, and Terry Hines & Associates of Burbank, California. Allied is the primary national newspaper agency for Twentieth Century Fox and Paramount. Terry Hines handles DreamWorks, Metro-Goldwyn-Mayer, Universal, and Warner Bros. Mainstream ad agency McCann Erickson handles newspaper ads for Sony Pictures. Various other ad agencies specializing in placing ads in newspapers tend to dominate various big cities outside the top 10 markets. For example, Grube-Guggenheim Advertising, with its affiliates, places movie ads in Houston, Kansas City, and New Orleans.

Magazines

The magazine category is segmented by the frequency of publications, ranging from the monthlies to the weeklies. Although magazines are a small part of movie advertising, magazine audiences are appealing because specialized publications deliver readerships that are tightly focused by demographic. For example, there are four national gay magazines, 23 pet magazines, and 53 magazines devoted to parenting. For a movie ad to make an impact, it should be designed for use in magazines and not simply be creative material really intended for newspapers.

The top magazines ranked by theatrical movie advertising revenue in 2003 are *People* ($2.4 million), *Time* ($2.0 million), *Entertainment Weekly* ($1.9 million), and *Newsweek* ($1.4 million), according to Nielsen Monitor-Plus.

Magazine ad rates are based mostly on circulation, both subscription and single sale on newsstands. These are estimates of readership, as numerous persons can read the same magazine. Media buyers affix the highest value to readers within the household for which the magazine was purchased, figuring these individuals will scrutinize the magazine closely, and less value to pass-along readers outside the primary household. As a selling point for ads, the magazine industry says consumers are very engaged in the medium because reading articles takes concentration; magazine marketers argue that consumers devote less attention to other media.

Out-of-Home Media

Advertising platforms outside the home are part of the movie advertising mix, although these platforms usually are slow load media in which audience impressions are made over long periods of time.

The out-of-home category includes big outdoor billboards, mass transit ads, in-store ads, and some oddities such as banner pulls, in which airplanes tow airborne signs above crowds at sporting events and crowded beaches. Mass transit ads include the exteriors of buses, interiors of buses and commuter trains, and signage at bus/train stops. Another out-of-home platform is billboards or television monitors in public places, such as waiting lines at airports and supermarkets.

Warner Bros. was the seventh biggest outdoor billboard advertiser in 2003, Walt Disney 13th, and Sony Pictures 18th, according to the Outdoor Advertising Association of America. Outdoor billboards are effective in reaching an urban in-city audience because this population is geographically concentrated.

Outdoor billboards are sold based on their audience exposure, called showings, in a specified time frame, which are the equivalent of rating points in television. A billboard with a 100-showings audience would be seen by the equivalent of the entire population in its market.

Film companies and Hollywood talent are fond of placing billboard ads on the West Side of Los Angeles, the heart of the movie business, to "speak" to the movie industry. This generates a buzz within the film community. The prime locations are the Hollywood–Beverly Hills–Santa Monica area. These Los Angeles billboards cost $10,000–$50,000 per month. On the Sunset Strip, a slice of this area, the prices range from $30,000–$40,000 per month.

In 2001, Sony Pictures placed an outdoor billboard in New York City and Los Angeles for action film *XXX* a year before the film opened in order to start a buzz for the action film. In August 2004, director Vincent Gallo made a bid for attention with a billboard ad in West Los Angeles in which actress Chloe Sevigny, star of his film *The Brown Bunny,* appears to be engaging in a sexual act with him. Protests resulted in the ad being taken down. The movie, about a motorcycle racer's search for true love, is distributed by Wellspring Media.

Media Buy/Interactive

The Internet is finally shaping up as a significant advertising platform, as moviegoers increasingly surf the Web with high-speed connections. Internet sites offer banner ads, which are billboards incorporated into the Web site, and pop-up ads, although many surfers now have automatic blockers.

Web sites can be entirely film specific or entertainment specific, or sections of a high-traffic Web site may have limited content devoted to entertainment (see Chapter 6). At the top of the film heap, Yahoo! Movies gets 10 million unduplicated visitors each month. Telephone and Web site movie directory services, which sell audio ads, are part of this category (see Chapter 8).

Of course, not all the ads go on movie Web sites. Nonmovie Web sites and pages that relate to a film's theme, such as animals, politics, or automobiles, reach very specific audiences that a film targets.

A July 2004 FTC report on film industry advertising noted that three distributors advertised R-rated films on Web sites with substantial youth audiences, which is an inappropriate audience given the film classification. The Web sites were *gamespy.com* (36% youth audience), *IGN.com* (40%), *MTV.com* (38%), *ugo.com* (44%), and *teenpeople.com* (53%).

History of Media Buying

Starting in the late 1950s, independent distributors innovated with the first saturation advertising campaigns that broke ground for the modern era.

Independents concentrated theater bookings in one city at a time and supported each opening with heavy spot television advertising. After an independent film played out in one city, its release prints were moved to another city that would get the same saturation treatment, until a film eventually covered the entire country. The independent pioneers included producer/distributor Joseph E. Levine, who released dubbed voice-track Italian import *Hercules* in 1959, the first of a string of "sword and sandal" period epics that were a foundation of Avco Embassy Pictures. Another notable indie distributor of the era noted for saturation television advertising was Sunn Classic Pictures, which released family films such as *The Life and Times of Grizzly Adams* in 1977.

In this era, the major studios did not embrace costly television advertising because their films did not saturate a city but instead played off gradually. Major studio films would open initially in the flagship theaters in a city's downtown area. After ending downtown runs, film prints would move to successive waves of second-run theaters in the same city. As a consequence, the major studios concentrated advertising in newspapers.

By the late 1960s, television programs were draining audiences away from cinemas, and the business model of the major studios no longer worked. To revive their business, the majors began adopting strategies used by independents, particularly wider distribution of films supported by television advertising campaigns. By the late 1970s, distributors such as Warner Bros. paid $4.2 million for television advertising for *Superman*, yet majors were still outspent by indie distributors such as Pacific International, which pumped $4.6 million in spot television to support *The Late Great Planet Earth*.

It's ironic how the tables have so completely turned. Today, the majors are the masters of the saturation booking/advertising strategy, with vast openings in thousands of theaters simultaneously. The independents now are marginalized into narrow advertising because it's no longer economically feasible to mount saturation regional rollouts. No film distributor can tie up a film in a succession of regional rollouts because that process would delay lucrative video release. Thus, independents are forced to distribute films nationally, where they are unable to achieve the mass scale of the deep-pocket majors.

A survey by the MPAA indicated that the major studios spent 68% of their advertising on print media (newspapers and magazines) in 1989. These days, print media spending by major studios is about 18%.

4 Promotional Tie-ins/ Product Placement

Ever since Clark Gable took off his shirt in It Happened One Night *and sales of men's undershirts plummeted, popular-culture entertainment has proven its ability to sell products and services, and to transform brands.*

Steven J. Heyer, Beverage Industry Executive

With Hollywood's major studios spending billions of dollars annually on release prints and advertising in the United States and Canada, there's pressure to enlist third parties to help carry the marketing load. Thus, film distributors turn to tie-in promotions, which are cross-marketing deals with consumer goods companies. In exchange, the consumer goods outfits get to associate their products with films, hoping that a little Hollywood magic will rub off.

Another type of promotion is the product placement, in which brand-name items are visible in the films themselves. Companies whose products are identifiable in films may provide some form of compensation, whether tie-in promotion support (promoting a movie in their own advertising), cash payments, and/or lots of free product to the film production.

The tie-in promotion and product placement fields are becoming increasingly sophisticated, as movie marketers and their consumer goods partners expand the scope of their alliances. One budding trend is for such alliances to continue beyond just theatrical release. The association of a consumer goods outfit with a film might continue to the downstream release windows of home video and television.

The involvement of consumer goods marketers can be striking. The DreamWorks romantic comedy *The Terminal* starring Tom Hanks is loaded with 40 stores in product placements for its centerpiece airport set. Retail outlets Burger King, Starbucks, the Discovery Store, Borders, Verizon Wireless, Auntie Anne's Pretzels, Swatch, and Godiva Chocolatier are highly visible in the film. Each company was responsible for building its own store—at an estimated cost of tens of thousands of dollars each—saving DreamWorks on set construction costs.

In addition, United Airlines, US Air, Air Canada, Asiana, All Nippon, and Star Alliance are seen in *The Terminal*. Actress Catherine Zeta-Jones portrays a uniformed United Airlines flight attendant who becomes romantically involved with the Hanks character.

In 2004, tie-in promotions experienced a downturn. Mass marketers channeled big chunks of their advertising budgets to costly summer Olympics tie-ins, which reduced marketing spending that was available for movies. Also, television programs are increasingly soaking up entertainment promotion tie-in money. For example, beverage giant Coca-Cola reportedly paid a $20 million fee to tie up with reality show *American Idol*, getting drink cups with its red logo placed on the desks of judges. Advertisers pay about $475,000 for a regular 30-second commercial in the show. Elsewhere, ABC Television carried a Pepsi Play for a Billion sweepstakes in Spring 2004.

Tie-in Overview

Film marketing executives at distribution companies are fond of saying that they've never met a movie producer who didn't want promotional tie-ins with consumer goods companies. The advertising firepower and reach in the marketplace of fast food restaurants, carmakers, national store chains, and mobile phone outfits are welcome support for theatrical release.

Consumer goods companies provide millions of dollars, and in some cases tens of millions of dollars, in advertising that simultaneously promotes their products and the movie. Tie-in partners seek a halo effect from a movie for their consumer goods or services (Fig. 4.1). Combining car, liquor, apparel, and other categories can marshal upward of $100 million in tie-in advertising support on a worldwide basis for big films such as the James Bond spy thrillers.

Figure 4.1 Partners by Industry Involved in Entertainment Marketing Programs

Rank	Category	Percentage
1	Fast food	22.0%
2	Retailers*	15.8%
3	Online services	9.7%
4	Soft drinks/water	6.1%
5	Packaged foods	6.1%
6	Beer/wine/spirits	5.5%
7	Consumer electronics	5.0%
8	Candy/snack foods	4.6%
9	Auto manufacturers	4.1%
10	Magazines**	3.5%
11	Apparel/footwear	3.5%
12	Health/beauty aids	3.5%
13	Games/toys	2.8%
14	Phone services	2.6%
15	Consumer goods***	1.9%
16	Associations	1.9%
17	Sports leagues/teams	1.9%
18	Hotels/motels	1.7%
19	Airlines	1.5%
20	Book publishers	1.1%
21	Credit cards	1.1%
22	Car rentals	<1.0%
23	Photo supply/services	<1.0%
24	Travel/tourism	<1.0%
25	Health care	<1.0%

Note: Percentage surpasses 100% because of multiple tie-in partners.
*Retailers include mass merchants, department stores, video chains.
**Magazines include comic books.
***Consumer Goods is a catch-all for everything from luggage to soap to watches to petroleum products.
Source: Entertainment Marketing Letter. © 2002 EPM Communications, Inc.; www.epm-com.com

In contrast, in 2003 Hollywood's major studios spent an average of $34.8 million of their own money on advertising and related marketing per film in the United States, according to the Motion Picture Association of America. There is a crucial distinction between advertising directly by the film distributor and ads of promotional partners. Film distributor ad campaigns present a creative message that is fully focused on the movie, unlike tie-in support where the movie message piggybacks on the consumer goods ads and mostly builds awareness for a movie.

Movie distributors require that tie-in ads arrive in the marketplace concurrent with theatrical release. Consumer goods outfits bicker over the quantity of consumer advertising/promotion they deliver and the extent to which the movie is pitched in those efforts. The consumer goods companies also negotiate for specified access to movie logo, footage, sounds, music, and, in some cases, actors for use in consumer goods ads.

"The emphasis right now is on finding ways to use technology to help in the ongoing battle of proving return-on-investment in promotional marketing," says Susan Nunziata, executive editor of the newsletter *Entertainment Marketing Letter*, which is published by EPM Communications in New York City. "Sweepstakes are one way to track consumer response, since you can show entry rates. Couponing is another. Also gaining popularity are things like free music downloads, LidRock CDs, and other types of CD/DVD premiums that direct consumers to put the discs into their computers, where they can access websites that give discounts, the chance to enter contests, opt-in for follow-up contact from the company, and numerous other features. The web connection enables the marketers to track usage and opt-in rates, gauge intent to purchase, and create a one-on-one dialog with a motivated consumer." LidRock provides CDs containing entertainment for marketers via lids on soft drink cups.

Consumer goods outfits plug movies in numerous ways, from sweepstakes to partnerships with media such as newspapers (Fig. 4.2).

A key issue for tie-ins is that a movie's audience matches the consumer base of the partner goods companies. It's an obvious point, yet occasionally there is a disconnect. For example, in 1998 when DreamWorks's *Small Soldiers* received a PG-13 rating instead of the anticipated PG rating, Burger King hurriedly revamped its tie-in promotion campaign so as not to target children, which would have been inappropriate given the film's classification.

To reach the all-important youth market, the top categories for movie-related promotions tend to be fast food restaurants (called QSRs, for quick service restaurants in the marketing vernacular), snack foods, and breakfast cereals. Automobiles and liquor are the big categories for movie tie-ins for the adult demographic. Soft drink beverages and mass merchants (such as Wal-Mart) are important categories straddling both the youth and adult demographics.

On the local level, radio stations are popular tie-in promotion partners for what are single-city efforts. Film distributors align their movies with radio outlets whose audiences are a good fit, arranging for private

Figure 4.2 Top Promotions in Entertainment Marketing Campaigns

Rank	Technique	Percentage
1	Cross-promotions	46.2%
2	Sponsorships	19.4%
3	Sweepstakes/contests	16.0%
4	Premiums	14.3%
5	Tour	14.0%
6	Direct mail	9.4%
7	Discount	7.9%
8	Cross-merchandising	6.0%
9	Licensed property	6.0%
10	Product placement	5.0%
11	Sampling	4.6%
12	Exclusivity	4.0%
13	Interactive	3.7%
14	Media partnership	3.3%
15	Rebate	2.0%
16	Street marketing	2.0%

Note: Results from all types of entertainment marketing programs, not just movies. Percentage adds up to over 100% because of multiple types of promotions used in each campaign.
Source: Entertainment Marketing Letter. © 2002 EPM Communications, Inc.; www.epm-com.com

screenings for a film prior to its general release. The radio stations give away screening tickets via on-air plugs for the film. Typically, the distributor arranges one screening, which costs roughly $5,000 per city for theater rental. Any multiple screenings are held back to back on the same day to reduce expenses.

Besides mass media, film marketers also are pushing into unconventional media platforms. Twentieth Century Fox arranged to promote its movies at shopping malls operated by General Growth, in what is an umbrella deal covering multiple movies. The studio's promotions will reach moviegoers in an out-of-home environment, and Twentieth Century Fox is the exclusive movie marketer at 125 of General Growth's malls.

The most sought after tie-ins are with family films, typically rated G (all ages) or PG (some content may not be suitable for children) on the five-point movie classification scale. The consumer goods partners are particularly sensitive that their movie tie-in ad campaigns don't push R or PG-13 movies to youngsters, after a 2000 report by the regulatory agency the Federal Trade Commission criticizing film distributors for doing so.

Consumer goods companies also like films that are sequels because their reception in the marketplace is easier to predict than original films. However, for film distributors, sequels probably are the least needy for promotional lifts because they are extensions of their well-known predecessor films.

Talent in Tie-in Promotions

A frequent sticking point in tie-in promotions is whether star talent will allow use of their likeness, which cements the connection in the public's mind between consumer goods and a movie. Animated movies are easier to work with than live action, given that actors only are involved to the extent of voicing.

Often, movie stars decline or seek extra compensation on the grounds that lending their names, likenesses, or voices is making an implied endorsement to a consumer goods product. Consumer goods marketers typically refuse to pay movie talent for participating in their movie promotions because the companies maintain they are already shelling out ad support (and possibly goods and services) for the movie itself.

Consumer goods outfits view working with actors as particularly sticky. In addition to their business representatives, stars often involve their personal hairstylists and wardrobe advisers, who can object to carefully laid plans for promotions simply on aesthetic grounds. When talent refuses to lend itself to a promotion, the consumer goods partner is left with using movie logos, props, and backdrops to communicate its association with a film.

For example, *Spider-Man* star Tobey Maguire doesn't allow his likeness to be seen in promotions of the Columbia Pictures release, so his character wears a mask or is pictured from the rear in materials of tie-in partners. However, co-star Kirsten Dunst is identifiable. Kevin Costner's refusal to allow his likeness to be used by Ralston Purina disrupted a big cereal promotion tied to *Robin Hood: Prince of Thieves* released by Warner Bros. in 1991.

There are other instances of stars lending their image to tie-in partners. Both John Travolta and Halle Berry let Heineken beer use their likenesses in a reported $10 million ad campaign supporting *Swordfish*, the Warner Bros. thriller from 2001.

For years, Arnold Schwarzenegger has been at the top of the list of promotion-minded actors, and his marketing savvy is credited with helping him become elected as the governor of California. "He really understands marketing and learned how to use it to the benefit of the movie and himself," recalls former entertainment journalist Anita Busch, the first reporter to cover entertainment marketing on a daily basis for the Hollywood trade papers. "He would spend the time to sit down with the merchandising and the licensing people involved to learn everything. He was a quick study." Schwarzenegger courted the press, granted likeness rights for promotions, worked with the film marketing team on implementation of merchandising, and even checked media buying strategies.

Tie-ins for Restricted Audience Films

Arranging tie-in promotions becomes more difficult as film ratings become more restrictive, such as PG-13 and R, because marketing to a children's audience would be inappropriate. Still, tie-in avenues are available for restricted films.

Warner Bros. lined up an estimated tens of millions of dollars of promotional support from Samsung for *The Matrix: Reloaded*, which was released in May 2003. The electronics firm received product placement for its cell phones in the R-rated film. Also, the PowerAde beverage contributed more than $10 million in promotional support for a tie-in for a *Matrix* film.

For the vampire action adventure film *Van Helsing*, the West Coast fast food restaurant chain Carl's Jr., which includes the Hardee's, La Salsa, and Green Burrito restaurant chains, signed up as a promotional partner with the film's distributor Universal Pictures. *Van Helsing* was not a family-friendly movie given its horror genre and PG-13 rating, although it did gross $120 million after its May 2004 release in the domestic (United States and Canada) market. The Carl's Jr. chain, with 3,200 restaurants worldwide, mounted regional blood drives in partnership with the American Red Cross, which was a cheeky association that played off blood-sucking vampires in the film. Star Hugh Jackman appeared in public service ads (PSAs) for the promotion. Carl's Jr. also offered 44-ounce collector cups and mint tins. Elsewhere, science fiction films, which on the surface can be too sophisticated for a children's audience, can work as movie tie-in promotions with giveaway plastic action figures of unusual characters.

For another seemingly tough-sell movie, Warner Bros. corralled up-market brands Diamond Trading Co. (De Beers Group), the 700-store Kay Jewelers, Kahlua (spirits brand from Allied Domecq), and Jaguar for its July 2004 release of *Catwoman*. In the PG-13 movie, the Catwoman character portrayed by Halle Berry puts a diamond ring on her right hand, which plays into the Diamond Trading ad campaign suggesting that single women wear rings in such a manner. The advertising tag line in the Diamond Trading ad is, "Your left hand says 'we.' Your right hand says 'me.' " Jaguar, which is the Ford luxury car brand, incorporated *Catwoman* footage in its television commercials. The film's theatrical release also had tie-ins with mainstream consumer product outfits Coca-Cola and imaging giant Eastman Kodak. Interestingly, star Berry is a presenter in Revlon advertising, although the cosmetics outfit is not part of the movie's promotional partners. Despite the promotions, *Catwoman* flopped at the box office.

An innovative tie-in with the 750-store Best Buy electronics stores is credited with making *Hellboy* a modest hit for Columbia Pictures and producer Revolution Studios. Some 500,000 promotional DVDs showcased the fantasy horror movie with film clips and talent interviews. *Hellboy*, rated PG-13, cost an estimated $66 million to make and generated a healthy $59 million in domestic box office after its April 2004 release. The DVD presents the romance, fantasy, action, special effects, and character pathos for 10 minutes and 25 seconds. The film's director, three actors, and creator of the comic book on which the film is based provided on-screen commentary.

A relatively new avenue for promoting films is delivering trailers to video players in homes. Personal video recorder outfit TiVo sends film trailers and other promotional materials via the Internet to its installed base of users for Twentieth Century Fox and other movie distributors. TiVo provides service to about 1.6 million TV households and is a relatively new medium, having started its service in 1999.

Film marketing executives are relentless in searching for new ways to promote what is the century-old medium of the motion picture. Blazing trails enhances personal reputations and career advancement for film marketing executives. Some innovations may stretch too far.

Columbia Pictures pushed the marketing envelope by convincing Major League Baseball to place *Spider-Man 2* logos on the bases and in the on-deck circles of 15 Major League parks over the weekend of June 11–13, 2004. Fans mounted an outcry that this went too far in commercializing the national pastime, so the placement of movie logos on the playing field was quickly abandoned. Other parts of the *Spider-Man* promotion with baseball did go forward. Reportedly, the baseball promotion would have cost the studio $3–$4 million as originally conceived, with chunks of the money going to the participating baseball teams.

Restaurant and Automaker Tie-ins

The up-and-down nature of the film business is cooling enthusiasm by restaurant chains, which are more cautious than a few years ago about putting their weight behind tie-in promotions.

The mighty McDonald's chain, which has exclusivity for Disney animated movies under a long-term tie-in deal, now says it wants to engage in fewer movie tie-in involvements, asserting they don't sufficiently build up the restaurant chain's image. "We no longer ask for stand-alone event or game or a licensed character tie-in just for the sake of having it," Dean Barrett, senior vice president of worldwide marketing at McDonald's, told the Promotion Marketing Association in May 2004. "When we market entertainment, we send mixed messages everywhere while our brand goes nowhere." McDonald's says that, in the future, it wants broader range of partners to include fashion, music, and sports, as well as movies.

With 13,609 restaurants in the United States and another 1,339 in Canada, McDonald's is a potent movie marketing partner whose exclusivity to Disney movies runs through 2007 via a 10-year pact. Under the deal, the restaurant giant reportedly has paid Disney $100 million in royalties since 1996 and has given tens of millions of dollars in movie tie-in ad support to Disney films. The McDonald's tie-in includes theme parks, television programs, home video releases, and theatrical releases.

McDonald's entered into the exclusive deal when Disney movies basked in the euphoria after the studio's 1994 animated release *The Lion King* proved to be a blockbuster at the box office and in promotions. McDonald's wanted to prevent Disney films from aligning with rival Burger King, which was the tie-in partner for *The Lion King* and Disney's *Toy Story*. Since McDonald's entered into the exclusive pact in 1996, Disney's animated films have experienced uneven performance. This includes 2002 flop *Treasure Planet*, with just $38 million in domestic box office, and 2001's *Atlantis: The Lost Empire*, with a moderate $84 million in domestic box office.

Although restaurant chains are more selective these days, given that some tie-in promotions underperformed in relation to expectations, they still are a significant force. Hollywood's other animation powerhouse, DreamWorks, maintains its ties to Burger King, whose 7,904 restaurants in the United States and 357 in Canada are a platform for movie promotions under a multipicture deal dating back to 2001. For DreamWorks's animated family film *Shark Tale* released in October 2004, Burger King gave away 10 different movie toy items over a 5-week period to support the film. Other *Shark Tale* tie-ins are in place with Coca-Cola for its flagship

Minute Maid and Hi-C brands, Pillsbury, Betty Crocker, Hewlett-Packard, and Krispy Kreme. Other large fast food chains, such as Wendy's (with 5,761 outlets), KFC, Subway, and Taco Bell, have not been particularly active in movie promotions, which is an indication of a cooling by retailers this decade from the peak in the late 1990s.

The automobile category is particularly lucrative because it is a huge business with commensurate ad and promotion spending. Car tie-ins are infrequent and are limited to adults, but when they are done they can be promotional gushers.

Ford reportedly provided $30 million in promotion support for MGM's James Bond spy film *Die Another Day;* Mitsubishi laid out $25 million in advertising to link to *2 Fast 2 Furious* from Universal Pictures; Jeep spent an estimated $10 million promoting *Tomb Raider: The Cradle of Life* from Paramount Pictures, including sponsored theater stand displays in cinemas; and Mazda spent $8 million on ads promoting *X2* from Twentieth Century Fox. The James Bond films distributed by MGM seem to perpetually change their commercial affiliations. Prior to the Ford link with 2002's *Die Another Day*, the James Bond film franchise agreed to a product placement for the then-new BMW Z3 roadster for the 1995 release of *GoldenEye*. BMW contributed an estimated $25 million in promotional support for that James Bond film.

For Twentieth Century Fox's July 2004 release *I, Robot*, German carmaker Audi adapted a futuristic concept car for use in the movie that was seen in Fox advertising for the film's opening. In the movie, actor Will Smith, who portrays a homicide detective, drives the silver Audi with butterfly doors around Chicago in the year 2035. The carmaker's corporate logo of interlocking rings is visible in a film trailer and in the movie on the steering wheel. Audi also displayed the vehicle at automobile shows, giving the movie another promotional boost. In most cases, car companies provide vehicles for use in filming, which alone can reduce production costs by hundreds of thousands of dollars.

Cell Phone and Other Tie-ins

The mobile phone business is a promotional partner category that currently takes a back seat to cars, beverages, and restaurants in the United States, but it is expected to grow in importance. Mobile phone service providers are pushing enhanced services, so they're expected to eventually deliver film clips and other entertainment content to new-generation video phones. This already occurs in Japan and South Korea.

"It seems that every six months, there's a major evolution," said Jeffrey Godsick, executive vice president of marketing at Twentieth Century Fox. "Wireless (cell phone) is now incredibly important to us, where just two years ago it wasn't." Wireless phones can receive text messages, and newer models can play back video downloads of film trailers.

Outside the United States, movie distributors mount some of their biggest tie-in promotions with cell phone companies in Asia and Europe. In those regions, teenagers and young adults are addicted to wireless phones because fixed-line service is poor. Another reason mobile phone tie-ins are bigger overseas than in the United States is that one or two service providers tend to dominate each foreign territory, making it easy to arrange for national coverage. "To cover the entire United States, you'd have to strike deals with the half dozen major service providers and this is tricky because they all want exclusivity," says *Entertainment Marketing Letter*'s Susan Nunziata.

In the United States, mobile phone partnerships with television programs are favored over partnerships with movies because the weekly frequency of television programs is ideally suited for interaction with mobile phones. They can be used for fan voting each week, as is the case for *American Idol*. Film marketers still are making inroads as Samsung did big product placement and promotional tie-ins with the second and third installment of the *Matrix* sci-fi films.

Among the major studios, Columbia is particularly active in mounting mobile phone promotions given that it has a large digital media division attached to the studio. Its parent company is directly in the cell phone business via the Sony Ericsson joint venture that manufactures handsets. However, service providers tend to be the preferred promotional partners for movie distributors because they are the conduits for daily phone service, whereas handset makers tend not to interact much with customers after the initial purchase of mobile equipment. In some cases, though, a tie-in with a handset manufacturer can give a movie marketer the added clout needed to attract a service provider, because most handset makers are aligned with one or two specific telephone service providers.

Theater circuits overseas are particularly active in mounting promotions with mobile telephones because of the desire to capture e-mail addresses of moviegoers near the theaters so they can send e-mail alerts about upcoming films. In the United States, the theater circuits emphasize Internet service using personal computers for e-mail communications to moviegoers because home computer penetration and usage are high.

Besides single-picture alliances, consumer goods companies also tie-up with studios on a corporate basis. For example, Universal Pictures has

10-year deals with Coca-Cola and Nestle and 5-year pacts with MasterCard and Kodak. The Universal link also extends to movies, television shows, video games, and theme parks. Carmaker Toyota holds an option for tie-ups with Universal movies. Disney has its own slew of long-term deals, including with Coca-Cola. Lucasfilm, the maker of the *Star Wars* movies, has a long-term promotion deal with Pepsi.

Even the independent sector is getting into the act with long-term commitments. New Line Cinema, which is classified as an independent although it is a corporate sibling to Warner Bros., signed a two-year promotional deal with Samsung Electronics in June 2004. The first film to receive Samsung cross-promotion support via a sweepstakes was the June 2004 release of the drama *The Notebook*, which has Samsung products visible in the film and which grossed $80.1 million domestically.

Miramax Films, the autonomous Disney-owned unit that also is classified as an indie, reached an agreement in August 2002 with Coors beer for a promotion/product placement alliance covering a range of future films. Coors reportedly is guaranteed product placement in a minimum of five films within three years. Using a bit of Hollywood movie magic in relation to a product placement, Miramax employed a special effects house to digitally replace the label of a Heineken beer bottle that gets screen time with a Coors label in *A View from the Top*, which Miramax filmed just before signing Coors. An element of the Coors tie-up is that Miramax reportedly is obligated not to use competing beers in its productions—it's either Coors or a fictional brand. Coors even finagled a commitment to designate 15 persons for nonspeaking, walk-on parts in movies, which can include contest winners.

Film festivals are a growing sector for tie-ins. Sundance, the top indie fest in the United States, receives hundreds of thousands of dollars for corporate sponsorships from outfits such as Hewlett-Packard, Volkswagen of America, *Entertainment Weekly*, and Microsoft. Such corporate sponsorship revenue covers 30% of the festival's operating budget. There is an excess of film festivals, with some mounted by cities simply to bolster tourism, so lesser fests in the crowded film calendar might not be particularly desirable promotion partners.

Tie-in Misfires

After being stung in the past, consumer goods outfits are careful to spell out specific rights and obligations for their film partners in Hollywood tie-ins. Perhaps most famously, Columbia delayed the release of *Radio Flyer* from summer 1991, leaving a tie-in promotion with Dairy Queen in a lurch. The restaurant chain opted to run the movie promotion on schedule in July 1991, which included $1 million in advertising, even though the youth drama eventually was pushed back to a February 1992 release date (making just $4.6 million in total domestic box office).

The film release shift highlighted the fact that the film industry could not always deliver as promised. In particular, movie schedules are subject to change because of production and postproduction delays, as well as competitive reasons in the jockeying for good release dates.

There was also the previously cited promotional scramble connected to the 1998 summer release of *Small Soldiers* by DreamWorks. Rather than receiving an anticipated PG rating, the film got a PG-13 classification, in part because toy characters in the film shot nails at each other. That scene made the film too rough for a children's promotion that was already planned by Burger King. DreamWorks did alert the restaurant chain two months in advance that the film was more intense than anticipated, so Burger King was not caught off guard. Burger King had sufficient time to revamp its promotion, such as not placing tie-in advertising in kids television shows, which would be inappropriate for a PG-13 movie. The restaurant chain also posted signs in stores alerting parents to the content of *Small Soldiers*. In another instance of a soured Hollywood connection, New Line Cinema sued Little Caesar's in 1999, claiming the restaurant chain didn't follow through on an agreement to mount a promotion for *Lost in Space*.

A common source of friction is conflicts with creative executives who make films. Taco Bell was hobbled after it put up an estimated $20 million in media support for a tie-in with the 1998 Hollywood version of *Godzilla*, released by TriStar Pictures, the Sony Pictures Entertainment unit. The restaurant chain found that the association was watered down when filmmakers insisted the Godzilla character could not be in advertising and in-store promotional items such as drinking cups until the film was in theaters. The secrecy was aimed at stoking interest in the new rendition of the monster, but the holdback undermined promotion. *Godzilla*, which cost between $120 and $150 million to make, generated $136.3 million in domestic box office.

The horror stories are rarer now since tie-in promotion partners have learned from their mistakes. If anything, the trend today is for closer alliances between film and licensees on a selective basis. Consumer goods marketers are pitched by Hollywood to provide promotional support for target movies in video and other release windows after theatrical release. "We can combine our [advertising] buys," Universal Pictures vice chairman Marc Shmuger told the EPM Entertainment Marketing

Conference in Los Angeles in late 2003. "We can synchronize our media and publicity plan to deliver billions of impressions, providing more concentrated exposure than any marketing plan ever, either movie or product." In the broadcast television window, the consumer goods partner can buy commercials and possibly mount tie-in promotions with the television channel telecasting a partner film.

In the broadest sense, movie marketers are offering a multimedia sponsorship to films with expanded tie-ins. It remains to be seen how effective this will prove to be, because there are risks. Excessive or inelegant commercialization of films will certainly irk consumers, which would defeat the goals of both film distributors and their partners in the consumer goods world.

Also, if a film proves to be unsuccessful in theatrical release, the consumer goods partner would be hitching its wagon to a vehicle that has poor prospects in video and television windows. Still, consumer goods marketers know that picking films is a hit-or-miss business, so they will have to endure some misses in order to latch on to hits that deliver substantial marketing benefits.

Some movie outfits suggest consumer goods marketers should pay up to help develop films—which would be a first—because being involved in a film's creation would allow partners to help shape the presentation of their branded products. That seems a stretch, however. Many film projects die in early stages, so consumer goods marketers would be forking over film development money that is totally wasted if a target film never gets out of "development hell."

Some consumer goods marketers grumble that if they are to provide foundation capital, then they are entitled to earn cash returns like any other equity investor. This has the potential to create a conflict and would distract from the original cross-promotion purpose of alliances for consumer goods outfits, which is to inject some movie magic into the marketing of consumer goods companies.

Product Placement Overview

Product placement is arranging for brand name items to receive exposure in films, television programs, and other media. This section is somewhat duplicative with the previously-cited tie-in promotions, since both involve film companies hooking up with consumer goods companies. But product placement—inserting brands in films—is a separate activity from tie-ins that promote brands outside of films.

Interestingly, film executives say that, in most instances, when a recognizable product lands in a movie it's without a formal placement contract. The product simply fit the needs of the movie's script. For example, the 1992 surprise comedy hit *Wayne's World* contained scenes in which characters tell a television executive they won't "sell out" and then are seen brandishing a Pizza Hut box, Doritos chips, and Reebok apparel. The film's distributor Paramount Pictures did not receive compensation for those satirical plugs.

Consumer goods outfits are increasing product placement efforts because they are worried that personal video recorders (PVRs) are enabling television viewers to skip their television commercials. PVRs (sometimes called digital video recorders) are easy-to-use, hard-drive video machines with VCR-like functionality, including fast forward capability. PVRs currently are in 4% of United States television households and penetration is expected to hit 30% in 4 years. Consumer goods outfits believe embedding their brands in films themselves (and television shows) will partly offset the anticipated loss of impact on consumers from skipping of television commercials via PVRs.

The industry custom is for film productions and consumer goods companies to work through a middleman—the product placement company. These placement brokers charge clients fees in the tens of thousands of dollars a year to place their branded consumer products in movies, television shows, and music videos. At least 20 such boutique brokers are located in the Los Angeles area, and some are divisions of big advertising agency conglomerates. Hollywood talent agencies also arrange for product exposure for consumer goods outfits that are clients, such as packaged goods giant Procter & Gamble, Coca-Cola, and brewer Anheuser-Busch. Product placement executive Brad Brown makes the case for using middlemen, saying, "You need to have someone who knows the landscape, who knows the people in Hollywood, and who knows what's fair and reasonable." Brown is executive vice president of both Davie-Brown Entertainment and Pepsi-Cola Entertainment in Los Angeles.

Often a product placement company—working on behalf of consumer goods marketers—simply provides the product and arranges any legal clearances necessary for its usage in a film. A case in point is the car caper film *The Italian Job*, which presented the Mini Cooper automobile in a starring role. Yet, Mini Cooper parent BMW simply supplied cars to the production and technical support in modifying cars for stunt scenes. Because the cars were selling briskly and already were in short supply, there was no promotional investment. The June 2004 release by

Paramount Pictures generated a robust $106.1 million in domestic box office (the crime caper is a remake of a 1969 film).

Product placement requires long-lead planning because it involves the production of the movie itself. In cases where deals are made late and if creative talent agrees to cooperate, short scenes with the branded product are shot after principal photography for inclusion in a film.

In many cases, the production may receive large quantities of product used in product placement, such as beverages, for cast and crew. A deeper relationship combines a tie-in promotion supporting a film's release with product placement. For example, actors in Miramax's live-action family film *Spy Kids 2: The Island of Lost Dreams* wore Payless ShoeSource shoes, and the footware chain with 4,952 stores supported the film with a national ad campaign. A *Spy Kids*-branded line of footware with the movie logo on the tongue of the shoe retailed for $14.99.

There is an effort to make the formal placement subtle and clever, of course. In Twentieth Century Fox's PG-13 comedy romp *Dodgeball: A True Underdog Story*, a sports arena is adorned with advertising placards that provide a touch of realism and also fakery for humor. Visible ads include Lumber Liquidators, which is a genuine company with a placement deal (providing flooring for the sets of Average Joe's and Globo gyms in the movie). The arena also has a placard ad for the studio's Fox Sports sister company and parodies a rival channel with a banner for ESPN 8: the Ocho, which plays off a gag in the film about television coverage of obscure sports.

Rare instances of cash payment typically involve only thousands or tens of thousand of dollars, and mostly from a few competitive product categories such as beer. Product placement executives say fee figures bandied about in public are often exaggerated. Also, payments are not made until after a movie is finished and going into release, just in case a crucial scene containing the branded product is dropped by the director or film company in final editing. The contractually specified payment typically is held in an escrow account.

Most of the time, consumer goods companies try not to call attention to their product placements so that they are subtle. Yet overt commercialization seems to work–if it is not expected–in other films. Audiences relish the cavalcade of brand-name glamour visible in the James Bond spy film thrillers. MGM's 2002 release of *Die Another Day* was loaded with product placements for the Ford Thunderbird automobile, Revlon cosmetics, the Norelco Spectra shaver, Bollinger champagne, 7-Up, Swatch/Omega wristwatches, Philips cell phones, Kodak, British Airways, Samsonite luggage, and Finlandia liquor.

Filmmakers can offer screen credit for providing products, but some consumer goods companies feel those screen credits are of little value because they appear at the end of a list of credits that audiences seldom watch. Also, some consumer goods outfits prefer keeping the formal association anonymous so as not to shatter the illusion that a branded product's appearance was anything but spontaneous.

For their part, stars often are unaware of a product placement deal, especially if there is no follow-on promotional tie-in in theatrical release. The product is simply on the set the day of shooting. If there is a tie-in promotion later, the consumer goods partner typically needs the talent's permission for use of personal images, voice, or persona in the tie-in ads.

An obvious requirement is that a brand name item fit in with a film's scenario, which is easy for many everyday products if films have contemporary settings. In MGM's 2001 thriller *Hannibal*, the homicidal villain portrayed by Anthony Hopkins breaks into an FBI agent's home and finds a cell phone that was a product placement for Verizon. The telephone company even provided a mock Verizon bill as a prop.

In other cases, a film's scenario may be a difficult fit for product placement, such as a historical epic, sci-fi film, or fantasy. Even contemporary films set in familiar surroundings can present problems. When movie stars portray characters who are placed in working-class neighborhoods, luxury products obviously are poor fits. For the assassination drama *In the Line of Fire*, a hardscrabble FBI agent portrayed by Clint Eastwood is seen eating supermarket-brand Breyers ice cream because an upscale ice cream would seem out of place for the no-nonsense character. Breyers got the placement for simply providing quantities of its product to the 1993 Columbia Pictures release.

Story-point Product Placement

For consumer goods marketers that cajole filmmakers to include their branded products in films, the holy grail is getting a *story point placement*. Here, the product is not just seen, but it is handled by actors, is integral to the story, or is referred to in dialogue. Consumer research indicates that brand recall for products in the background is about 25% but shoots to greater than 50% for story point placements.

A Lincoln-Mercury's Navigator sports utility vehicle in Fox Searchlight's road comedy *Johnson Family Vacation* is referred to as Mr. Hip Hop in the film, which was released in July 2004. In New Line Cinema's 1999 wacky comedy *Austin Powers: The Spy Who Shagged Me*, the lead character portrayed by Mike Myers says at one point, "Get your hand off my Heinie, baby," which plays off Heineken beer that is a promotional partner of the film. In Twentieth Century Fox's 1988 comedy *Big*, a playful character portrayed by Tom Hanks extracts a soft drink from his private Pepsi vending machine without paying. "I rigged this up so you don't need quarters," brags the character portrayed by Hanks. The vending machine is prominently framed in scenes of his apartment, which is furnished like a playground.

Glad trash bags ran a sweepstakes in conjunction with 1987 film *Million Dollar Mystery* to guess the location within the film of a plastic garbage bag containing $1 million. Though this was a story point placement, the release from defunct De Laurentiis Entertainment was a bomb, not even grossing $1 million domestically. This chilled the notion of integrating contests within movies themselves. Glad's parent company First Brands spent an estimated $4 million in the *Mystery* tie-up.

Leading product placement firm Norm Marshall & Associates (NMA), based in Sun Valley, California, reads 600–800 scripts per year provided by film companies and studio production resource teams, according to NMA president Devery Holmes. She says that scripts are evaluated scene by scene to determine where product placement opportunities for natural client integration may exist. "Ninety percent of what we do is provide product that simply cuts below-the-line expenditures," says Holmes. Below the line is the cost of physical production and excludes the salaries of cast, director, and producers.

As another service, product placement firms stock vintage versions of branded products that may be hard for producers to find for films in historical settings, providing what are essentially antiques as props. "If a production needs an item, we give it to the production free of charge," says Steve Ochs, principal of Hero Product Placement in Sun Valley, California. "That's standard operating procedure." Product placement companies are careful not to place products whose sale is restricted in films that children will see. "With alcoholic beverages, we are very mindful of the audience that the property is going to reach," says Ochs. "So needless to say, we're not going to give Jagermeister [liquor] to *Power Rangers*."

A much sought-after product placement is automobiles, because car companies have huge marketing budgets to mount tie-in promotion campaigns to support theatrical release. Mercedes Benz reportedly paid $5 million to get its then new sports utility vehicle into *The Lost World: Jurassic Park 2* released by Universal Pictures in 1997. This placement included a tie-in promotion that supported theatrical release. Mercedes replaced Ford, which reportedly paid just $500,000 to have its Explorer sports utility vehicle (SUV) chased by dinosaurs in the 1993 release *Jurassic Park*.

Elsewhere, the Cadillac CTS, which has a futuristic angular body style, received extensive exposure in *The Matrix: Reloaded* for a freeway chase scene, which was a key placement given the demographic target for the General Motors brand. Cadillac is focusing on attracting young adults as car buyers, so the sci-fi *Matrix* audience fit its goal. Lincoln-Mercury's Navigator SUV got heavy exposure in the road-trip comedy *Are We There Yet?* from Revolution Studios/Columbia.

A contemporary setting is the best platform for product placement for cars because automakers can showcase their current lineup. Films set in the future can be a springboard for automakers to display so-called concept cars, which are forward-looking designs that are showcased at car shows. For Twentieth Century Fox's sci-fi thriller *Minority Report* in 2002, Lexus paid for construction of the branded futuristic concept car that was driven by Tom Cruise in the movie.

Product Placement Conflicts

Product placement executives say that, besides arranging favorable appearances for clients' products, another function is to serve as radar, providing advance warning to clients of instances in which their branded products are being used in an unfavorable light. In general, companies have a legal basis to request that their branded products be removed from a film if the product is misused in an unsafe manner. An example is a movie character who gets drunk from a bottle of branded spirits and then causes a car accident. The remedy would be for the film not to display recognizable brands in scenes of unsafe usage.

However, if products are used in a safe and appropriate manner, there's little legal recourse for consumer goods outfits. United State trademark law allows for "fair use" of brands by media such as news outlets and films, even though those trademarks are the property of others. The existence of this trademark law doesn't deter consumer goods companies from sending out stern letters anyway, warning of infringements of their trademarks, figuring there's no harm in being assertive. Still, fair use typically prevails. Miramax's black comedy *Bad Santa* from 2003 shows a character swilling vodka from a bottle with a red label somewhat similar to Stolichnaya, whose maker Allied Domecq Spirits refused permission for an official product placement.

Film distributors sometimes find themselves on the receiving end of complaints of misappropriation of trademarks. Resort operator Club Med filed a lawsuit that attempted to block the February 2004 release of horror spoof *Broken Lizard's Club Dread* by Fox Searchlight, in an effort to get the title changed. The film opened as planned with the name unchanged. When MGM released *Harley Davidson and the Marlboro Man* in 1991, both the motorcycle and cigarette makers sent letters to the studio complaining about their names appearing in the title. As owners of valuable trademarks themselves, studios aren't inclined to pick fights with others but get dragged into tiffs to back up their filmmakers.

A subtle part of the business is that product placement firms attempt to place products of competitors to be used by villains while heroes are seen with their clients' products. Further, they advise clients not to mount tie-in promotions with raunchy or violent films that would put products in an unfavorable light.

A common element of product placement deals is a non-disparagement clause in which film productions agree not to denigrate brand name items of their partner consumer goods companies. This is sort of a "bear hug" whereby a film production gets benefits of access to partnerships with consumer goods companies but is limited regarding product depiction. Having an automobile suffer a breakdown in the movie, perhaps accompanied by characters disparaging the car, is an obvious no-no. If a carmaker has a product placement deal with a film in which a vehicle is seen in a bad light, the usual remedy is for the carmaker to provide a vehicle from another manufacturer. Typically, identifying badges are removed or replaced with markings of a made-up brand.

No-disparagement clauses became standard features of contracts after several consumer goods outfits were burned in product placement deals. Perhaps the most talked about examples of product placement backfiring involved uplifting sports drama *Jerry Maguire* starring Tom Cruise and Oliver Stone's crime spree drama *Natural Born Killers*.

Sports apparel company Reebok sued Sony's TriStar Pictures in 1997 over *Jerry Maguire*, alleging it breached a product placement/promotional support contract. In the movie, a football player expresses frustration over not being able to get a Reebok endorsement deal, swearing at one point, "[Expletive] Reebok. All they do is ignore me, always have." Reebok said that it learned just weeks before the film's release that an upbeat scene in which the athlete character finally gets the Reebok contract ended up on the cutting room floor.

Reebok asserted that it invested more than $1.5 million in support of *Jerry Maguire*, creating the special television commercial that was supposed to be in the movie and providing products. Some Reebok television and radio ads for the movie had already run. At the time, the studio said that the scene with the Reebok commercial featuring the athlete was dropped because it turned out that it didn't fit creatively.

In the Warner Bros. release *Natural Born Killers*, Coca Cola reportedly was stunned to find its television commercials intermixed with mayhem. The soft drink marketer agreed to the placement in the Oliver Stone film from 1994 believing the ad would be in the background during a non-violent scene. Elsewhere, Wham-O filed a lawsuit involving *Dickie Roberts: Former Child Star*, the Paramount release from 2003, claiming its trademark Slip 'N Slide plastic water toy was visible and defamed. In the movie, a character forgets to wet the yellow backyard water slide before taking what turns out to be a painful slide.

Smoking products, which cannot advertise on television, are another controversial category. Under a 1998 lawsuit settlement, major cigarette makers agreed not to pay for product placement and attempt to prevent their products from being displayed. Public interest groups and government regulators are on the lookout for cigarette placement, particularly where they would be seen by children. Filmmakers don't always comply with attempts to prevent making brand name cigarettes visible, saying that using recognizable products is necessary to achieve realism.

In past decades, cigarette companies had been among the most aggressive in arranging for product placement in movies, often paying hefty cash incentives. Health groups complained that paid-for exposure didn't carry health warnings that are supposed to accompany advertising. According to Congressional testimony in 1989, Philip Morris paid $350,000 to get Lark cigarettes placed in the James Bond spy film *Licence to Kill*.

Tie-ins at Theaters

Movie theaters are increasingly a battleground for marketing, as cinemas solicit advertising not connected with movies. The courting of nonfilm advertisers for on-screen ads and lobby promotions sets up a showdown with movie distributors, which want to use those spaces to promote their films.

Already, there has been one high-profile clash. Regal Cinemas balked at allowing lobby stand displays for *Lara Croft Tomb Raider: The Cradle of Life*, which also promoted tie-in partner Jeep Wrangler in June 2003. Regal cited a policy against giving free theater access to third-party brands without receiving financial compensation. Paramount Pictures, which is the distributor of the movie, reportedly shifted bookings from 47 Regal cinemas to other theaters that cooperated by allowing access for the Tomb Raider/Jeep promotional materials.

Exhibitors—movie theater operators—sold 1.5 billion tickets in 2003 in the United States, which has one of the highest per capita attendance ratios in the world. Theaters tout the ability to mesh on-screen advertising with some kind of linked consumer promotion in their lobbies, such as a sweepstakes, contest, or coupon programs. Even the rival pay television medium is invading theaters. In summer 2004, pay television service Starz! mounted a sweepstakes that included distributing scratch-and-win cards at theaters.

"In-theater advertising and in-lobby promotions look to grow as marketers push to connect with out-of-home ads," said Susan Nunziata, executive editor of *Entertainment Marketing Letter*. "Besides regular advertising, promotions such as in-theater giveaways with refreshment purchases and sweepstakes will likely increase, for both movie and non-movie advertisers. Because of the desire to capture consumers outside the home, I think you'll see more premium giveaways such as LidRock CDs in theaters and promotions such as sweepstakes. These are most often done in tandem with on-screen advertising that runs prior to the films, as part of an integrated effort to build brand impressions or drive sales." In June 2004, Regal Cinema, which is the largest theater chain in the United States with 6,045 screens, signed a deal for LidRock promotions placing CDs on soft drink lids.

Theater circuits are betting that national advertisers will embrace in-theater placement because traditional television advertising suffers from audience fragmentation. These days, on-screen ads are presented as moving pictures (referred to as "rolling stock" by exhibitors), not just the still-slide shows that were prevalent in the past. Also, cinema audiences are touted by theaters as being particularly valuable to advertisers by representing consumers with above-average incomes who are extremely mobile and light television viewers. Although the regular television medium may be losing effectiveness, there's no guarantee national advertisers will pile into cinema advertising or that audiences won't rebel down the road with complaints of overcommercialization. A survey released in November of 2004 by InsightExpress indicates that 27% of moviegoers claim to reduce their patronage of theaters with screen ads and 53% want screen commercials to stop.

History of Tie-ins and Product Placement

In the 1970s, tie-in promotions began to proliferate as restaurants, soft drinks, and other consumer goods marketers sought to attach their products to movies. Promotional tie-ins with movies peaked in the late 1990s, especially after the 1999 sci-fi epic *Star Wars: Episode I–The Phantom Menace* fell short of expectations. The film's producer Lucasfilm had negotiated a rich five-year deal for Pepsi to provide hundreds of millions of dollars in promotional support. In a one-picture deal, *Episode I* had a tie-in with the restaurant chain that owns Pizza Hut, KFC, and Taco Bell. However, when sky-high expectations for movie tie-ins weren't met, consumer goods companies turned cautious about Hollywood, and film deals became less lucrative.

Still, the value of tie-ins has mushroomed over the decades, even after sliding back somewhat over the past five years. In the 1980s, the most media support a consumer goods outfit such as a restaurant chain would provide to a movie was a few million dollars. These days, automakers, cell phone outfits, and restaurants can provide tens of millions of dollars each to the same film (Fig. 4.3). This is the value of advertising that copromotes a movie and also point-of-purchase promotion such as signage in stores or restaurants.

In the early 1990s, studios tried bundling multiple films in the same promotion. However, such efforts fizzled when marketing partners felt some films did not mesh with their audience target. For example,

Figure 4.3 Top Ad Media in Entertainment Marketing Campaigns

Rank	Media	Usage
1	Internet	93%
2	Consumer magazines	67%
3	Cable television	67%
4	Radio	67%
5	In-theater	53%
6	Newspapers	47%
7	Network television	47%
8	Trade publications	27%
9	Outdoor billboards	20%

Note: Covers all types of entertainment marketing, not just movies. Total surpasses 100% because of multiple ad media used in each campaign.
Source: Entertainment Marketing Letter. © 2004 EPM Communications, Inc.; www.epmcom.com

Paramount assembled Kmart, Chrysler, and Goodyear for a sweepstakes promotion dubbed Passport to Summer Entertainment supporting groupings of films in the early 1990s. Filmgoers buying adult tickets to Paramount movies received a scratch-and-win card, with instant prizes such as soft drinks at theaters or videos redeemable at stores of the studio's promotion partners. The big prizes included a Chrysler Le Baron car and vacation cruises.

Over the years, the relationship between Hollywood and Madison Avenue for advertising tie-ins has been rocky at times. McDonald's caught flack from parents for its 1992 tie-in with Warner Bros. release *Batman Returns* over complaints that the PG-13 rated film was too intense for the kids who were targeted with a Happy Meal promotion.

As for product placement, brand name goods were seldom seen in the early days of film. Liquor was poured out of decanters without labels, and cigarette packs had nondescript packaging. Branded products started to appear in daytime serial dramas on network television because those programs were owned by packaged goods companies. In film, the New Hollywood movement of the 1960s and 1970s emphasized realism, so props needed to have visible brand names to appear genuine.

Film outfits embraced placement for branded products by the 1980s, often negotiating for promotional support from consumer products companies to help push theatrical releases. Clever brand placement goes back decades. In MGM's 1984 release of the sci-fi drama *2010*, a futuristic television ad was an arranged product placement for an airline with this voiceover: "So if your business takes you out of this world, enjoy the speed and comfort of a Pan Am space clipper with convenient non-stops to the moon and all major space stations. At Pan Am, the sky is no longer the limit." The airline, Sheraton Hotels, Apple Computer, Budweiser beer, and *Omni* magazine all were visible in the film and contributed promotional support to the theatrical release. With promotional support hanging in the balance, major studios increasingly specify in employment contracts with filmmakers that certain product placements make the final cuts of films.

Perhaps the most celebrated product placement of all time came in the 1982 blockbuster *E.T. The Extra-Terrestrial*. The marketer of Milk Duds candy rejected an opportunity for a story point placement when the candy is used to lure the alien. Instead, Hershey Chocolate lent its Reese's Pieces—then a second-tier candy brand. Once the movie became a blockbuster, Reese's Pieces experienced a sudden 65% hike in sales. The product placement broker for Milk Duds explained later that the E.T. character gets sick at another point in the movie, so the feeling was that the placement would make their candy seem unappetizing. That probably was a legitimate concern at the time, given that consumer goods marketers are very protective of their images.

Another landmark came when the James Bond movie character ordered a martini with vodka in 1962's *Dr. No* (with instructions it be shaken, not stirred). The liquor industry said the scene was a catalyst for a wholesale consumer shift away from gin. In recent years, the highly coveted vodka product placement in the James Bond spy films shifted between Smirnoff (seen in *Dr. No*) and Finlandia.

Some noteworthy backfires have occurred in the recent history of product placement. As cited earlier, sports apparel outfit Reebok sued Sony's TriStar Pictures in 1996, alleging the studio's *Jerry Maguire* breached a product placement agreement. In 1990, electric tools outfit Black & Decker sued Twentieth Century Fox and another company for claiming it was left out of *Die Hard 2* despite having a product placement deal.

In the 1980s and into the early 1990s, Hollywood's major studios attempted to squeeze cash out of product placement by contracting directly with consumer goods companies. They sought $10,000–$60,000 per placement, but those efforts fizzled for several reasons.

One problem is that film companies have divided loyalties. They typically have deeper relationships with Hollywood creative talent, so film companies may be reluctant to intervene when filmmakers ridicule products or cut scenes with product placement. As a result, independent placement boutiques prevailed because they are more sensitive to the consumer goods companies. Also, the independent brokers could monitor all of Hollywood's film output, while each studio could only serve up its own limited slate of films. Finally, in-house studio efforts to arrange product placement resulted in a barrage of news stories that made the film companies look crass, which also was a catalyst for studios to lower their direct involvement.

5 Merchandising

This is the Buzz Lightyear aisle (at this toy store). Back in 1995, short-sighted retailers did not order enough dolls to meet demand.

Tour guide Barbie doll in Toy Story 2

The above quote, which is a clever inside joke from a scene in the Disney-distributed animated hit *Toy Story 2*, highlights a common dilemma in movie merchandising. A talking Barbie doll that is giving a tour of a store points out that toy companies missed a bonanza by not immediately jumping on the first *Toy Story* movie, as she gestures to ample merchandise from the second movie. The original *Toy Story* far exceeded industry expectations, grossing a blockbuster $192 million domestically in its 1995 release, leaving licensed movie merchandise in short supply.

Tour guide Barbie's comment in *Toy Story 2* is an apt metaphor for a chicken-and-egg quandary for new properties. Up to one year's lead time is necessary for design, manufacture, and sales of merchandise to stores. Thus, the merchandising industry must decide on whether to embrace a new film before it is finished and, in many cases, before the first scene of a movie is even shot.

Merchandising companies may have a script and know the talent involved (actors, director, and producers). It's a big decision because retail sales of licensed merchandise—coming from all sources and not just movies—was a $71.4 billion business at retail in 2003 for the United States and Canada (Fig. 5.1).

Figure 5.1 Total Licensed Merchandise Sales by Category, 2003

Category	Retail Sales ($ bil.)	Percentage of Total
Accessories	$6.20	9%
Apparel	$9.00	13%
Domestics	$4.05	6%
Electronics	$0.95	1%
Food/beverages	$7.70	11%
Footwear	$2.10	3%
Home furnishings	$1.75	2%
Gift/novelties	$5.85	8%
Health/beauty	$4.20	6%
Housewares	$2.50	4%
Infant products	$3.35	5%
Music/video	$1.50	2%
Publishing	$5.00	7%
Sporting goods	$1.65	2%
Stationary/paper	$3.60	5%
Toys/games	$7.30	10%
Videogames/software	$4.50	6%
Other	$0.20	<1%
Total	**$71.40**	**100%**

Note: Data covers the United States and Canada in U.S. dollars.
Source: The Licensing Letter. © 2004 EPM Communications, Inc.; www.epmcom.com

Licensed merchandise companies, which make products such as key chains and towels with movie logos and characters, and retail stores are reluctant to buy into movies based on a totally new concept. Originals have burned them too often, such as the box office disappointment *The Last Action Hero* in 1993. And nothing has come close to the $1.5 billion retail merchandising haul from Walt Disney's 1994 theatrical release *The Lion King*, which holds the all-time record for an original property.

Merchandisers prefer to wait for video release, sequels, and embrace new films based on properties adapted from other media, such as books or video games. But even that's not an insurance policy. The big budget, English-language *Godzilla*, which was based on the famous Japanese movie property, was a merchandising disappointment in 1998.

Since the bonanza from *Star Wars* in 1977, merchandising mushroomed as a source of revenue for Hollywood. Today at the top end of expectations, a major studio film that is aimed at the family audience and is a big holiday-season theatrical release earns $5–$15 million for studios from merchandise rights. The movie merchandising business actually peaked in the late 1990s but has fallen back since then because retailers—burned by underperforming movies—turned cautious. These days, there's something of a feast or famine for films. Some films get little merchandising interest while others line up hundreds of deals.

Merchandise licensing conveys the right to manufacture products with theme elements based on movies (and can include the creation of movie-themed services for companies that do not make durable goods). Typically, films are represented directly by movie companies, although in some cases the producers, star talent, and/or owner of underlying property rights, such as a comic book publisher, also are involved.

To reach the mass market with merchandise, three critical retailers are used: Wal-Mart, with 3,550 United States and 235 Canadian stores; Target, with 1,475 United States stores (including some up-market outlets); and Kmart, with 1,511 United States stores (Kmart is buying Sears). Wal-Mart, which rings up a staggering $256 billion in annual worldwide sales, accounts for roughly one third of DVD and VHS video sales in the United States. Some pundits say that increasing concentration of marketing power in these three discount chains is one factor in a trend to lower merchandising rates for movie property in recent years.

The biggest headache remains trying to sort out the hits from the misses in advance. Entertainment stock analyst Lee Isgur famously mused years ago that one never knows what to expect even when accomplished filmmaker George Lucas creates a movie with cute characters. It could turn out nicely like *Star Wars* or badly like *Howard the Duck*. "Despite all the publicity and early reviews, no one really has any idea whether a movie will be a box office smash or a dud," Isgur said.

Preexisting Properties

For movies based on preexisting properties, such as comic books, the owner of the underlying property usually has its own merchandising effort. The promise of a big-budget Hollywood film will be a catalyst for even more merchandising. As a result, the film distributor and property owner arrange a formula to split royalty revenue and divide responsibility for management of merchandising.

A prolific source for comic book properties is Marvel Enterprises, which has 450 merchandise licensing deals of its own. For licensing the rights to its Spider-Man property, Marvel reportedly receives a few percentage points from all the film rental streams of the *Spider-Man* movies that Columbia Pictures distributes, which would be from theaters, video, and television. The studio makes an upfront payment for each film—the minimum guarantee—and pays more if the movie's revenue pushes Marvel's cut above the minimum guarantee. Marvel reportedly received $20 million from this contract provision for the first *Spider-Man* movie.

For its comics that are made into films, Marvel stated in a 10-K disclosure filing that it "generally retains control over merchandising rights and receives not less than 50% of merchandising-based royalty revenue" from film exploitation. Marvel properties include *Spider-Man, X-Men*, and *Daredevil*, which have been made into movies.

The movie merchandising field is mostly the domain of major studios and their specialty units distributing independent films, such as New Line Cinema, which is a sister company to Warner Bros. and made the *Lord of the Rings* trilogy. The majors and their affiliates have the deep pockets to produce and widely distribute the highest-profile films, which of course are most sought after by merchandising outfits.

Besides licensing properties from outsiders, Hollywood's major studios are eager to make movies based on intellectual properties from within their own corporate family. For example, Paramount Pictures released feature films based on cartoon television series *Rugrats, Jimmy Neutron*, and *SpongeBob SquarePants* from sister cable network Nickelodeon. Paramount and Nickelodeon are part of Viacom, the sprawling media entertainment conglomerate with $27 billion in revenue.

In listing the most promising films of 2004–2006, *The Licensing Letter* newsletter came up with 42 movies, of which three fourths are based on some kind of preexisting property. These movies include sequels such as Lucasfilm's *Star Wars: Episode III—Revenge of the Sith* and Miramax's *The Green Hornet*, which is a live-action film based on the crime-fighting comic superhero.

The sequel syndrome is widely derided because sequels have a history of generating less box office revenue than their predecessor movies. Although perhaps not as successful as prior movies of the series, sequels tend to be a sure bet to make a predictable impact with consumers, which is a comfort to merchandisers and stores that must estimate volume of movie product sales.

In addition, children are generally receptive to what is familiar, which gives a boost to sequel products. Finally, there are the movie memorabilia collectors, which are a dependable buying group for sequel merchandise. Because sequels have something of a bad rap, merchandise licensing executives in Hollywood try to avoid the word, instead referring to follow-on movies as "a continuing merchandising franchise" or "a brand extension."

Preexisting properties can be a source of other headaches. A tug of war surfaced over the *Spider-Man* movies distributed by Columbia Pictures, which is part of Sony Pictures. In 2003, Marvel Comics, which owns the underlying property, filed three related lawsuits against Columbia over royalties. A June 2004 settlement made Marvel the lead party in licensing deals for a joint venture with the studio. The settlement means all merchandising royalty revenue will flow through Marvel, which will increase sales at the publicly traded company, even though a big chunk of that money automatically is paid to Columbia.

Marvel takes charge for *Spider-Man 3*, which is planned for 2007, as well as the studio's other upcoming Marvel adaptations, *Luke Cage* in 2005 and *Ghost Rider* in 2006. Marvel had said that it would receive at minimum $8 million from Columbia for *Spider-Man 2*, prior to the film becoming a blockbuster in its June 2004 release.

Financial Terms

Royalties for licensing—fees that movie rights owners receive from merchandise companies—can range anywhere from 3% to 20% of wholesale prices of products. Today most fall in the range from 8% to 14%. The category paying the lowest rate on a percentage basis is food/confectionery at 3% to 8%. Typically, the merchandising company makes an upfront payment that is an advance, which is deducted from future royalty obligations.

For a film based on popular preexisting properties, movie rights can cost the filmmaker 1% to 5% of film rentals from theatrical, video, and television distribution. That's a small cut of a potentially huge revenue stream, and the movie company almost always shoulders the entire cost of production and marketing. Merchandising rights to the film are subject to a separate but related contract.

It's important to remember that news reports typically cite retail sales of movie merchandise, which is a measure of consumer spending. But this is not the benchmark for licensing royalties. Licensing payments are pegged to wholesale revenue, which in round numbers is about 50% of the retail level. If merchandise from a film racks up $250 million in retail sales, the wholesale figure would be about $125 million and the royalty rates would be applied to that lower wholesale figure.

Licensing contracts can have sliding percentage rates that initially are low and then climb higher. Categories that shoulder large product development, such as video games and toys, often pay low initial royalty rates to film companies that rise if merchandise sells briskly. The low rates are designed to let the merchandise company cover their expenses for product development with the first wave of sales.

Another element of licensing contracts is mandating that some royalty payments go into a common marketing fund, which the master licensing entity—typically the film company—administers to promote a movie's overall merchandise sales. This may be a 1% royalty on initial sales up to a predetermined amount, after which no more payments are made.

Movie merchandising contracts specify a time frame and geographic exclusivity, in addition to financial terms. Film licenses typically are made for two-year terms, although sales to consumers usually are concentrated in the weeks around theatrical and video release. "Movies today are being treated as essentially six to eight week promotion events, as opposed to an on-going merchandising opportunity," said Martin Brochstein, editorial director of EPM Communications, the New York City-based publisher of newsletter *The Licensing Letter*. "That's a function of the open-wide, make-the-first-week-big release patterns that you see. Years ago, it took a while for everybody to see a movie that they were interested in but now movies don't play very long."

The major studios each have merchandising arms whose job is to line up deals for new films as well as milk old films—and characters—in their movie libraries. Since the early 1990s, major studios have looked upon licensing revenue as multimillion-dollar revenue streams that are figured into the profit-and-loss statements of their mass market movies. Before that time, the studios viewed merchandise revenue as gravy that was not a critical part of a film's initial revenue projections.

Travails

A decade ago, Hollywood's major studios plunged deeper in merchandising by creating properties and keeping more business in-house, rather than parceling out rights to outsiders. In recent years, the studios have pulled back from direct merchandising ventures, preferring to work with third parties.

One idea that fizzled was packaging original movies with a comic book flavor to eliminate the need to pay royalties to third parties. However, films following this template stumbled. For example, Disney's 1930s period adventure *Rocketeer*, which was a PG movie released in 1996, was one disappointment. In another studio foray into merchandising, Universal Pictures lost several million dollars years ago from making a direct investment in a company that made toys based on its blockbuster *E.T. The Extra-Terrestrial*.

As a consequence of such travails, studios today are willing to license established properties from third parties, figuring its worth the expense to get preexisting name recognition and the built-in base of fans from the book, comic, or television show. In another benefit of this strategy, the studios collect upfront payments that are minimum guarantees from third-party merchandising companies. The payments are a financial cushion for films that later fall flat.

In what cooled interest in movie properties, the merchandising industry overextended for the 1999 theatrical release of *Star Wars: Episode I—The Phantom Menace*. Lucasfilm, the sci-fi fantasy film's creator, orchestrated a well-structured merchandising campaign, and the space adventure yarn ultimately generated an estimated $1 billion in merchandise sales at retail. That amount would be a success for just about any other movie but was short of expectations of around $3 billion, on which minimum guarantees and product manufacturing volume were based. The result was piles of unsold *Star Wars* merchandise that had to be discounted for clearance. Twentieth Century Fox distributes *Star Wars* to theaters.

Another stumble came with a decision by filmmakers to keep merchandise off store shelves for *Godzilla* until the 1998 release from Sony's TriStar Pictures was in theaters. Normally, movie-related merchandise is in stores a few weeks earlier, and by some estimates about 30% of sales occur before a film opens. However, the filmmakers were trying to keep secret their particular vision of the well-known monster, which was the subject of 20 Japanese-language B-movies.

Those two merchandising disappointments, the dot-com recession that started in 2000, and an inability of later animated films to match the success of Disney's *The Lion King* prompted movie licensing to cool. Royalty rates declined and merchandisers became more selective after the late 1990s peak. "I don't think you will see those days again for some time," says Al Ovadia, former executive president at Sony Pictures Consumer Products.

Strategies

Orchestrating a successful merchandising campaign is something of an art. Movie marketers want plenty of merchandise to generate royalty revenue and lots of signage at stores to support theatrical release. At the same time, merchandising shouldn't be so excessive that consumers are turned off. It's also something of an art gauging what merchandising is appropriate for a movie and what goes too far.

"Publishing, video games, and toys are key categories" because of high revenue potential for a movie property, merchandising executive Al Ovadia said during a 2004 seminar at the International Licensing Industry Merchandisers' Association (LIMA) trade show.

To give a sense of scale, the $9.5 billion in 2003 box office for the United States was eclipsed by the toy industry, which generated $20.7 billion in retail business in the same year, according to The NPD Group, the Port Washington, New York–based researcher. The 2003 toy sale figure was down 3% from the prior year. About 60% of toy sales occur around the Christmas holiday.

Printed books and magazines are other key categories. At the top end, *James Cameron's Titanic*, a $50 book, sold more than one million copies. Its publisher HarperCollins is a sister company to Twentieth Century Fox, which originated the big-budget disaster film. A more realistic sales figure is moving tens of thousands or hundreds of thousands of copies of a movie-related book that is loaded with photos. Film distributors often give away such books to voters for film awards as promotions when films are a contender. For movies based on books, the book publisher typically keeps its preexisting merchandising separate from any related films, because the movie deal eventually will expire.

Movie merchandising sometimes stumbles when it is in the shadow of a preexisting property. For example, Universal Pictures' live-action kids film *The Flintstones* rolled up a hefty $130.5 million in domestic box office when the film was released in 1994. However, toy sales were weak, with some analysts saying children associated the property more with its original television cartoon series than the newer live-action movie with human actors.

In other instances, television exposure is helpful. The theatrical release of *Ghostbusters* in 1984 was a big hit at the box office, but its licensed merchandise did not sell well until the animated television series *The Real Ghostbusters* followed later. As a result, *Ghostbusters* generated an estimated $200 million in retail toys sales. Warner Bros. is preparing a merchandising blitz for its summer 2005 release *Batman Begins* and counts on marshalling support from television incarnations of the property. A new animated television series *The Batman* is telecast on the studio's sister outlets Kids WB and Cartoon Network.

A promising original film property with broad family appeal—one not based on a book, television show, or other preexisting property—can be expected to snag merchandising deals with upward of 100 merchandising companies (one merchandiser might make multiple related types of products). A sequel whose previous movie was a big hit or movie based on a popular preexisting property with family appeal can nab several hundred merchandisers. Not all movie licensing is for durable goods. For example, technology companies have licensed *Star Trek*—which portrays mankind as being noble and tech savvy in the future—for ad campaigns targeting a business audience and for use at trade shows. Such licenses can generate cash payments in the tens of thousands of dollars per year.

Movie merchandise marketers sometimes try for a generic positioning to enlarge sales potential. For instance, Universal Pictures and Steven Spielberg's Amblin Entertainment succeeded in staking out the entire dinosaur category for *Jurassic Park* in 1993. The film presented scientifically accurate dinosaurs, which provided another selling point for its creatures in merchandising. "We think *Jurassic Park* products will make all other dinosaur products extinct," the head of Universal's merchandising division joked at the time. The 1993 release had 100 companies making more than 1,000 types of products, which is a huge merchandising campaign. There are about 100 broad categories that are key for movie merchandising, and each category is subdivided into numerous product lines (Fig. 5.2).

The best merchandising prospects are for family films rated G or PG, because those films target the children's market that embraces popular-culture fads and merchandising. A PG-13 classification cuts into the children's audience, and an R rating eliminates children. Even having

Figure 5.2 Movie License Categories for Consumer Merchandising

Apparel & Accessories
Adult/casual footwear
Adult/headgear & outdoor
Adult/jackets & outerwear
Adult/swimwear
Backpacks & bags
Children/costumes
Children/shoes
Children/infant clothing
Children/jackets
Children/sleepwear
Children/swimwear & outdoor
Children/underwear
Jewelry/steel & 14K gold charms

Jewelry/high end
Keychains & metal accessories
Headwear & rainwear
Luggage
Lunch pails
Pet accessories
Sunglasses
Tee-shirts
Watches/children's
Watches/adult

Beverage & Food
Candy/general
Candy/novelties and empty containers

Figure 5.2 *Continued*

Cookies
Drinks/juice and non-juice
Fruit snacks

Gifts & Collectibles
Die-cast vehicles
Coasters/drink holders
Plush dolls
Playing cards
Vending items/rubber balls, vinyl items

Health & Beauty
Bandages
Brushes/hair
Shampoo/lotions
Soaps (hand)
Toothpaste

Home & Housewares
Clocks/clock radios
Coolers
Chairs (folding)
Cups/cup dispensers
Dinnerware/children
Handkerchiefs
Lamps/lighting products
Linens/sheets & pillow cases
Lunch kits
Pens/writing instruments
Radios/portable
Sleeping bags
Umbrellas/sun & rain

Interactive
Video game console
Video game handheld
Toy video game
Cell phone game

Publishing
Book/children's print
Book/children's sound
Book/making of
Book/novelization

Magazine/souvenir
Sticker book
Wall calendars & mini-calendars

Stationary
Arts & crafts supplies
Address labels/personal checks
Greeting cards
Mouse pads
Paper/letter & envelope
Paper/pads
Party goods/ornaments
Pencils & pens/packages
Photo images/digital
Posters
Stickers/adult

Toys & Games
Assembly kits/snap together
Assembly kits/glue models
Assembly kits/wood & other
Backyard & inflatables
Cards/trading
Characters/bobble head
Characters/plastic action figures
Games/board & puzzle
Games/hand-held electronic
Infant toys
Inflatables/large indoor
Kites/flying toys
License plates, waste baskets, etc.
Medallions, bracelets, etc.
Pool/water
Props, masks & busts
Scooters/in-line skates
Skateboards/body boards
Sports equipment
Stickers/children
Vehicles/die-cast metal
Vehicles/plastic

Wireless
Phone games, ring tones & images
Cell wall paper

Source: *Marketing to Moviegoers*

intriguing cartoon characters in a youth film is no guarantee of success. Disney's *Who Framed Roger Rabbit* was a blockbuster, grossing $154 million in domestic box office, which was staggering for a 1988 release. Although the film was rated with a family-friendly PG and enjoyed acclaim for its breakthrough technique of combining cartoon characters with human actors, its toy merchandise sold poorly. Pundits said that the wisecracking lead cartoon character did not connect with children.

Talky contemporary dramas, historical epics, and adult-skewing films with PG-13 or R ratings have limited merchandising prospects because they don't appeal to the youth market that is crucial to mass merchandising. Those types of movies have a small range of merchandising prospects. Religious blockbuster *The Passion of the Christ* managed to originate some licensed merchandise including one unusual item: a single nail made of pewter that's a $17 pendant with a leather necklace. Other *Passion* merchandise included a book, crucifixes, lapel pins, and cards.

An early effort at pricey merchandise was a $2,250 Special Edition knife for *Rambo III*, the R-rated film released in 1988. However, such expensive merchandise is not widely sold, so the cross-promotion benefit to the movie is limited.

One new trend is to simply attach a movie license to preexisting products that are appropriate. For example, Twentieth Century Fox's animated 2004 release of *Garfield: The Movie* licensed Ashley Furniture Industries for its reclining chairs retail priced at $300–$500. The easy chairs are a good fit with a movie that features a lazy cat.

With the uncertainties of a new film in theatrical release, merchandising companies increasingly prefer to wait for movies to reach video release, which comes roughly two to five months after theatrical opening. Retailers "are building bigger programs for DVD release than for the theatrical launch," notes Disney Consumer Products chairman Andy Mooney. "This is really a new phenomenon post-*Finding Nemo* and it is building."

Home video is attractive because, after popularity is established in theatrical release, merchandisers find they can correctly estimate the demand for film merchandise and not get stuck with overstocks. Since retail stores sell the movie DVDs, VHS tapes, and movie-themed merchandise, there's cross promotion within the same store.

Mass merchants such as Wal-Mart seek low-cost movie merchandise such as key chains and hats with logos to accompany a video release. This kind of movie-associated merchandise can be stocked on pallets—standardized shipping platforms—placed in aisles and at the ends of shelves. The movie merchandise helps create a short-term event of several weeks that accompanies video release, and stocking pallets are easily removed to make way for the next in-store event. The video event merchandise tends not to be placed on store shelves, which are less visible than pallets in aisles and are reserved for items that are more year-round sellers.

It remains to be seen if the trend to wait for video release of a film significantly erodes merchandising support for theatrical releases down the road. Film distributors prefer that the cross-promotion coincide with the theatrical opening, which establishes a marquee value for a film that will be carried through other release windows such as video and television.

Involving Movie Talent

Movie merchandising is becoming more complicated as actors increasingly build a business exploiting their own persona and thus may not allow their images or voices to be used outside of the movies themselves. Top actors are directly promoting themselves from personal Web sites from which they may sell licensed merchandise and interact with fans. In some instances, they also line up their own product endorsements, which may conflict with partnerships arranged by their movie.

The team of Mary-Kate and Ashley Olsen, who are teenage television stars dubbed The Olsen Twins, is one of the biggest such talent juggernauts. The duo generate $1 billion per year in licensed merchandise tied to their personas. The Olsens starred in the Warner Bros. family comedy *New York Minute*, although the film mustered just $14 million domestic box office after a May 2004 release.

Tom Cruise and Robin Williams are among the top-tier actors who are known to be dead set against letting their likeness or voice be used outside their movies. This list also used to include Robert Redford, but he did a United Airlines voiceover in 2004 in what was his first mass market commercial.

On the other hand, youth market heartthrob Vin Diesel allowed his likeness to be used in the video game *The Chronicles of Riddick: Escape From Butcher Bay*, which came out at the same time that Universal Pictures released a *Riddick* movie in June 2004. A Diesel-owned company is cocredited with creating the video game from Vivendi Universal Games.

Merchandising Classic Films

Film studios increasingly pluck characters and films from their vaults for merchandising unrelated to new movies. Dusting off old properties attempts to wring fresh revenue from what's sitting on the shelves at film studios. This type of merchandising usually isn't intertwined with a current theatrical release but extracts revenue from old movie properties.

A case in point is Disney Consumer Products, which generates $14 billion in sales from merchandising all its parent company's properties. Its top characters are Mickey Mouse and Winnie the Pooh, which together account for $9 billion of licensing revenue. In 2000, Disney embarked on a strategy of developing new products using its properties, so that it would no longer rely heavily on third parties to hatch merchandise concepts. Among its successes is the Disney Princess doll, which is expected to ring up a staggering $2 billion in retail sales in 2004 in numerous product categories connected with the property.

Also milking its film library, Metro-Goldwyn-Mayer orchestrated a summer 2004 merchandising blitz for The Pink Panther, which is a 40-year-old character, and the promotion will give a running start to a new film scheduled for release in 2005. The Pink Panther animated character was updated and licensed to 20 companies to make 200 products. Licensees include Thomas Pink for women's apparel; JEM Sportswear and Jerry Leigh for T-shirts and tops; Vespa for scooters; Global Tour Golf for sports accessories; World Trade Jewelers diamond and pink sapphire charms; and E-Watch for timepieces.

This fits nicely with today's trend of consumers embracing "retro" (retrospective) properties, particularly from the 1950s. Unfortunately for the movie marketer with visions of collecting big bucks, the reality is merchandising companies may feel children's bed sheets adorned with Hostess Ding Dongs cake logos are a safer bet than a new and untried movie.

In another bid to milk old film property characters, Universal Studios Consumer Products Group tapped into nostalgia with a 2004 line of clothing, toy, and game products based on vintage films. The films include 1973 teenager coming of age drama *American Graffiti* and 1978 college campus farce *Animal House.*

Taking another tack in exploiting existing characters, Universal Pictures made its horror release *Van Helsing*, which grossed $120 million in domestic box office after its May 2004 release, into a showcase for characters it owns. The studio lays claim to character rights from the Wolf Man and Frankenstein, which both figure prominently in *Van Helsing*.

Video Games

Video games based on films cover a broad swath of movie marketing. They can impact merchandising, because game companies make licensed products based on the movie, and they can be springboards for promotional tie-ins, because game releases get their own big pushes in advertising for which there is rub-off on the movie. A big marketing campaign for a game launch can amount to $10 million in advertising and promotion and is climbing yearly.

Video game licensing is a big chunk of overall merchandise revenue for sci-fi, fantasy, and action adventure movies aimed at the youth audience. A minimum guarantee for game adaptations from big films runs $1–$8 million because hit games can sell one million copies at $30–$50 retail price. Licensing deals typically have escalators if unit sales surpass targets, which generate additional payments beyond the minimum guarantee.

Hardcore gamers, which are the youth and young male demographic, are cautious about titles based on movies because they have been disappointed by film-based games in the past. Still, the potential exists for a good adaptation because the video game software industry generated retail sales of $5.8 billion in the United States during 2003, according to researcher The NPD Group.

A successful game can account for 15–20% of a major film's total merchandise licensing revenue, according to *The Licensing Letter*. If a film does not have a big overall merchandising program but the game license is rich, the game contributes upwards of 75% of total merchandising revenue, estimates the New York City-based newsletter.

Game companies try to lock up bundles of films by making long-term, exclusive licensing deals with studios and other property rights holders. For example, Activision's license for *Spider-Man* is via the comic book outfit Marvel Enterprises in a deal that expires in 2009. Sony-owned Columbia Pictures, which makes the *Spider-Man* movies, shares in licensing revenue. Activision also has a long-term deal with DreamWorks covering computer graphic movies (and any sequels) for *Shrek 2, Shark Tale*, and *Madagascar* due in 2005 and *Over the Hedge* due in 2006.

Elsewhere, Electronic Arts has video game rights to the James Bond 007 franchise through 2010, via a deal with MGM Interactive and Danjaq, which is the producer of the James Bond films. Electronic Arts reported that the *Everything or Nothing* game based on James Bond property sold more than two million units worldwide. Nintendo sold more than five million game units for Nintendo's N64 platform based on the spy franchise's *GoldenEye* movie, which is the biggest game seller for a single game platform based on a single movie title, according to NPD Group (Fig. 5.3).

More recently, a huge success in the Hollywood–Silicon Valley alliance are games based on New Line Cinema's *The Lord of the Rings*

Figure 5.3 Top Selling Film-related Video Game Titles by Platform in the United States 1995–June 2004

Overall Rank*	Title (Platform)	Publisher	Introduction Date	Unit sales (mil.)	Average Retail Price
4	GoldenEye 007 (N64)	Nintendo	Aug-97	over 5.0	$50
40	Spider-Man: The Movie (PS2)	Activision	Apr-02	over 1.8	$37
44	Star Wars: Shadow of the Empire (N64)	Nintendo	Dec-96	over 1.7	$61
53	A Bug's Life (PS)	Sony	Nov-98	over 1.5	$28
57	Star Wars: Episode 1 Racer (N64)	LucasArts	May-99	over 1.4	$32
63	Tomorrow Never Dies 007 (PS)	Electronic Arts	Nov-99	over 1.4	$32
65	Lord of the Rings: The Two Towers (PS2)	Electronic Arts	Oct-02	over 1.4	$44
67	Bond: Agent Under Fire (PS2)	Electronic Arts	Nov-01	over 1.4	$40
72	Star Wars: Rogue Squadron (N64)	LucasArts	Dec-98	over 1.3	$48
83	Enter the Matrix (PS2)	Atari	May-03	over 1.2	$44
94	Harry Potter and the Sorcerer's Stone (PS)	Electronic Arts	Nov-01	over 1.1	$36

N64, Nintendo 64; PS, Sony Playstation; PS2, Sony Playstation 2
*Rank among all titles including non-film
Note: Based on sales data compiled from 1995 to June 2004
Source: The NPD Group

that sold an estimated 5.5 million units for Electronic Arts, or more than $100 million at retail. That figure is based on three movies. The video game industry's all-time sales leader is the NFL football title marketed under the name of television sportscaster John Madden that has sold 37 million copies over 15 years for Electronic Arts.

The leading independent video game companies are Activision, Atari, Capcom, Eidos, Electronic Arts, Konami, Namco, Sega Enterprises, Take-Two Interactive Software, THQ, Ubisoft Entertainment, and Vivendi Universal Publishing. The three makers of video game consoles—or platforms—also are big game makers: Sony (PlayStation), Microsoft (XBox), and Nintendo (GameCube). Representing another format, Nintendo makes Game Boy, which is the popular hand-hand platform. Sony's PlayStation 2 format is the biggest draw for game software. The three console game makers tend to favor their own platforms in software sales, which is why film companies often license to independents that are neutral and thus service whatever platform has the highest sales potential. Video game licenses almost always are granted on an exclusive basis, with game companies typically making games for multiple platforms.

Majors in Game Merchandising

With big money at stake, major film studios have tried to enter the game business directly, but with mixed results. Several studios had affiliates pursuing ambitious game-making businesses for a time, but the businesses were unprofitable and scaled back. Vivendi Universal Games, a sister company to Universal Pictures, struggles. It cut one third of its workforce in June 2004, reportedly amid two consecutive unprofitable years. There's another Hollywood connection to the game business in that Sumner Redstone, chairman of Paramount Pictures–parent Viacom, is controlling shareholder of Midway Games. That's a personal investment separate from Viacom, although Viacom may buy the company someday.

Despite setbacks, a goal of film studios is to carve out a bigger position in the video games business. They see video games as vehicles to extend film merchandise selling beyond the brief eight-week window around theatrical release for other types of licensed movie products, such as T-shirts and caps. Research indicates consumers play a favorite video game for an average of 50 hours, creating a potential depth of engagement not associated with other licensed merchandise from a movie. Another goal of film companies is to create video game adaptations that are so compelling that the game adaptations will be hits even if the films on which they are based fare poorly in cinemas.

The ideal scenario is to release video games based on big films concurrent with theatrical release to cross-promote the film. For example, THQ's *Finding Nemo* game arrived at stores three weeks ahead of the Disney/Pixar family animated film's May 2003 theatrical release. Activision's *Spider-Man: The Movie* video game made its debut at the same time as the Columbia release in May 2002.

Notable points of friction have occurred between video game outfits and film marketers. In June 2003, Activision sued Viacom. Activision alleged the conglomerate's Paramount Pictures studio did not adequately maintain the Star Trek franchise, after Activision signed a 10-year video game licensing deal in 1998. Only one *Star Trek* movie has been made since the pact was signed. Several weeks later, Viacom later filed a cross-complaint suing Activision. The lawsuit revealed Activision agreed to pay $20 million in advance royalties and warrants and then make additional payments based on game sales. In late 2004, Viacom licensed the rights to make a massive multiplayer game based on *Star Trek* to startup Perpetual Entertainment, while the Activision litigation continued.

The release of games at the same time or in advance of theatrical release represents a dramatic shift in thinking within the movie business over the past two years. A few years ago, the video game license was seen simply as a component of the overall movie merchandising campaign. Now, it's something of a standalone proposition because of the big money involved.

Video games are among the most demanding product licensing category because games are placed into development months before a movie starts production. Video game companies need about 18 months of lead time to create and market a game, so they begin the process even before a movie's script is finished in some cases. More typically, a game license is arranged once a film is approved for production. Game companies base their decision on whether to license a movie in part on the extent they'll be able to utilize likenesses of actors and other recognizable elements of a film.

One factor in choosing a video game company is its track record in marketing games on schedule, because the movie distributor is counting on the game release to support the theatrical opening. In general, the video game industry has a spotty record making deadlines. In some cases, a film is required to shoot footage for use in making the game, although that practice is becoming less prevalent as computer graphic technology improves.

Talent in Game Merchandising

Hollywood talent agents take the position that licensing the likeness of their actor clients for video games is a right to be acquired separate from the actor's performance in a film. With film productions in line first and already pocketing licensing fees, game companies are cautious about making additional payments for actors for use of their likenesses and voices. To get around movie star demands for likeness fees, game companies simply create characters in their games based on films that do not look exactly like the actor playing the movie role.

In other cases, video games sometimes are allowed to use actual likenesses of movie talent but they employ third-party "voice actors" for dialogue. In *The Lord of the Rings* video game, actor Elijah Wood provides voice for the Frodo character, but soundalikes represented other characters portrayed in the film by Orlando Bloom and Viggo Mortensen. In a high level of movie-to-game involvement, the writer–directors of *The Matrix: Reloaded*, the brothers team of Larry and Andy Wachowski, shot scenes for the video game published by Infogrames (which is a sister company to Atari) during movie photography. They were credited as the game's creators.

Video game companies have become increasingly selective, choosing to put their resources around fewer titles in bids for blockbusters. For example, Atari reportedly invested well over $10 million to make a game based on the Warner Bros. film *The Matrix: Reloaded*. The blockbuster mentality is also a byproduct of skyrocketing engineering costs. A sophisticated video game costs $2–$10 million to create today, more than double a few years ago, amid escalating salaries for game makers.

The best prospects for video game adaptations based on films are family, action, adventure, sci-fi, thriller, and comedy genres. The audience for these films is a good fit with the games demographic of children and young males. Obviously, some film genres are not suitable, such as dialogue-driven dramas for sophisticated audiences, because this demographic is not in the game player market.

Interestingly, video game outfits mount their own promotional tie-ins with consumer goods companies. For example, beverage PowerAde got a product placement in Atari's *The Matrix: Reloaded* as part of the Coca-Cola product's $10-plus million tie-in promotion with the movie. PowerAde, which is part of the Coke beverage empire, created tie-in ads with a made-up character known as Agent Johnson, who is seen in the backdrop of the movie. PowerAde also launched a new flavor based on *The Matrix*.

Video Game Platforms

Video game companies typically sell their wares on a worldwide basis. The United States, which is the biggest territory, usually accounts for slightly less than half of all sales; all the other international territories make up the balance.

Video game companies say they expect to make their products compatible for new wireless platforms, such as cell phones, in the future. At the moment, the big platforms in the market are Sony's PlayStation 2 console (introduced in North America in October 2000) and the original PlayStation; Microsoft's Xbox console (introduced in North America in November 2001); the personal computer format; Nintendo's GameCube console (introduced in North America in November 2001); and finally Nintendo's handheld Game Boy and Game Boy Advanced (Fig. 5.4).

Consoles are devices made specifically as platforms for video games, unlike personal computers, which can play game software but are designed primarily for nongame uses. Sony, Microsoft, and Nintendo are developing next-generation game consoles that probably will reach the market in late 2005 or more likely in 2006.

In the United States, the big retail outlets for games are Wal-Mart (which accounts for 20% of revenue at Activision), Best Buy, Blockbuster, Circuit City, Electronic Boutique, GameStop, Target, and Toys R Us. In 2004, THQ set its suggested retail prices for game cartridges in the United States at $20–$55 for PlayStation 2, XBox, and GameCube; $20–$35 for Game Boy Advance titles; $10–$55 for personal computer games; $10–$15 for the aging PlayStation; and $20 for the Game Boy Color handheld.

Figure 5.4 Activision's Video Game Software Sales by Platform

Platform (Manufacturer)	Percentage	
PlayStation 2 (Sony)	43%	
Xbox (Microsoft)	22%	
Personal computers	20%	
GameCube (Nintendo)	8%	
Game Boy (Nintendo)	4%	
PlayStation (Sony)	3%	

For fiscal year ended March 31, 2004
Source: Activision

Video game companies develop something of a brand name identification based on how their products are received. Because games are individually engineered products, a degree of commonality exists within a company's products, which the more savvy game players can distinguish. Looking at the economics of the games business, software and product development accounted for 22% of expenses in fiscal 2004 at THQ, which markets games based on movies *Finding Nemo* and *Polar Express*. About 11% of its expenses were payments for intellectual licenses, such as movie rights.

Music

Music is one element of the creative process that almost always is flogged in marketing efforts to support theatrical release. The music business is a willing but battered partner. Worldwide retail sales of music experienced a 7.6% decline for 2003, slipping to $32 billion, and have been shrinking since 1999.

The United States accounts for about 37% of global music sales at retail ($11.8 billion in 2003) and Canada 2% (US$676 million). The Big Four music companies are SonyBMG, Universal Music Group, Edgar Bronfman Jr.-led Warner Music Group, and EMI Group. Together these four account for 75% of global music sales.

Movie soundtracks go back decades, yet some new twists are emerging as the album for *Spider-Man 2* broke new ground. There were 11 different soundtrack albums for the *Spider-Man 2* movie, each customized for a geographic region by the studio's sister company Sony Music. Each regional album has somewhere between 15 and 19 songs, with Sony Music working in a mix of its artists around the world in an effort to build their popularity. For instance, *Web of Night* by TMR is only on albums in Japan, Portugal, and Brazil. The band Killing Heidi performs *I Am* on the album for its home country of Australia.

The soundtrack album from the first *Spider-Man* movie sold a lofty two million units worldwide and included the hit single *Hero* from Nickelback. Top-selling film soundtracks in the United States over the years include *The Bodyguard* from 1992 with 11.7 million albums, *Titanic* from 1997 with 10 million albums, and *The Lion King* from 1994 with 7.7 million albums (Fig. 5.5). The soundtrack from escape comedy adventure *O, Brother, Where Art Thou?* almost seemed like a bigger hit than the Disney movie of 2000, selling 6.8 million albums.

Most movies register more down-to-earth sales for their albums. Music from Disney's teenage surreal drama *Holes,* which was a surprise

Figure 5.5 Top Selling Music Albums Based on Films

Rank	Title	Units (mil.)	Year of Movie
1	*Bodyguard* Soundtrack	11.8	1992
2	*Titanic* Soundtrack	10.0	1997
3	*Lion King* Soundtrack	7.6	1994
4	*O Brother Where Art Thou?* Soundtrack	6.8	2000
5	*City of Angels* Soundtrack	5.4	1998
6	*Grease* Soundtrack	5.1	1978
7	*Waiting to Exhale* Soundtrack	5.0	1995
8	*Space Jam* Soundtrack	4.7	1996
9	*8 Mile* Soundtrack	4.6	2002
10	*Forrest Gump* Soundtrack	4.4	1994

Note: Sales data covers 1991 to July 2004 in the United States only
Source: Nielsen SoundScan

hit in 2003 with domestic theatrical box office of $67 million, generated shipments of 120,000 album units in its first two weeks of release. Radio Disney estimated that 3.1 million young people listened to radio play of *Holes* songs per week on its service alone. The film was cheap by major studio standards, costing just $30 million to make, versus the majors' average of $63.8 million.

Advertising for movies sometimes includes plugs for the album in cross-promotions. For example, newspaper ads for Columbia's *Not Another Teen Movie* in 2001 carried large text saying "Soundtrack featuring *Tainted Love* by Marilyn Manson and music by Orgy, Saliva, Muse and Mest."

Consumer goods marketers are always eager to arrange promotional tie-ins with movie music. For DreamWorks' animated film *Shark Tale*, Coca-Cola adapted a song from the soundtrack into television commercials running 30 and 60 seconds. The song is Mary J. Blige's new version of *Got to be Real*, which is a remake of a 1978 Cheryl Lynn hit.

Geoff Cottrill, group director–entertainment marketing at Coca-Cola, said the Mary J. Blige song meshes nicely with beverage giant's current ad campaign Coca-Cola Real. "This is a good example of what I would call a value-for-value proposition," said Cottrill. "We committed to specified numbers for (movie-themed product) packaging, promotional weight, and media weight for this campaign." In exchange, Coke gets to use movie-themed music. Coke mounted other big movie tie-ins with *The Grinch*, *The Matrix: Reloaded*, and two of the *Harry Potter* movies.

A lot of the action in music now focuses on securing play of music videos. Music videos tend to be a mixture of scenes from a movie combined with special footage. The special footage can be of the music artists, who are not seen in the film itself, and/or actors from the movie in scenes shot specifically for the video. A common point of friction is that music channels desire exclusivity for airplay, although granting exclusivity limits exposure.

A breakthrough in using the music video to promote a movie came with the 1983 release of the slick coming-of-age drama *Flashdance*, whose sexy dance sequences received extensive television exposure. The 1992 comedy spoof *Wayne's World* got a plug via a one-hour MTV special in which its main characters presented a series of music clips, including The Top 10 Bands that Sound Like Diseases. The distributor of both movies is Paramount, which is a sister company to MTV.

History of Merchandising

The first protection for consumer product brands in the United States became possible in 1870, when a federal law established a trademark registry. Walt Disney Co. issued what is believed to be the first movie merchandise license in 1929 for the rights to put a Mickey Mouse character on a children's writing tablet, which according to legend was granted for a $300 fee. By 1932, Disney set up a licensing division—the first of its kind by a film studio—and remained the most active among studios for decades. Ingersoll-Waterbury sold the first licensed Mickey Mouse-themed watch in 1933.

"In addition to Disney, names like Little Orphan Annie, Jack Armstrong, and Bugs Bunny infiltrated American households in that era," notes LIMA. "One of the very early licensing successes during this period was the unprecedented sale of Shirley Temple look-alike dolls." The child actress was under contract to Twentieth Century Fox.

In the early sound era of film, the first important sound tracks came from musical films. A breakthrough occurred in 1937, when songs from the Disney animated feature *Snow White and the Seven Dwarfs* garnered widespread radio airplay, particularly for songs *Heigh Ho! Heigh Ho! It's Off to Work We Go* and *Whistle While You Work,* according to *Motion Picture Marketing and Distribution: Getting Movies in a Theatre Near You* (Focal Press, 1991) by Fred Goldberg.

The impact of film was demonstrated when undershirt sales plummeted after Clark Gable appeared bare-chested in the 1934 romantic comedy *It Happened One Night*. By the 1940s and 1950s, television programs dominated the business with merchandise from children's favorites Hopalong Cassidy and Howdy Doody.

Movies joined sports, fashion, and books as mainstays of the modern licensed merchandise industry. The current age for movie merchandising erupted with Twentieth Century Fox's *Star Wars* in 1977 and Warner Bros.'s *Superman* in 1978, which both proved to be blockbusters in merchandise sales. In a famous turn of events, *Star Wars* writer–director George Lucas agreed to reduce his salary as a filmmaker, which reportedly amounted to $100,000, in exchange for personally getting the film's merchandising rights and other lesser noncash consideration from Fox.

The *Star Wars* saga has generated billions of dollars in retail merchandise sales over the years from its multiple films. The Lucasfilm property actually appeals to two different market segments. First is the regular children's market, which is tapped by all pop culture movies. Second is a following among adults who are both nostalgic—because they remember the first film—and sci-fi aficionados.

Revenue from merchandising grew steadily in the 1980s. By the early 1990s, merchandising moved from just ancillary revenue to being a budgeted line item in a film's financial plan. This intensified pressure on studio merchandising executives to wring lucrative deals from the licensing industry.

Stoking both Hollywood and the merchandising industry were hits such as Disney's 1994 tsunami of a blockbuster *The Lion King*, which rolled up $313 million in domestic box office and $1.5 billion in retail merchandise sales. Warner Bros.'s *Batman*, which was released in 1989, reportedly generated $500 million in retail merchandising sales, translating into $50 million in revenue for Warner Bros. Some 30 million black T-shirts with the Batman logo were sold, creating an apparel-industry shortage of black T-shirts for a time. Until then, successful family films did just tens of millions of dollars in merchandising at retail, with some exceptions such as *Star Wars*.

The licensing industry looked past occasional stumbles in this era, such as *Dick Tracy*, which was the Disney release of 1990 starring Warren Beatty and Madonna. Although the movie grossed a satisfactory $104 million in domestic box office, *Dick Tracy* merchandise sold poorly, probably because its source comic strip was dated and because Beatty did not connect with contemporary youth culture.

Another misfire was the fantasy action adventure *The Last Action Hero*, which Columbia Pictures released in 1993. Columbia–parent Sony kept merchandising in-house as much as possible in a bid for corporate synergies. A Sony MiniDisc player, cell phones, and other electronics products were peppered in the movie, which cost $80 million to make. Sony music artists contributed to the soundtrack album. Promotions included plastering the film's name on a NASA rocket launched into orbit. The film starring Arnold Schwarzenegger mustered a disappointing $50 million in domestic box office.

The high water mark in movie merchandising business came with *Star Wars: Episode I—The Phantom Menace*, the 1999 Twentieth Century Fox release that was a licensing disappointment. Its estimated $1 billion in retail sales of merchandise was handsome by most measurements but was short of the $3 billion expected. Filmmaker Lucasfilm had crafted a well-received program to revive licensed merchandise and signed lucrative deals. For example, toy company Hasbro committed to pay a reported $590 million in minimum royalties and granted warrants to Lucasfilm for 7.5% of its stock, as part of a 9-year pact for three *Star Wars* movies. The Hasbro deal covered toys such as action figures, vehicles, and board games. In 2003, Hasbro's minimum payment was renegotiated to $505 million and its toy license extended to 2018.

In a sign of the current climate of licensee caution, toy companies backed away from open-ended commitments for multiple movies. These days, the trend is for merchandise outfits to sign for individual movies.

6 Publicity

It is not enough to conquer; one must learn to seduce.

Voltaire

Publicity is the most cost-effective but is among the least predictable disciplines in film marketing. The task of film publicists is rather simple: make every one of their films seem exciting and interesting, even the films that are not.

The traditional publicity campaign relies on media outlets to cover a film with stories, gossip column items, reviews, or posted content. The objective is to create a buzz in the marketplace that mushrooms. "You must penetrate the population culture," said Jeffrey Godsick, executive vice president of marketing at Twentieth Century Fox. "You must hear from the inner friend base, the outer friend base, the DJ, from the news."

Film marketers don't control the extent of press coverage, whether positive or negative, or the timing of its dissemination. However, when everything clicks, a publicity campaign saturates the marketplace with subtle third-party endorsements of films via upbeat media coverage (Fig. 6.1).

Publicity campaigns cost tens to hundreds of thousands of dollars per film. Publicity is the big area of opportunity for film marketers because of the emergence of the Internet. Film marketers can get Web sites to post raw movie materials because entertainment content is in demand by consumers. Furthermore, film marketers and their agents can interact directly with consumers online, who may not necessarily know they have hooked up to a film's publicity machine.

131

Figure 6.1 Giving a prominent platform to *The Last Samurai*, the *Chicago Sun-Times* presented its newspaper logo being sliced in half by the film's star Tom Cruise in December 2003

Source: *Chicago Sun-Times*

Publicity in Production

Each film has a unit publicist, whose job is to work at or near the set during principal photography of a theatrical film, which typically runs 7 to 16 weeks. For most films, the unit publicist's salary and expenses are included in the budget of the film and are considered a production cost. Even at this early stage, a defined marketing strategy should be in place for a given film so that the unit publicist can lay the groundwork to achieve goals.

The unit publicist prepares biographies of key creative talent (top actors, director, producer, cinematographer, etc.), a synopsis of the film, and other materials to be included in a press kit. The unit publicist usually oversees taking of still pictures and, in some cases, video recordings for later use in publicity efforts (Fig. 6.2). Principal photography is the ideal venue because the cast is available on the set and is in costume and in thematic backgrounds. If on-set interviews of talent are part of the marketing plan, the publicist can arrange the interviews with journalists during production in order to start a ripple of publicity.

A separate but related marketing person is the unit photographer, who shoots still photos during principal photography of a movie. Usually, the photographer works only selected days and is not on the set every day, as is the unit publicist.

Figure 6.2 Press Kit Inventory

- **Lead** – Two page overview description of movie written in a quasi-news style that describes a film's plot and genre and lists top creative talent in brief
- **Production Information** – No more than five pages of description of where principal photography occurred and when, with some interesting anecdotes
- **About the Cast** – Mini biographies of main cast and creative talent, including other film credits and personal information
- **Cast and Credits** – a full list of cast, crew and producers; this should be flagged as being preliminary
- **Long Biographies** – More detailed biographies of stars and any other significant talent
- **Clips** – reprints of favorable articles about the film, such as from film festivals
- **Photo Log** – inventory of still photos that are included or available
- **Video Clips** – DVD of video clips

Source: *Marketing to Moviegoers*

Getting high-quality and compelling still photos is perhaps the most important objective for marketing during principal photography. Newspaper editors and magazines publish striking photos from obscure films over mediocre photos from famous films, so high-quality photos are one way small films get attention. "You can't underestimate what good stills can do," said Nancy Gerstman, co-president of distributor Zeitgeist Films. "They are very powerful marketing tools."

A key security issue is that the still photographer's work is under control of the production. Star talent often has approval rights of photos as part of employment contracts. In a typical scenario, after the top talent approves a pool of photos, all photo prints, film negatives, and digital files of unapproved shots are destroyed to ensure they don't pop up later by mistake or are misappropriated.

Major studios traditionally produced 5,000 press kits per movie for delivery to newspapers, magazines, broadcast news, and other media outlets. With digital technology and the Internet, studios have set up online digital press kits from which journalists using passwords can download materials. This practice is catching on because journalists receive materials in a digital format that is easily adapted to their media. With conventional press kits, media outlets must convert analog materials such as glossy picture prints to digital. As a result, press kit duplication is down to 2,500 units at the major studios. Independent distributors tend to duplicate 750 to 1,500 press kits per significant film.

Screenings

The publicity campaign cascades in waves following a standard chronology for just about every film. Long-lead media outlets such as monthly magazines are serviced first and short-lead media such as daily newspapers last. Journalists from each category screen films together, often at parallel screenings held in Los Angeles and New York. Reviewers from the same media outlets screen movies separately closer to premiere.

For the news/feature/editor crowd, press screenings for monthly magazines are scheduled four to six months in advance of a film's premiere, assuming a mostly completed film or big blocks of footage are in presentable form. If a film is not sufficiently assembled, this first wave is skipped. In some cases, a film may be 90% finished, which is suitable in most circumstances, but the film's director argues that the film should not be shown to journalists until it is finished.

Monthly magazines, such as *Vanity Fair*, *Esquire*, and *Premiere*, commission feature stories three months before publication, so editors must be impressed early to get the stories into their editorial planning cycles. Approximately 60 monthly publications are potential berths for film stories.

Press screenings for weekly magazines, such as *Entertainment Weekly*, *Newsweek*, *People*, and *Time*, tend to be held eight weeks before film release. The weeklies can include editors from big Sunday entertainment sections of dailies, entertainment guides, and alternative press, such as New York's *The Village Voice*, which tends to have weekly frequency. The daily newspapers and electronic media screen films two to six weeks in advance of release.

Efforts to book film talent on television shows, such as *The Late Show with David Letterman* on CBS Television, starts months before show premieres. Besides network television talk shows, syndicated television shows with national reach, such as *Entertainment Tonight, Access Hollywood*, and *The Oprah Winfrey Show*, interview movie stars or do features on films.

"If we have a film that we are gung-ho about, we'll invite the daily editors with the monthlies (in the very first screenings)," said Shannon Treusch Goss, a partner at New York City-based film publicity agency Falco Ink. "They may not all come, but at least this puts the film on their radar screens. If you have a good film, there's no reason to hide it."

If a film has a shot at landing a cover placement, the lead time required by the media outlets is longer. For a film that does not have realistic potential to get a cover or big feature write-up in a print publication, the screenings should at least generate capsule write-ups in summary sections of new films.

A film typically gets 10 to 20 mass press screenings in Los Angeles and New York City over a six-month period prior to premiere. "An independent film may not be at the top of editors' lists, so we hold a lot of screenings to give editors a lot of options," said Janice Rowland, partner at Falco Ink.

Movies that appeared in film festivals have already been seen by some critics and perhaps have received some press attention. "At festivals, you don't want to get too much coverage by the general press, because that means light coverage when the film hits theaters later," said Zeitgeist's Nancy Gerstman. "But once your film is booked in theaters, there is no such thing as too much publicity."

Industry trade shows are another platform for screenings to reach both the consumer press and the film trade. *Men in Black*, the oddball 1997 comedy that became a blockbuster grossing $251 million for Columbia

Pictures, is an example. The film had little profile with journalists when a block of footage was screened at ShoWest convention for movie theater operators in Las Vegas four months before the film's theatrical premiere.

"All we had was 10–12 minutes of footage, but it was enough," said Marvin Levy, marketing chief at Amblin Entertainment, Steven Spielberg's company that made the film. "We showed it and, wham, it worked. People really got the idea that this would be something special. This was March and the movie was coming out in July." A smaller film clip presentation that had been made to New York journalists a few weeks earlier also helped seed press efforts.

Reviewers tend to have separate screenings that also are held in succession for media with monthly, weekly, and daily frequency, which come after their news and feature colleagues have seen the same film. Prestige films and films aimed at sophisticated adult audiences live or die by reviews. A film that targeted this adult audience but turned out poorly typically is scheduled for reviews at the last possible moment.

Some films are not screened at all for reviewers prior to release, which results in what some call a "cold opening." A cold opening is always a sign to media outlets that the distributor is worried about the critics' response. Films released in summer 2004 without pre-release review screenings included *Alien vs. Predator* and *Paparazzi* from Twentieth Century Fox, *Exorcist: The Beginning* from Warner Bros., and *The Cookout* from Lions Gate Releasing. The absence of a pre-release critic screenings means that, at best, electronic media can get a review out the same day a film opens and daily morning newspapers on the following day.

Mainstream reviews have a small or no influence in the youth and children's market. Film critics panned the contrived cartoon comedy *Space Jam*, horror character extravaganza *Van Helsing*, and steel mill music video yarn *Flashdance*, but those films were "review proof" because they became hits anyway.

Publicists place embargoes on review publication dates. The embargoes are generally honored by media, but which day a review should appear to be useful to moviegoers is not always clear. With theaters opening some big films just moments after midnight on Wednesdays or Fridays, some newspapers want their reviews to run two days earlier. Another scheduling quandary involves films that open Wednesdays at some theaters and then open more widely on Fridays.

Occasional dust-ups occur between film publicity executives and journalists when journalists break review embargoes. Often, a point of friction is comments by on-air entertainment news presenters in broadcast media. They can banter that they've seen a certain film and, while saying they are obliged not to discuss it, nonetheless go on to make short commentaries that make it clear whether they think the film is great or disappointing.

Publicists usually take a hard line against offenders who run reviews before embargo dates, even if the reviews are positive. Publicists reason that if breaches become commonplace, more media outlets may disregard embargoes and chaos will ensue. Publicists can always threaten to completely ban offenders from specified future screenings, although that punishment hurts the box office prospects of films.

Independent publicity agencies often perform a significant amount of the work for publicity campaigns, even for major studios that have big in-house publicity operations. Outside agencies handle geographic areas, such as servicing New York media for a Los Angeles-based distributor. The agencies also can handle specific media, such as the Internet, or various ethnic groups. Fees can range from tens to hundreds of thousands of dollars. Outside agencies tend to be hired for several weeks to six months, depending on their task.

Film distributors target ethnic groups for special marketing, especially the large Latino audience that composes 13% of the United States population but accounts for a estimated 20% of cinema admissions. Spanish-language television channels, radio, and print media are outlets for star interviews and other coverage. Latin World Entertainment, using estimates from its studio clients, says that Latinos composed 34% of the opening weekend box office for Columbia/Revolution's youth actioner *XXX* and 24% of the opening weekend for Disney/Pixar's animated family film *Monsters Inc.*

Planting Exclusives

Although mass mailings to blanket media journalists are standard procedure, so are the one-on-one initiatives. Movie marketers use a lot of discretion—the art of publicity—in steering exclusive stories and content to media outlets to trigger maximum coverage. Journalists want to be ahead of the pack, so an early look at a film or exclusive access to talent can be a catalyst for splashy coverage.

The wooing process starts with determining which journalists from important publications most likely will embrace a given film. This determination requires knowledge of the press corps. Once a candidate is identified, the pitch is made for a private screening with an important caveat. If the journalist does not like the film, the journalist promises not to discuss the film with others until the film goes to a general press screening. Otherwise, the journalist can start an early ripple of bad word of mouth that dogs the film. Publicists and journalists work together for a succession of films, so they are motivated to maintain a trusting relationship.

In one example of this strategy, *American Beauty* received an enthusiastic, out-of-the-blue write-up in the *New York Times* approximately 10 weeks before the film's premiere in 1999. The newspaper has national reach and is followed by other media outlets, so other journalists quickly took notice of the DreamWorks film. The *New York Times* looked smart because the quirky drama about middle-aged angst in the suburbs went on to win the Oscar for Best Picture.

The media world is segmented into an array of niches, each of which provides an opportunity for exclusive placement. For example, one of the national news weekly magazines can be pitched exclusive access, with the understanding that the movie has a shot at a cover position or photo inset on the cover teasing a story inside. The news weekly exclusive does not impact monthly magazines, daily newspapers, or electronic media. Publicists can pursue exclusive placements in some media segments while taking a general saturation approach for the rest.

The late-night broadcast television talk shows hosted by Jay Leno on NBC Television and David Letterman on CBS Television are hotly competitive with each other, so they'd never book the same guest. The early-morning network magazine shows—ABC Television's *Good Morning America*, CBS Television's *The Early Show*, and NBC's *Today*—are separate booking opportunities, but again the shows are competitive with each other, so just one appearance may be possible. The late-morning syndicated talk shows are another booking opportunity that doesn't interfere with appearances on earlier network morning shows.

Several considerations are involved in deciding whether to pursue the exclusive placement. The exclusive strategy is useful for films that are a hard sell. The ploy is used assuming that the films, without some extra push, will garner little attention even in a well-executed broad publicity blitz. The hard-sell film could have a problematic genre, such as a drama with elderly characters, which media outlets might routinely downplay given their pursuit of the youth culture. Also, if a film turns out particularly well, it's a good bet that any journalist getting an early exclusive screening will quickly file a report, which hopefully will start a positive buzz.

One downside of exclusives is that media outlets sometimes back out at the last minute, often because of unforeseen breaking news that takes a slot promised to a movie. At that point, the publicist is free to pitch the film elsewhere, but it may be too late to start the whole process from scratch. For this reason, some publicists try to avoid exclusives because they can fall apart through no fault of either party.

For booking talent for television appearances, the most sought after placements are news magazines in prime time on broadcast networks and Oprah Winfrey's syndicated afternoon show. One reason the show is popular is its reputation for not canceling at the last minute, so the show is a dependable booking. Another attraction is that Oprah Winfrey's interviews are in-depth, and both publicists and talent feel the placement is impactful. A drawback is that the audience may not be a direct demographic match with a film. Still, the exposure is valuable given that a paid 30-second advertisement on *The Oprah Winfrey Show* is approximately $80,000 for an original episode (not a repeat).

Actors Tobey Maguire and Kirsten Dunst made a joint appearance on *The Oprah Winfrey Show* in June 2004 just before Columbia's release of *Spider-Man 2*, in which they starred. The show presented film clips and the host talked up the technical wizardry of the movie. "Filmmakers wanted their hero of fly higher, their villain to be more terrifying, and their stunts to look seamless," Winfrey said for a lead-in to one clip. Going for the personal touch, she quizzed Maguire on the demands of dieting to bulk up for *Spider-Man 2* after slimming down for his role in horse racing drama *Seabiscuit*. Winfrey questioned Dunst on the famous upside-down kiss in the first *Spider-Man*, for which Dunst recalled, "I was freezing... and I had to act romantic."

The idea of exclusive placements sounds so simple, but plenty of competitive zeal among journalists and sometimes surprising rivalries exist. For example, in late 2001, Warner Bros. clashed with *Entertainment Weekly*, which is in another division of its parent Time Warner. *Entertainment Weekly* published a big story on *Harry Potter and the Sorcerer's Stone* without cooperation from Warner Bros. and just ahead of studio-arranged stories by other publications. According to *The Wall Street Journal*, the studio retaliated by not running movie ads in *Entertainment Weekly* for three months and not inviting the magazine's film critics to screenings until both sides patched things up.

Junkets and Talent

Star talent is a magnet for media coverage, whether one-on-one access with journalists from top media outlets, mass interviews in what are called press junkets, or barnstorming via publicity road tours.

The junkets are the most impactful because they are cost efficient and can be conducted quickly. The word *junket* comes from an era when studios paid expenses of traveling journalists, although these days most media outlets either won't accept or limit freebies. In general, the bigger the media outlet, the more likely its journalists will pay their own expenses because their employer has deep pockets. Smaller media outlets are more inclined to accept and even expect freebies. The financial arrangements can be a mix where out-of-town journalists pay their own travel expenses such as airfare, but the film distributor pays for meals (including for in-town press). Which side pays for hotel bills of out-of-town journalists varies depending on circumstances. For example, if the junket is in an exotic or offshore location, the film company often is expected to provide hotel rooms because journalists may find the rooms difficult to book directly.

These press events are held at a single location—hence the efficiency—where talent sits for interviews and photos for rotating waves of journalists. In Los Angeles, the popular hotel for press events is the Four Seasons in Beverly Hills. In New York, the venues often are Essex House and the Regency Hotel. Such press events can run 2–3 days and accommodate 50–300 journalists. "Today, we have to think globally," said Amblin's Marvin Levy. "On press junkets, it used to be half day or a day for international press while domestic press would get two or three days. Now it's evened up. For most movies, you know that you are not going to get another chance with the international journalists."

The junkets are particularly useful for hooking up movie talent with out-of-town press and journalists from second-tier publications whose media outlets are not significant enough to be accorded one-on-one interviews. Journalists from top media outlets sometimes don't participate because they have the clout to obtain solo interviews.

Distributors typically promote several films at one junket. Two distributors may run junkets in concert, which provides more movies and thus is a bigger magnet for press participation. In a typical arrangement, one distributor gets the electronic press one day and then print media another day, so journalists are hosted by the same distributor for a full day. Shorter, less elaborate mass press events are referred to as roundtables, where press spends a few hours interviewing in a single day.

The junket structure calls for small groups of print media journalists to be allotted a series of interviews up to a half hour each. When one mass interview is over, the group moves to another room to conduct a new mass interview with different film talent. Thus, the actors, directors, and other movie talent who give the interviews stay in the same room to speak to numerous groups of journalists back to back during the course of a day. Television journalists usually get 5–10 minutes for one-on-one interviews. This eliminates having multiple voices asking questions, which would confuse viewers when the footage is televised.

In some instances, top talent insists that journalists promise in writing to adhere to ground rules that limit the scope of questions and restrict what journalists can report. The taboo subjects can be talent's political or religious beliefs, family life, or a past unpleasant incident. Actor Tom Cruise is among those who insists on written ground rules as a condition for many of his interviews.

The agreements typically specify that no "bloopers" from electronic interviews be disseminated and, for both print and electronic, no "derogatory" coverage be published. However, the very top tier of media journalists are exempt because they have clout and their employers enforce strict rules against such agreements. Interviews with top-tier media journalists often are one-on-one and carefully choreographed by publicists, who do their best to steer journalists away from sensitive topics in advance.

The majority of journalists from smaller media outlets don't have clout, so they are pressured to sign as a condition of their participation in junkets. The agreements are an ethical quandary for journalists. Freelancers who are hungry to exploit interviews over multiple publications often are required to sign because they may stretch material in order to sell a story. For their part, publicists maintain the purpose of the interviews is to discuss a new movie and talent's movie career, so written agreements spelling out ground rules simply ensure journalists will stay on the subject.

The best laid plans of film publicists can be derailed by talent that balks at participating in press events and interviews. Occasional heated behind-the-scenes battles occur between distributors and personal publicists of actors, who oppose marketing ideas for films or act as surrogates for talent in presenting objections.

Curiously, it is the custom for a movie production to pay personal publicists of top-tier actors for several months as part of the employment contracts with the actors, even though the personal publicists later may resist movie marketing plans. For example, the personal publicist may get $5,000 per month for 3 months. Whenever film companies have the leverage, they negotiate into the talent employment contract provisions that require talent to participate in specific publicity efforts.

Internet Introduction

The biggest opportunity for film marketers is the Internet, which enables entertainment-hungry moviegoers to feast on movie content via high-speed connections. Movie sites present film trailers, additional footage, talent interviews, Making Of documentaries, and comments and mini-reviews by moviegoers themselves.

High-speed broadband was in 20% of television homes in the United States at the start of 2004, up from 5% in 2000. With broadband, Internet subscribers can view moving video almost instantly, unlike narrowband dial-up that requires long waits for a download and generally presents jerky and poor-quality video.

Most broadband allows only a small video image—meaning a portion of a computer screen. However, within that small size frame both the audio and video quality are very good. "Finally, we're able to replicate the cinematic experience on the computer," said Doug Hirsch, general manager of Yahoo Movies, the leading Internet film site. "Today I can watch the first three or five minutes of the films. I can consume about as much of the movie as I want."

A centerpiece of Internet marketing is the official movie Web site, which typically costs $20,000 to $100,000 to build. At the very high end, the major studios can spend as much as $500,000. Audiences for sci-fi, horror, and fantasy films tend to be early adopters of technology and expect movie Web sites to be elaborate.

The Web sites incorporate many of the elements found in press kits—star biographies, pictures, and story description—but are geared for moviegoers and not professional journalists. Web sites also list film classification information prominently (which is mandatory for films rated in the United States), theater playdates, trailers, sweepstakes/contests, games, and downloads of movie-themed images and audio. Once a film opens, critic reviews may be posted as well. The trend-setting *The Blair Witch Project*, the 1999 blockbuster that created an enormous buzz from Internet marketing, pioneered the strategy of adding new content gradually to its official movie Web site over time. This gave Web surfers an incentive to return to peruse the new material.

Visitors can register for e-mails about the movie. E-mail provides film marketers with an avenue to directly contact moviegoers and can be used again when a film hits video release. In another interactive application, Web sites can solicit online sales of movie-themed products such as caps and T-shirts.

The ability of film distributors to communicate directly to consumers is unique to the Internet. In earlier decades, film marketers always faced a buffer in consumer communications, whether it was movie theaters or media outlets such as television channels on which movie ads were placed.

Internet Buzz

With Web sites aching for unique entertainment content and millions of moviegoers surfing the Web, publicity campaigns directed solely at the Internet have become a standard component of movie publicity campaigns.

Major studios and independent distributors tend to rely on one or more outside publicity agencies to execute Internet publicity campaigns. Internet publicity agencies used by film companies, which are clustered in Los Angeles, New York, San Francisco, and Boston, charge fees ranging from $10,000 to $100,000 per film. Internet publicity agencies structure their services much like mainstream advertising agencies by working through an account team that marshals other services within the agency, such as the creative department and the media buying department.

Film marketers who hire Internet agencies increasingly seek some measurable response rate to quantify results, which was difficult years ago when Internet marketing was embryonic. These days, marketers can count e-mail responses, Web site hits, and pickups of movie materials by third-party Web sites. In Internet lingo, a hit is the request for a file made to a server.

The planning for Internet campaigns ideally begins six to nine months before a movie premieres. The lengthy lead time is necessary to produce Web-specific materials. The campaigns themselves tend be mounted in waves that start a few months before a film opens, with each successive ripple becoming more pronounced and more specific to the film. The Internet efforts reach a fevered pitch four to six weeks before a film opens, hopefully propelled by earlier waves.

Given that Internet marketing is a form of grass roots communications, Internet campaigns often are supplemented by street teams. The street teams consist of marketing foot soldiers organized to spread commercial messages by posting handbills, passing out promotional items at events, and even chatting up people in public places. Organized and systematic street team campaigns can cost $10,000 to $20,000 in several big cities.

Many publicity opportunities lie outside a film's official Web site. For independents, the trend is to place big portions of films on third-party Web sites to create a buzz and induce moviegoers to see the whole movie at theaters.

Yahoo Movies, the most popular movie site with 10 million unduplicated visitors per month, is a prized platform. It has posted large slices of Sony Pictures' *Darkness Falls*, Lions Gate Films' *Cabin Fever*, Fox Searchlight's *28 Days Later*, and Fox Searchlight's' *Brown Sugar* prior to their theatrical release.

"It gives you whole chunks of the movie, a real taste," said film marketing consultant Jeff Dowd of the strategy. "It's not just quick cutting-trailers." For Dowd, use of pre-release slices is a proven technique borrowed from the past when he worked at a Seattle arthouse theater years ago. He showed the first reel of *Harold and Maude* during screenings of other movies in what helped build word of mouth that made the offbeat 1971 comedy a hit.

Another concept is introduction of episodic content crafted specifically for placement on the Internet, dubbed Webisodes. The episodic structure emphasizes a continuing story, so moviegoers who have seen the first episodes presumably will want to catch the subsequent segments to see where the narrative leads. Supporting the IFC Films release in July 2004 of rock band documentary *Metallica: Some Kind of Monster*, an arc of nine episodes running several minutes each was placed on music Web site *fanscape.com* and the official movie Web site.

The major studios, which have higher-profile films than independents, are less inclined to let big chunks of their films float around cyberspace to stoke marketing. The big stars in major studio films also discourage uncontrolled dissemination of their images and voices. Indeed, many studio-mounted promotions use soundalikes for stars' voices heard in interactive marketing promotions.

The Internet marketing of *The Blair Witch Project*—the scripted mystery drama about supposedly missing documentary makers—was an Internet marketing milestone. The release of snippets of the mock documentary on the Internet and the resulting buzz propelled the 1999 release to a staggering $140.5 million in box office from the domestic (United States and Canada) market. Artisan Entertainment, which now is part of Lions Gate, distributed the film, which was made on a shoestring budget of just tens of thousands of dollars.

In the immediate aftermath of *The Blair Witch Project*, pundits heralded the Internet as a dependable platform for impactful viral marketing, but few other movie phenomena of this ilk followed. Viral marketing is communications that encourages recipients to pass on messages or materials to others in order to achieve a peer-to-peer snowball effect. Other films could not match the Internet success of *The Blair Witch Project* because the film's mystery seemed real at the time, not calculated manipulation. *The Blair Witch Project* enjoyed a novelty, which evaporated when other film campaigns attempted to duplicate the strategy. Verifying that the thrill indeed was gone, the sequel *Book of Shadows: Blair Witch 2* generated just $26.4 million in domestic box office.

British sci-fi import *28 Days Later* is considered the next most celebrated film whose success can be traced primarily to Internet marketing. The yarn about bloodthirsty zombies overrunning the United Kingdom cost $8 million to make and rolled up a sizable $45.1 million in domestic box office. Its advertising campaign from distributor Fox Searchlight minimized traditional ad spending in television, even though *28 Days Later* opened broadly at 1260 theaters in June 2003.

The distributor spent an estimated $1 million in Internet advertising such as banner ads and mounted *28 Days Later* sneak previews in 28 cities, supported by Internet publicity, to build word of mouth. Fox Searchlight posted clever messages urging moviegoers to attend the sneaks wearing red and rewarded those who did with movie-themed merchandise.

Internet film campaigns often launch with a first wave of anonymous content but then transition to revealing the source, as with *September Tapes*, a low-budget scripted drama presented in documentary style. The film, which was distributed theatrically by First Look Pictures in September 2004, is the first feature made in Afghanistan by a Western outfit after the defeat of the Taliban regime. New York-based Internet publicity outfit Special Ops Media, which handled the campaign, seeded the Internet with dramatic combat footage from the R-rated *September Tapes*. When directed to a nondescript Web site with first wave, consumers saw a cryptic message from someone named Eric Bruderton, who urged them to watch the clip and "show it to your friends." Later waves are attributed to the movie.

Although the source of the first wave of material is murky, "it's not that much of a stretch because some of the footage was actually shot in Afghanistan, which is a real war zone," said Special Ops partner Christian Anthony. "This not something you just put out there and see what sticks. For *September Tapes*, we leaked select information and clips to build early stages of a buzz. Then the official website is launched. More clips are leaked and this builds a backstory. For users who really liked the material, they will find clips and information already released."

General film sites are platforms to place materials and create buzz in chat rooms. The mainstream movie sites include *yahoomovies.com, iFilm.com, imdb.com, entertainment.msn.com/movies*, and *boxofficemojo.com*. More specialized venues are *aintitcool.com, rottentomatoes.com, filmthreat.com, CountingDown.com, filmforce.ign.com*, and *bloodydisgusting.com* (for horror films).

Some Internet publicity is not placed at movie Web sites but rather special-interest Web sites and pages that tie into a film's theme. Movies that deal with animals, travel destinations, fashion, or car racing aim publicity at Web sites on those topics.

Movie Web sites have blossomed into substantial businesses as evidenced by Internet giant IGN Entertainment's acquisition of *rottentomatoes.com* in June 2004, reportedly for approximately $10 million. *Rottentomatoes.com* was founded in August 1998. IGN was attracted by the movie Web site's young audience, which IGN covets to bolster Internet advertising sales. With paid advertising on the rise, movie Web sites probably will become less antagonistic to film marketers and less inclined to post unflattering material, given a desire attract banner advertising. They also will want to participate in distributor-sanctioned promotions.

Internet Pitfalls

Although movie Web sites can be a positive force, they also can create headaches for film marketers. A major problem occurs when moviegoers post reviews of films after test screenings, in essence evaluating a film that is merely a work in progress before theatrical release. Given the anonymous nature of e-mail addresses, verifying who wrote a given posting and if the person actually sat through a test screening is difficult.

Anonymity is a curse, but it also is a blessing because film marketing executives and their agents can fan out on the Internet, spreading word that a movie is fantastic. By simply using nondescript e-mail addresses, these film praisers can conceal their hidden agendas in chat rooms and film commentaries. The ethics of such disguised promotions are questionable, and the film industry is full of apocryphal stories of clever publicists supposedly roaming the Internet incognito to stoke movie publicity.

A potential source of future friction within the industry is movie marketers—under the cloak of Internet anonymity—who target inappropriate audiences, given a film's rating. After films are rated by the Classification and Ratings Administration for the United States, advertising materials are subject to review by the related but separate Advertising Administration to ensure the material conforms with the audience restriction.

Material surreptitiously circulated on the Internet to promote a movie could sidestep review, especially if the material's source is hidden. The issue is complicated because Internet campaigns usually start before a film is finished and classified. Materials of unrated films are not subject to review, of course.

Aggressive Web sites can go off in tangents not appreciated by film marketers, which is another downside of the Internet publicity shuffle. It's well established that media outlets have a right of "fair use" of copyrighted material, such as snippets of film images, for journalistic purposes but not for commercial usages. For journalism, it's legal to present small pieces of protected material in journalistic endeavors.

Film distributors have won legal actions blocking commercial usages. In 2003, two federal courts ruled in favor of Walt Disney that Video Pipeline, a home video retailer, could not stream unauthorized short previews over the Internet. The case is significant because Video Pipeline is a legal video distributor that simply prepared its own marketing materials using movie images instead of Disney-supplied images. Video Pipeline began streaming its own previews for Disney movies when Disney yanked studio-supplied promotion materials.

E-mail Publicity

Telephone calling trees are an old concept in which one person rings up several others who do the same to pass on a single message, creating a mushroom effect. The Internet elevates the calling tree to new heights because of the ability to pass on original messages in the form of e-mails. Films with social or political messages are ideal for such grass roots marketing, where a motivated base of persons sends out e-mails widely.

A case in point is *The Corporation*, a documentary that dissects the role of big companies in society. Good Company Communications, a Vancouver-based marketing outfit hired by the film's distributor, sent out 12,000 e-mails to persons with progressive political views and estimates that pass-ons resulted in the message reaching 300,000 persons. *The Corporation* was distributed by Zeitgeist Films in the United States and by Mongel Media in Canada.

Film distributors create their own e-mail lists, soliciting Web surfers to register at movie Web sites for follow-up information on video release and other films. Overall, the e-mail industry's response rate for replies ranges from 2–25%. This technique is still in its early days, and movie distributors have not yet marshaled mailing lists to any big marketing successes. Maintaining up-to-date e-mail lists is costly because respondents change addresses and demand to be removed from lists, which is a right under privacy laws.

Although film companies collect personal data when respondents sign on, the information is sketchy. Therefore, culling precise demographic sublists from big lists that have little or no demographic focus is difficult. Some major studios e-mail general promotions touting their entire film slates, but this approach looks to be ineffective. Such e-mail promotions have the effect of pushing a film catalog that is simply a grab bag, which sidesteps the capability provided by the Internet to engage in target marketing.

Promotion via Video

A growing trend is to use home videos to support a theatrical release. One tactic is issuing a special short (5–25 minutes) promotional video that contains clips and background material from a soon-to-be released film. Another strategy applies to sequel films, where the theatrical release of a new film in a series coincides with a video release of an earlier installment.

In March 2004, Columbia Pictures enlisted electronics/appliance retailing giant Best Buy to give away 500,000 special DVDs containing a preview of the April 2 release of *Hellboy*, the stylish horror film that went on to gross $59 million domestically. The DVD contained exclusive content: a 10-minute preview of *Hellboy*, talent interviews, and behind-the-scene footage. It also contained trailers for two other upcoming Columbia releases: *Spider-Man 2* and *Resident Evil: The Apocalypse*. Elsewhere, Twentieth Fox distributed promotional DVDs via electronics retailer Circuit City to support theatrical release of its 2003 action-adventure film *Daredevil*.

DVD giveaways are on the upswing because DVD hardware penetration passed 73% in the United States at the end of 2004, a fast takeup after its introduction in 1997. DVD households tend to have higher incomes, which is a key attraction. In comparison, the aging VHS videotape format has higher household penetration, 91% at the end of 2003 in the United States. However, VHS tapes are bulkier and more expensive, do not have the ability to instantly address sections, and offer less technical quality, which is an important consideration when showcasing high-gloss movies.

In large volumes exceeding 100,000 units, the manufacturing cost is 50 to 75 cents per DVD with simple packaging for promotion giveaways. In DVD giveaway tie-in promotions, the film distributor's partner generally pays for advertising and promotion to consumers. Deals vary as to which side pays for duplicating DVDs.

Before the DVD format made its splash, publicity efforts used CD-ROMs and enhanced CDs that plugged into personal computers, which created an Internet link to consumers. Film marketers used CD-ROMs for in-home computers as a vehicle to engage in e-mail communications with moviegoers. However, CD-ROM playback devices are not designed to present lengthy motion video.

On the other hand, DVDs distributed for film publicity tend to be played on regular television sets, not personal computers. The advantage is that an entire family typically is available to watch around a television set, but a television in the living room lacks an Internet link, according to *The Entertainment Marketing Letter* newsletter. A method to establish a communications link is to run a sweepstakes that is promoted with the DVD.

The other type of DVD tie-in involves timing the theatrical release of a sequel to coincide with video release of predecessors. In one sense, this type of tie-in is easy to arrange because the distributor usually controls both theatrical and home video release. However, a sequel can take more than a year to create, so its earlier installment has already been distributed on video. One strategy is packaging a video release as an enhanced version or as a boxed set.

Columbia TriStar Home Entertainment released a special DVD version of the original *Spider-Man* film on video on June 1, 2004 to stoke interest in the sequel *Spider-Man 2*, which arrived in theaters on July 2. In a new wrinkle, the DVD included a coupon for a cinema admission to *Spider-Man 2*.

Another noteworthy example of theatrical–video synergies is *Kill Bill Vol. 2*, which followed closely on the heels of its predecessor because both films were made at the same time. Miramax released the video of *Vol. 1* just three days before *Vol. 2* arrived in theaters on April 16, 2004, creating a publicity bonanza. "The marketing for both releases included plugs for the other," wrote Scott Hettrick, editor-in-chief of *Video Business*. "[Filmmaker Quentin]Tarantino was plugging both the new movie and the DVD in every newspaper interview and on every talk show, and even in an appearance as a judge on *American Idol*."

Promotional Documentaries

With expansion of cable television outlets and the Internet, mini-promotional documentaries are becoming increasingly useful in marketing movies. Mini-documentaries run anywhere from 5–49 minutes and typically cost tens or hundreds of thousands of dollars to make. These mini-documentaries go by many names, such as The Making Ofs or Featurettes. Besides supporting theatrical release, mini-documentaries are included with DVD releases of a film.

The challenge is in planning. A special filming crew is responsible for recording events during principal photography of a movie. The mini-documentary needs to follow a script that presents a point of view that fits into the film's overall marketing plan. However, a film's marketing objectives are not always clear at the principal photography stage.

Television channels can produce their own film tie-in programs, enlisting studio cooperation. In one example, Warner Bros. partnered with documentary channel Discovery for a two-hour program televised just days before the May 2004 release of the historical epic *Troy* starring Brad Pitt. Discovery's *Troy Revealed: Unsolved History* presented film clips from the movie, interviews with talent from the movie, and behind-the-scenes footage mixed with a historical examination of the 3,200-year-old story. Actors Pitt, Peter O'Toole, and Eric Bana and director Wolfgang Peterson gave interviews.

Troy, which cost $175 million to make and collected over $133 million in domestic box office, got a boost as both entertainment and a slice of history. The narration in the Discovery special noted that the filmmakers "took special pains to portray bronze-age equipment accurately" and the movie "tells a story that virtually defines the word 'epic.' " Movie clips were accompanied with an on-screen text credit "courtesy of Warner Bros.," and at commercial breaks the narration stated that the Discovery program is "brought to you in part by Warner Bros." Warner placed regular film ads in commercial blocks. Discovery Channel averages 588,000 viewers, according to Nielsen Galaxy Explorer.

Twentieth Century Fox's sci-fi yarn *I, Robot* got plugs in four television programs prior to its July 2004 premiere. MTV, the music television cable network, put *I, Robot* in its first telecast of *Never Before Scene*, a special that is a prototype for a possible regular series devoted to movies. The half-hour MTV pilot show presented movie clips, behind-the-scenes footage, and an interview with star Will Smith. MTV's audience averages 563,000 viewers, according to Nielsen Galaxy Explorer.

I, Robot also received extensive promotion by being featured on two episodes of *American Chopper*, the television series about motorcycle construction that is the most popular program on Discovery Channel. Finally, the film received special coverage on Home Box Office (HBO) and Fox Broadcasting, the studio's sister outlet.

To promote these kinds of shows, occasional excesses occur. The Sci Fi Channel admitted it hyped promotion of a three-hour documentary on filmmaker M. Night Shyamalan in July 2004. The Sci Fi Channel touted *The Buried Secret of M. Night Shyamalan* as revealing a "disturbing" secret about the Hollywood filmmaker. However, in fact, Shyamalan cooperated to plug his Disney release of *The Village*, and Sci Fi Channel later backed away from its earlier claims in news reports.

Perhaps the most curious The Making Of involved the feature film *The Man Who Killed Don Quixote*, a $32 million European coproduction that was abandoned during principal photography in 2000 because of a lead actor's illness. A crew shooting footage for a sanctioned mini-documentary used its insider access to instead produce an 89-minute feature-length documentary that received theatrical release—*Lost in La Mancha*. The documentary grossed $732,393 in box office via IFC Films in 2003. The documentary filmmakers had drafted a simple contract that contained no exclusions, such as a termination clause in the event the feature film wasn't made. Thus, the filmmakers were free to pursue the full-length documentary that recounted the travails of the aborted movie.

Oscar Campaigns

Oscar campaigns are publicity drives whose objective is getting awards that, in turn, can be promoted to consumers and the press. Oscar campaigns contain a big paid-media component because they typically include advertising in film trade newspapers. Such ads are aimed at movie professionals because the general public does not read the movie trade press.

The Academy of Motion Picture Arts and Sciences (AMPAS), which confers the Oscars, has just over 5,800 voting members, who are mostly clustered in Los Angeles. New York City is the only other city with a sizeable population of AMPAS voting members.

Campaigns for an Oscar cost from $200,000 to $3 million and often are managed by independent publicity consultants who specialize in such marketing. Campaigns include private screenings for academy members, events such as cocktail parties with filmmakers and cast, direct mail (via both e-mail and postal service), and ad campaigns in trade newspapers.

Separate but parallel award campaigns can target other organizations that confer awards, because recognition elsewhere can create momentum in Oscar voting. The Screen Actors Guild, Directors Guild of America, and Writers Guild of America give out prestigious awards in their crafts, and most of their members are not in AMPAS. Other film organizations, such as the Independent Feature Project, also honor film excellence with its Spirit and Gotham awards.

The various organizations of film critics, who are members of the press but are not filmmakers, are another component of the film award cavalcade. The most significant is the Hollywood Foreign Press

Association, which confers the Golden Globes. This award is highly sought because it is a harbinger (with 70% correlation) of the film that later wins the Best Picture Oscar and the Best Actress Oscar.

One consequence of awards marketing is that film distributors tend to advertise movies more heavily for theatrical release in Los Angeles media if the movies have awards prospects. The ads are nominally aimed at the general public, but film marketers know the ads also reach the pool of Hollywood professionals who vote for film awards. Outdoor billboards are favorites in this dual consumer and industry marketing.

The Oscar campaigns are sketched out a year in advance, in part to select theatrical release dates after sizing up the cinema market and rival films. The official Oscar selection process occurs in a compressed period running barely two months (Fig. 6.3).

Realistically, six to eight films have a shot at the five Best Picture nominations in any given year. The final planning is done in early autumn and kicks off around Thanksgiving, aiming to influence voting for nominations.

In February 2004, the main Oscars telecast averaged a whopping 43.5 million viewers in the United States, according to Nielsen Media Research. When *Titanic* was the big winner for 1997, 55 million people watched the awards telecast.

Figure 6.3 Official Oscar Chronology 2004–2005

Date	Event
Nov. 1, 2004	Deadline for entering animated features
Dec. 1, 2004	Distributors must file final screen credits for films
Dec. 27, 2004	Mail out of nomination ballots
Dec. 31, 2004	Deadline for completing qualifying theatrical run
Jan. 15, 2005	Nominations polls close at 5 p.m. PST
Jan. 25, 2005	Nominees announced at 5:30 a.m. PST
Feb. 2, 2005	Mailing of final ballots with nominees
Feb. 7, 2005	Nominees Luncheon at Beverly Hilton Hotel
Feb. 12, 2005	Scientific and Technical Awards Presentation at Regent Beverly Wilshire Hotel
Feb. 22, 2005	Final voting closes at 5 p.m. PST
Feb. 27, 2005	77th Annual Academy Awards at the Kodak Theatre at Hollywood & Highland televised live by ABC Television Network beginning at 5 p.m. PST

Source: *Marketing to Moviegoers*

Effective for the 2004 telecast, AMPAS moved the main awards ceremony forward one month to late February. This time frame is now a fixture, designed to reduce the window for Oscar lobbying and lessen the opportunity for influence by other awards.

The schedule compression puts more pressure on the last quarter of the year, which is the busy season for prestige films to position their theatrical debut for an Oscar run. The thinking is that, to be fresh in the mind of voters, a movie with awards potential should not be released early in the calendar year.

Despite conventional wisdom, films released early in the year occasionally clean up at the Oscars. Focus Features' quirky drama *Lost in Translation*, a September release, was selling briskly in video and—oddly enough—still was playing strongly in theaters shortly after the film received four Oscar nominations in January 2004. *Gladiator*, the DreamWorks release domestically, won the Best Picture Oscar for 2000, even though the film premiered in early May.

The academy nominally prohibits its members from overtly lobbying for votes, for example, by requiring cocktail parties saluting films not be limited just to Oscar voters. AMPAS even has an Oscar compliance czar Ric Robertson, Academy executive administrator, whose job is to advise marketers how to stay within guidelines—referred to as Academy Standards—and crack down on violators. The standards attempt to keep Oscar voting dignified, without excessively infringing on free speech. The AMPAS guidelines are available at *www.Oscars.org/regulations*.

In reality, the well-oiled Oscar marketing machines attempt to influence voters and go to the very edge of compliance with academy rules. Not lobbying increases the likelihood that rival films and talent with aggressive marketing campaigns will prevail in voting.

Much is at stake because the careers and salaries of Hollywood creative figures climb with Oscar nominations and soar with wins. Actors who win Oscars often see their salaries double, triple, or quadruple for their very next film because they are temporarily very hot. Their salaries may slide back over time but will remain well above their pre-Oscar levels.

Best Picture, Best Actor, and Best Actress awards can significantly lift a winning film's box office, particularly for arty films that open slowly late in the year. Those Oscar categories are magnets for adults who are light moviegoers but will patronize serious films that receive critical acclaim.

As a rule of thumb, a Best Picture win adds somewhere between $15 and $40 million to domestic box office. For small films released late in the calendar year, a clutch of Oscar nominations and later wins can be catalysts to enlarge existing theatrical runs by booking more theaters or to even resume a theatrical run for a film not then in theaters. Oscar-winning films also get a big boost in international box office because they mostly premiere overseas later. On the other hand, mainstream commercial films, such as New Line's *Lord of the Rings: Return of the King* in 2003, tend not to receive big boosts domestically attributable to Oscar wins, because they typically have already cleaned up at the box office. In recent history, the Best Picture Oscar winners have generated a sizable domestic box office (Fig. 6.4).

A new rule for the Oscar class of 2004 is that advertising for one nominee may not "cast a negative or derogatory light" on others, according to AMPAS. Also, for the first time, the film distributor can pass out free tickets to voters for entry to commercial theaters to see nominated films. Film marketers routinely hold free private screenings open to all academy members, but these screenings are not as convenient as being able to go to any performance at a commercial theater.

In the 2002 Oscar race, Miramax placed newspaper ads quoting former AMPAS president Robert Wise, an Oscar-winning director, as saying Martin Scorsese had his vote for Best Director for *Gangs of New York*. Miramax's action drew a rebuke. AMPAS instructed Miramax to pull the ad because academy members are not supposed to make implied endorsements of nominees (in any case, Roman Polanski won that year for *The Pianist*).

In the run-up for the 2001 Oscars, a flurry of column items and news stories said that an Oscar smear campaign was targeting Universal's troubled genius drama *A Beautiful Mind*. Word circulated about unsavory aspects of the movie's real-life subject, a Nobel Prize-winning mathematician. The whispering campaign, whose source was never identified, erupted after the film received eight nominations but before final Oscar voting was completed. Still, *A Beautiful Mind* won the Best Picture Oscar.

Independents, which are overwhelmed by the major studios in box office, can stand toe to toe in competition for Oscars and other kudos. The edgy and serious films of independents resonate more with AMPAS voters than do glossy studio fare. Lately, the independents have stepped up with box office hits that also are favorites with high-minded film reviewers. Newmarket Films distributed *The Passion of the Christ*, which is a foreign language film to boot, and Lions Gate Releasing and IFC Films jointly handled Iraq war critique *Fahrenheit 9/11*.

The master of the Oscar campaign is Miramax, which is the New York-based distributor owned by Walt Disney but classified as an indie. Miramax, whose Best Picture winners include *Chicago* in 2002 and *The*

Figure 6.4 Best Picture Oscar Winners 1980–2003

Year	Title	Distributor	Box Office	Oscar Wins	Release Date
2003	The Lord of the Rings: The Return of the King	New Line	$377,027,325	11	12/17
2002	Chicago	Miramax	$170,687,518	6	12/27
2001	A Beautiful Mind	Universal	$170,742,341	4	12/21
2000	Gladiator	DreamWorks	$187,705,427	5	5/05
1999	American Beauty	DreamWorks	$130,096,601	5	9/17
1998	Shakespeare in Love	Miramax	$100,317,794	7	12/11
1997	Titanic	Paramount	$600,788,188	11	12/19
1996	The English Patient	Miramax	$78,676,425	9	11/15
1995	Braveheart	Paramount	$75,609,945	5	5/24
1994	Forrest Gump	Paramount	$329,694,499	6	7/06
1993	Schindler's List	Universal	$96,065,768	7	12/15
1992	Unforgiven	Warners	$101,157,447	4	8/07
1991	The Silence of the Lambs	Orion	$130,742,922	5	2/14
1990	Dances With Wolves	Orion	$184,208,848	7	11/09
1989	Driving Miss Daisy	Warners	$106,593,296	4	12/15
1988	Rain Man	MGM	$172,825,435	4	12/16
1987	The Last Emperor	Columbia	$43,984,230	9	11/20
1986	Platoon	Orion	$138,530,565	4	12/19
1985	Out of Africa	Universal	$87,071,205	7	12/20
1984	Amadeus	Orion	$51,564,280	8	9/21
1983	Terms of Endearment	Paramount	$108,423,489	5	11/23
1982	Gandhi	Columbia	$52,767,889	8	12/10
1981	Chariots of Fire	Columbia	$58,972,904	4	9/25
1980	Ordinary People	Pararamount	$54,766,923	4	9/19

Source: Box Office Mojo (www.boxofficemojo.com)

English Patient in 1996, allocates significant funding for trade ads and cocktail parties. It covers travel/living expenses for out-of-town talent to reside in Los Angeles for weeks during the Oscar season to advance campaign objectives.

Publicity Screeners

In recent years, film distributors sent out videos—either DVD or VHS—to voters for the Oscars and other awards to ensure their films were considered. Video distributions to a small circle of industry professionals and press often came before the public video release of the films, which might still be in theaters.

After seeing that industry "screeners"—videos for consumption by voters—were becoming a source for film piracy, the Motion Picture Association of America (MPAA) briefly banned its members from sending out the videos in September 2003. Independent producers opposing the action won a court injunction by December. The court said a sweeping ban from the trade group was anticompetitive. Distributors that are MPAA members now set their own policies (AMPAS was not involved because it is not directly involved in distributing screeners).

In the firestorm that ensued when the screener ban was announced, independent distributors complained the main impact of the ban was to help big high-profile films, which are the domain of the majors, and to diminish the chances of indies. The MPAA edict also extended to indie arms of majors such as Miramax, New Line, and Fox Searchlight. Interestingly, independents with no major studio ties, including Lions Gate, IFC Films, and Samuel Goldwyn Films, were free to continue to send out screeners.

In the aftermath, film distributors instituted tighter controls on screener circulation, including cutting out some press organizations. Authorities later traced two incidents of piracy to screeners sent to academy voters, which supports the MPAA's original justification for dropping screeners. Other incidents of movie piracy have been traced back to screeners going out to other voters for other film awards.

History of Publicity

The studio system that emerged in the 1930s developed with well-oiled publicity machines that carefully orchestrated placement of news stories and items yet simultaneously kept unsavory missteps of stars out of the press. MGM's legendary head of publicity in that era—Howard Strickling—wielded enormous power over film journalists because he controlled access to the most star-laden studio.

Through the 1940s, most American cities had many newspapers. Thus, it was relatively easy to get coverage of publicity stunts, which the major studios generated via their own networks of field marketing offices and press agents. The studios would hatch easy-to-cover publicity stunts in the morning and, if it was a slow news day, get some pictures and stories in the afternoon newspapers, most of which have since folded, merged, or converted to morning newspapers.

By 1948, the studio system's stranglehold on Hollywood began to unravel with the court-ordered break up of studio–theater combinations, which divorced distribution from exhibition. In the aftermath, the movie business became more of a free-for-all. The first independent press agents—hired by stars, powerful producers, and indie movie companies—appeared in the 1950s. By the end of that decade, the rising popularity of foreign films and the emergence of strong independent producers led filmmakers to embrace gritty reality for subject matter.

With the switch, much of the fantasy appeal and glamour of studio-generated publicity faded. The anti-establishment ethos that came out of the Vietnam War made the press more eager to search out sensation by the late 1960s and less willing to go along with Hollywood hype. At the same time, the press started to take a more sophisticated approach to film by covering behind-the-camera filmmakers, such as directors and producers, as they did star actors.

By the 1970s, the major studios became attached to big conglomerates, which curbed the publicity excesses of their Hollywood outlets for fear of creating an investor or consumer backlash that would injure the parent. Studio field publicity offices began to fade in this era with the emergence of big chain media conglomerates whose journalists cover the film industry from offices in Los Angeles or New York City.

These days, film publicity materials can be sent digitally to distant news outlets. This method is supplanting an early 1980s innovation of the electronic press kits that included videocassettes, which aimed to drum up publicity on local television stations that are coveted placements for publicity. The videocassettes included star interviews and other film footage that local broadcasters could televise. Film marketers also used satellite feeds to deliver video to television channels *en masse*.

In the new millennium, the challenge is to promote movies in an age when activist film stars get press attention for their politics instead of their film roles.

7 Distribution to Theaters

There is no bad time to release a good movie.

Industry Adage

Marketing to Moviegoers focuses on the United States and Canada, which for the purpose of theatrical distribution are considered a single territory called the domestic market. Films almost always open simultaneously in both countries because of the common language (with the exception of French-speaking Quebec province) and because most of Canada's 32 million population lives along the border, giving that population access to mass media originating from the United States. In particular, United States television channels—with their salvos of movie advertising—are carried by Canadian cable systems along the border.

Overview

Despite growing competition from movies on home video and television, United States cinema achieved steady growth with 1.574 billion admissions in 2003, up from 1.262 billion in 1995, according to major studio trade group the Motion Picture Association of America (MPAA) (Fig. 7.1). In 2003, there were 473 theatrical releases, which declined from a peak of 510 in 1997. Of the 473 theatrical releases, 194 were new films from major studios, 265 were new movies from independents, and 14 were reissues from both majors and indies, which is shorthand for independent distributors.

Figure 7.1 Admission Growth in United States 1983–2003

Year	Admission (mil.)	% change prior year	% change 2003
2003	1,574.0	−4.0%	−
2002	1,639.3	10.2%	−
2001	1,487.3	4.7%	5.8%
2000	1,420.8	−3.0%	10.8%
1999	1,465.2	−1.0%	7.4%
1998	1,480.7	6.7%	6.3%
1997	1,387.7	3.7%	13.4%
1996	1,338.6	6.0%	17.6%
1995	1,262.6	−2.3%	24.7%
1994	1,291.7	3.8%	21.9%
1993	1,244.0	6.0%	26.5%
1992	1,173.2	2.9%	34.2%
1991	1,140.6	−4.0%	38.0%
1990	1,188.6	−5.9%	32.4%
1989	1,262.8	16.4%	24.6%
1988	1,084.8	−0.3%	45.1%
1987	1,088.5	7.0%	44.6%
1986	1,017.2	−3.7%	54.7%
1985	1,056.1	−11.9%	49.0%
1984	1,199.1	0.2%	31.3%
1983	1,196.9	−	31.5%

Source: Motion Picture Association of America

In distribution, a movie booked at a theater is called a playdate or engagement. Because films from major studios increasingly open wider, that is, they have more playdates, the benchmarks used to define various magnitudes of saturation in films' releases constantly change. Films open increasingly wider to maximize the benefit of costly and broadly focused advertising campaigns.

- An *exclusive run* involves just one theater per city, typically in just a few major cities nationally. Some film executives suggest exclusive could be up to three playdates in New York City, given its giant size.
- A *limited release* is just a few theaters per city.
- A *wide* pattern is 600 to 1,999 playdates nationally.

- *Saturation* is 2,000 to 2,999 playdates.
- With playdates on the rise, some pundits have added the category *super saturation* for films that premiere with at least 3,000 playdates.
- A *regional* release is limited to a specific geography and thus is not national.

Films typically open on Fridays in the United States and Canada, so the films are fresh in theaters to take advantage of the peak weekend moviegoing period. Sometimes major films open on a Wednesday—a doldrums period—if the distributor feels good word of mouth from small midweek audiences will energize the peak weekend box office.

A film that received the midweek premiere treatment in May 2004 was DreamWorks' *Shrek 2,* which collected a mind-boggling $164.7 million in its first 9 days of release. Walt Disney's *Pirates of the Caribbean: The Curse of the Black Pearl*, which premiered July 2003, is another example of a Wednesday opening that went on to be 2003's second-highest grossing film at $305.4 million. In an 11th-hour change, Twentieth Century Fox convinced some theaters in New York and Los Angeles that had booked the Denzel Washington action film *Man on Fire* to move up the premiere from a Friday to a Wednesday in April 2004. The objective was to jump start word of mouth in those influential cities. The film already was locked into a Friday premiere with a total of 2,980 playdates, where it took a hefty $22.7 million in box office for its 3-day opening weekend.

Interpreting box office success is tricky and varies depending on whether a film is in wide or narrow circulation. If a film is in exclusive engagements—perhaps a dozen engagements nationally—less than $10,000 per playdate per week usually is a disappointment. At that level, the film probably is not covering marketing expenses—mainly newspaper ads—and has poor prospects if the film goes wider. Films in such narrow exclusive release can gross in the multiple tens of thousands of dollars per playdate per week.

At the other end of the spectrum, the more playdates a film has, the more likely the film's per engagement average will be diluted because each additional wave of theater bookings cannibalizes the audience further. Also, the higher the playdate count, the more a distributor needs to book low-grossing theaters. A film that averages $5,000 per playdate on a three-day weekend with 2,500 engagements, which is a saturation release, translates into $12.5 million in box office. A film with $5,000 per playdate for a three-day weekend that has 100 engagements generates just $500,000 in total box office.

For three-day figures that often are cited in newspaper reports, films that don't average at least $2,000 per playdate usually are considered commercial disappointments, no matter how wide their release patterns. Looked at another way, a $3,000 per playdate average for a weekend with 3,000 playdates can be fine for a film but would be a disaster if the film had just 30 playdates.

Competing companies, such as Nielsen EDI, Rentrak, and Exhibitor Relations meticulously collect and collate box office revenue figures on a daily basis for film distributors, although admissions (head count or unit ticket sales) is not tracked carefully. Online services such as *Boxofficemojo.com* also compile cinema information. Box office for the peak weekend is subject to news reports, sometimes as early as Saturday, that are three-day projections from only the Friday actual figures. Somewhere between 70% and 90% of theaters provide quick, computerized box office figures. Film distributors take those figures and then estimate the uncounted balance from nonreporting theaters, which typically are low-grossing cinemas without computer equipment. Putting together the two pieces of information provides a total weekend box office figure, which is partly an estimate.

A week later, the main box office services have film distributors check their original flash figures, which were rushed, for any revisions. Theaters send film distributors their own tally on a six-week lag basis. If film distributors have auditors doing spot checks of ticket sales at theaters, those figures will be compared against tallies submitted by theaters for any sign of undercounting.

Using box office revenue as the main barometer for film performance results in the shortchanging of children's films in the rankings because kiddie tickets are priced lower than adult tickets. For example, the R-rated drama *Minority Report* from Universal was the top grossing film for the June 21–23, 2002 weekend at $35.7 million, although Disney's animated *Lilo & Stitch,* which opened the same day and tallied at $35.3 million box office gross, certainly sold more tickets when adjusting for children's prices.

Common Benchmarks

It's a longstanding rule of thumb in exhibition that a week-to-week decline of 40% or more from a constant pool of theaters is deadly for a film, indicating audience interest is evaporating. The constant pool counts only theaters that played the movie both weeks and excludes the impact of increasing or decreasing total screen count.

For very wide releases, the benchmark is slightly higher, perhaps 45%, because wide releases tap a large audience immediately. In an example of steep falloff, Universal's *The Hulk* grossed $132 million domestically, which would be wonderful for most films. However, the live-action movie, which cost approximately $140 million to make, is considered a disappointment because—after a boffo $81.7 million opening in its first full week in June 2003—its box office plunged an astronomical 67% to $27 million in its second full week.

Films in different genres follow consistent patterns. Films that appeal purely to the teenage and young adult audience, such as horror/slasher movies and gross-out comedies, tend to fade quickly because the moviegoers arrive the first weekend. Dramas for sophisticated audiences and romantic comedies hold steadier over many weeks because their adult audience reacts slowly to building word of mouth from the first wave of moviegoers. Also, the adult audience waits to digest reviews from critics. Kiddie films tend to run long because parents, who must bring their children to the theater, are sometimes slow to jump on a bandwagon.

For mainstream films, an ideal scenario is to segue to secondary crossover audiences after the film was first carried by other primary audiences. For example, adults may come in later weeks to see what the excitement is all about for films that initially were hits with a youth audience and received upbeat reviews from critics. A case in point is the top-grossing film of all time, *Titanic,* which generated a mind-boggling $601 million in domestic box office after a 1997 release. The youth audiences immediately embraced the teen love story between stars Leonardo DiCaprio and Kate Winslet and the hit theme song *My Heart Will Go On* by singer Celine Dion. Because of the booming box office and good notices from serious film critics, adults followed in later weeks, hence becoming a crossover audience. The original *Shrek* in 2001 also had crossover appeal. The family audience, which is heavy with children, was a big part of the film's $42.3 million opening weekend in May 2001. Teenagers and adults, drawn by reports that praised the film's campy humor, came in force later, helping boost the domestic box office to $268 million.

Another rule of thumb is that sequels typically don't match the box office of their predecessors. Although Columbia's *Stuart Little 2* was just as heartwarming and clever as its predecessor, the sequel grossed $65 million, versus $140 million for the first edition, an example of sequel falloff. Universal's three *Back to the Future* films showed a steady dropoff. The 1985 original grossed $208 million, the second $118.5 million in 1989, and the third $87 million in 1990. A common problem is that whatever came across as fresh and unique in the original is not so intriguing the second time around. There are occasional exceptions to the rule, however. Twentieth Century Fox's *X-Men: The Movie* generated a healthy $157 million in its 2000 release, whereas *X-2* soared to $215 million in 2003 (a third installment is in the works for 2006).

Movies with political orientation, whether overt or subtle, were considered an anathema to United States moviegoers, based on past experience. However, *Fahrenheit 9/11* and *The Day After Tomorrow*—two films with political messages—were big hits in the summer of 2004. Lions Gate Releasing and IFC Films jointly distributed Michael Moore's Iraq war critique *Fahrenheit 9/11,* which cost just $6 million to make and grossed over $119 million. Twentieth Century Fox's *The Day After Tomorrow,* the glossy disaster film that sounded a politically correct alarm against global warming, piled up an amazing $85.8 million in its first four days after a May 2004 premiere. The special effects extravaganza cost a reported $125 million to make and was directed by Roland Emmerich, who made the American flag-waving doomsday blockbuster *Independence Day* for the same studio in 1996. *The Day After Tomorrow* generated $187 million in total box office.

Still, in past years films with a political dimension fared poorly. An example would be *The American President*, the high-minded romantic comedy that critics held out as a paean to popular then-president Bill Clinton. Despite a stellar cast led by Michael Douglas and Annette Bening, the $60 million production mustered just a third-place ranking for its opening weekend in November 1995. The Columbia release finished the year ranked a disappointing 29th at the box office.

Release Dates

Picking release dates, which is the job of film distributors, is the intersection of science (statistical analysis of the marketplace) and art (gut instinct coupled with subjective judgments based on past experience). Many argue that the quotation opening this chapter—suggesting there's always plenty of room for good films—is merely a nice sentiment affirming the importance of quality in films. In reality, however, good films can fail miserably because of poor distribution plans, and mediocre films can generate robust box office because of good positioning in the marketplace.

The peak periods for moviegoing are the summer, when the youth audience is out of school; Christmas–New Year; Thanksgiving; President's Day; and Easter. The May through August summer period, which accounts for 33% of the calendar year, generates about 43% of box office. Big studio films open during the holiday weekends, or a week or two in advance, so that they are positioned as carryover films when the holiday starts. Release dates after peak holidays are perhaps the least attractive because the holiday hits continue to hold screens and moviegoers presumably have temporarily satiated their film appetite. Box office tracking services sell lists of school holiday vacation periods with details available down to individual school districts. Film distributors use the lists to plot release dates and theater booking strategies.

The majors trot out their biggest films in the summer. These films have production costs well above the 2003 major studio average of $63.8 million per film. In 2004, Universal's special effects horror extravaganza *Van Helsing* (with an estimated $160 million production cost) opened on May 7; Warner Bros.' sword-and-sandal epic *Troy* (thought to cost $175 million) on May 14; DreamWorks' animated sequel *Shrek 2* (estimated $80 million cost) on May 19; Twentieth Century Fox's environmental disaster drama *The Day After Tomorrow* (roughly a $125 million cost) on May 28; and Warner Bros.' *Harry Potter and the Prisoner of Azkaban* (the prior Potter film cost an estimated $140 million to make) on June 4. Columbia had planned to release *Spider-Man 2* on May 7 but moved the comic book actioner to June 30 to give the $200 million production more time needed for completion. *Van Helsing* then jumped into the vacated May 7 slot.

With major studios generating over half their total revenue from home video, the video release window is now a consideration in choosing a theatrical premiere. The Christmas gift season is a boom time for video, so June and July are great theatrical slots to position for video release four months later. Universal's *Seabiscuit* posted a satisfactory $31.6 million its first week in July 2003 and moved quickly to a video release in mid-December after collecting $120 million domestic theatrical box office. The horse racing drama ranked a lowly fifth its opening weekend but turned out to be the year's 16th highest grosser.

Another reason summer is a peak cinema period is that United States theaters have long been equipped with air conditioning, allowing moviegoers to escape summer heat. (In contrast, Europe's peak cinema season is autumn, in part because cinemas in its warm southern region only now are being fitted with air conditioning.) The Thanksgiving–Christmas period is another lucrative time frame to launch prestige films angling for Oscar and other critic awards. The end-of-year films are freshest in the minds of award voters.

Film marketers keep a close eye to the calendar, avoiding film releases at times its prime audience is distracted. For example, action films appealing to males are not scheduled for Super Bowl weekend. Other sports championships also are avoided. At election time, television and radio ad rates soar—increasing marketing costs—because of political ads.

Independents often are forced to take less desirable release dates because the prime slots are seized by majors. The indies also counterprogram versus the majors and calendar events. For example, an indie might release a movie with strong female appeal during a sporting event weekend to court women at a time men are glued to the television screen. Independents mostly target niche audiences—kids, teens, ethnic groups, or sophisticated adult audiences—because their films typically don't have the star power or production values of mainstream studio releases.

Films Colliding

Film distributors, which choose release dates, jockey for the best positions but also try to avoid suicidal confrontations. With the 473 films released in the United States in 2003 under classification ratings, multiple titles premiered in each of the year's 52 weeks. Films with similar profiles—action adventure, children's, documentary, etc.—try to avoid each other because they would carve up the same audience.

However, occasional showdowns occur. Lions Gate Films staked out an April 16, 2004 premiere for its actioner *The Punisher* long in advance, eventually lining up 2,649 playdates. Then in December 2003, Miramax moved its Quentin Tarantino-created martial arts actioner *Kill Bill Vol. 2* to the same date at 2,971 screens. Originally, *Kill Bill Vol. 2* was going to be a February release.

Thus, two hard-action R-rated movies collided, and both aimed for the young male audience. Miramax also timed the home video release of *Kill Bill Vol. 1* just days before the theatrical release of the sequel, enabling the theatrical and video marketing campaigns to double up and cross-promote each other. *Kill Bill Vol. 2* did best, grossing $25.1 million its opening weekend (compared to $22.1 million for the first installment) to beat the $13.8 million for *The Punisher,* whose opening was nonetheless satisfactory given the film was less heralded. Still, each is thought to have suffered diminished box office as a result of the clash.

In a showdown of highly anticipated animated films, DreamWorks (and Paramount) attempted to stake out November 5, 2004 as the premiere for *Shark Tale* (titled *Sharkslayer* at one time). Then Disney picked the same date for the superheroes romp *The Incredibles,* which it distributes for hit factory Pixar Animation Studios (*Toy Story* and *Finding Nemo*). DreamWorks then shifted *Shark Tale* forward to October. DreamWorks, with its two *Shrek* blockbusters, is Disney's arch rival in animation family films. The two distributors also are competitive because DreamWorks co-founder Jeffrey Katzenberg, the onetime Disney studio chief, had an acrimonious falling out with Disney chairman Michael Eisner.

However, the tendency among film distributors is to be collegial. Distribution executives job-hop so everybody has friends at other studios, which lessens competitive zeal. Also, a distributor that whacks a rival can expect the same treatment in return in the future, which everyone knows is bad for business.

Although competition exists for prime premiere dates, distribution executives know that consumer consumption for films is elastic. There's always hope of getting a big crowd on any weekend. A moviegoer may go to multiple movies in a month, depending on the quality of releases and the moviegoer's personal schedule. That's a far cry from other businesses where, for example, a consumer buys just one tube of toothpaste every month or an automobile every three years, regardless of what's offered in the marketplace.

An exception to the rule that there's plenty of box office for everybody involves films that audiences perceive as having nearly identical plots (as opposed to just being in the same broad genre). In such cases, history shows the first film to open usually does best. An example is the great volcano-film eruption of 1997. Universal's *Dante's Peak* hit the screens first on February 7, finishing with $67 million in domestic box office. Twentieth Century Fox's *Volcano*—with a reported $100 million production budget, making it the more expensive of the two eruption flicks—premiered April 25 and ended up with a disappointing $49 million in box office.

In the most conspicuous example to the contrary, however, among four comedy movies released between October 1987 and June 1988 about miraculously being transferred into another body, the last movie proved to be the biggest grosser. The highest grosser of the quartet—Fox's *Big* starring Tom Hanks—generated a blockbuster $115 million after its June 1988 debut. Of the three earlier releases—Columbia Tri-Star's *Like Father, Like Son;* Columbia's *Vise Versa;* and New World Pictures' *18 Again*—next best was *Like Father, Like Son* with $34 million. This film was first into the marketplace, opening in October 1987.

A 1998 showdown of big-budget yarns about asteroids threatening the earth also proved an exception when the second of two films did the most business. Launching second, Disney's *Armageddon* extravaganza starring Bruce Willis opened July 1, 1998 and collected a blockbuster $201 million in total domestic box office. Its less-regarded rival from DreamWorks/Paramount, *Deep Impact,* raced to an earlier premiere on May 8, 1998 and eventually grossed $140 million, which was a more than anticipated haul that was credited to reaching market first.

For films penciled in during off-peak periods, late date changes sometimes are made to avoid being rolled over by a surprise hit that opens ahead. A recent out-of-the-blue hit was Mel Gibson's *The Passion of the Christ,* which was released in February 2004 and played for weeks, generating $370 million in domestic box office. In the scramble to step aside as *Passion* held theaters, DreamWorks quickly moved its comedy *Envy* from April 2 to April 30. Late date shifts mostly work with smaller films. Larger films have tie-in promotions with fast food restaurants and merchandise licensees, each with separate but related marketing campaigns that are difficult to move *en masse* on short notice.

Film Ratings Overview

The film classification process in the United States is entirely voluntary and somewhat understood, even within the film industry. Under the First Amendment to the United States Constitution dating back to 1791 protecting free speech, the government does not attempt to run a national film censorship entity, although some local jurisdictions do enforce restrictions, mainly as child protection measures. As a result, the United States has one of the world's few nongovernment national film rating systems—the Classification and Ratings Administration (CARA).

CARA is an autonomous unit associated with the MPAA. The MPAA, which traces its origins to 1922, is the trade group for Hollywood's seven major studios. The MPAA president picks the CARA chairman but otherwise is not involved in operating the film rating board. The MPAA's major studio members and their indie-style affiliates, such as Warner's New Line Cinema and Fox Searchlight, agree not to distribute any film to theaters without a CARA rating and agree to have the key marketing materials for their films checked for compliance with ratings.

Independents that are not MPAA members, such as Lions Gate Films and IFC Films, are free to bypass the CARA. Most independents choose to have their films classified, partly because some theaters and outlets for film advertising such as newspapers don't want to be involved in promoting unrated films.

CARA ratings consist of the famous five-point scale:

- G: General audience—all ages admitted
- PG: Parental guidance suggested—some material may not be suitable for children

- PG-13: Parents strongly cautioned—some material may be inappropriate for children under age 13
- R: Restricted—under age 17 requires accompanying parent or adult guardian
- NC-17: No one 17 and under admitted

In accordance with the agreement to have a film rated by CARA, the distributor also agrees to abide by guidelines established by the MPAA and to have marketing materials approved by the related Advertising Administration. The principal function of the Advertising Administration is to ensure that movie advertising, with the exception of restricted trailers, is suitable for general audiences and that such advertising contains nothing that most parents would find offensive for their children to see or hear.

In 2000, placement of advertising became a hot issue in Washington, DC. Public interest groups complained that substantial amounts of advertising content inappropriate for children reached the kid audience. In particular, critics said that violent and sex-laden films were marketed to teenagers.

In response to pressure from the United States Congress and the Federal Trade Commission (FTC), the MPAA formulated a voluntary 12-point plan to address FTC concerns about media placement practices, promising that its member companies would scrupulously follow the guidelines. The plan came after the FTC in September 2000 issued a report that was critical of movie industry marketing practices. The report cited specific examples of saturating inappropriate audiences and left film distributors somewhat embarrassed.

Since then, complaints have faded as the film industry became more careful about ad placement. Of course, whereas the Hollywood majors and their affiliates are bound to the 12-point plan, independent film distributors are not.

The voluntary 12-point plan for major studios consists of the following:

- Each studio requests that exhibitors not show trailers for R-rated films in screenings of G-rated movies (in addition, trailers for R-rated films are not to be previewed on home video versions of G-rated movies).
- Pre-release test screenings of films that eventually may be rated R for violence must exclude moviegoers under age 17 unless they are accompanied by a parent or adult guardian.

- Studios will not market and advertise films with R ratings for violence to children.
- Each studio appoints a senior executive as compliance officer.
- The MPAA reviews each studio's compliance annually.
- The MPAA encourages theater owners and video retailers to improve compliance.
- Studios provide additional descriptive reasons a film received a certain rating in its print advertising and official movie Web sites.
- The MPAA established or help set up Internet sites that provide film classification information to the public, *www.mpaa.org, www.filmratings.com,* and *www.parentalguide.org.*
- Studios include text explanation for film ratings on video versions of films.
- Video ratings direct readers seeking more information to *www.filmratings.com.*
- The MPAA and studios encourage theater owners to provide explanations at their customer-call centers for ratings of films they exhibit.
- Studios furnish newspapers with the reasons for the ratings and request that newspapers include those reasons and capsule summaries of films in their movie reviews.

One unusual aspect of the CARA panel based in the Los Angeles area is that only the panel's chairman is publicly identified. The identities of the other members are kept secret to protect them from industry lobbying. The full CARA panel consists of 8 to 13 persons who work full time for varying periods. The only known qualification is having served in a parenting experience so as to be sensitive to children.

Film distributors pay a fee—based on a sliding scale—to have their films rated, and the fees make CARA self-sufficient. The fee scale is a formula based on the cost of making the film and the total revenue of the submitting party, which CARA says enables small films from independent distributors to pay less. The fee covers all editing through certification. A nominal administrative fee is charged to submit a film for appeal.

The MPAA consults with the exhibitor trade group National Association of Theatre Owners on film classification issues. In examining the implementation of film ratings, it's important to note that movie theaters are, of course, the enforcers of audience restrictions because the theaters interface with consumers.

If a film is R rated, it's up to theaters to ensure that under-aged youths are admitted only if they are accompanied by an adult guardian. Indicating that the ratings system is voluntary, the 268-screen GKC Theaters allows parents to give blanket consent for their children to be admitted to R-rated movies, according to a *Variety* news story. The R-Card, which was introduced in 2003, is controversial because the R rating specifies children should be accompanied by an adult guardian.

The CARA ratings system has been in place since 1968. In 2003, 940 features were rated, of which 473 achieved theatrical release (Fig. 7.2), according to the MPAA. Titles that were rated but did not go theatrical likely went direct to video or became television premieres. Besides submitting an entire film, distributors must provide to the Advertising Administration ad materials to ensure the materials are suitable for viewing by persons of all ages.

"Trailers are an important aspect of the program," notes former MPAA chief Valenti in his 2000 description of ratings. "They are approved for 'all audiences,' which means they may be shown with all feature films, or for 'restricted audiences,' which limits their use to feature films rated R or NC-17. There will be, in 'all audience' trailers, no scenes that caused the feature to be rated PG, PG-13, R or NC-17." Trailers restricted to accompanying R-rated films are color coded in red, which exhibitors refer to as "red band" previews that are audience restricted.

Marketing Implications of Ratings

For film distributors, the biggest gap is between PG-13 and R films. An R film excludes teenagers ages 14–16 who are unaccompanied by parent or adult guardian, thus losing a big chunk of the heaviest movie-going

Figure 7.2 Feature Films Made, Rated & Released in United States 1996–2003

Year	Produced	Rated	Released
2003	593	940	473
2002	543	786	467
2001	611	739	482
2000	683	762	478
1999	758	677	461
1998	686	661	509
1997	767	673	510
1996	735	713	471

Source: Motion Picture Association of America

demographic. According to the MPAA's 2003 movie attendance study, ages 12–20 accounted for 16% of the population but 27% of movie admissions that year.

In contracts with directors and other creative talent, movie companies routinely specify that filmmakers are obligated to craft a film that will achieve a specified rating, whether G, PG, PG-13, or R. Such a provision came into play with *Team America: World Police,* the risqué animated film that spoofed terrorism, according to trade press reports. Paramount Pictures, which released the film in October 2004, and filmmakers spent weeks sparring with CARA to avoid getting an NC-17 rating for *Team America* over what was said to be simulated sex involving puppets. Finally, the film was edited sufficiently to receive an R rating, which carries the descriptive text "graphic, crude and sexual humor, violent images and strong language all involving puppets."

In other instances, talent contracts may say the film must be crafted simply to avoid the most restrictive NC-17, whose films have a history of poor box office. The highest grossing NC-17 rated movie was MGM/UA's 1995 release of *Showgirls* with $20 million in box office; Universal's 1990 release of *Henry & June* at $12 million; and Miramax's 1990 release of *The Cook, the Thief, His Wife & Her Lover* at $8 million. For *Showgirls,* the NC-17 rating cited "nudity and erotic sexuality throughout, and some graphic language and sexual violence."

Hollywood is an industry whose creative workers earn reputations with edgy R-rated films, although R-rated films have an uneven track record in box office. Because R-rated films are popular with movie critics and on the film festival circuit, they reap more than their share of awards for their actors and other creative talent. Among films released in 1991–2000, eight of the 10 Oscar winners for Best Picture were R rated, starting with *The Silence of the Lambs* and running through *Gladiator.* After that, the next three consecutive Best Picture winners were PG-13 films.

There's a definite trend toward PG-13 films, which accounted for 60% of ratings (out of five categories) conferred in 2003, versus 20% for R ratings, according to the MPAA. Looking back farther through history, R-rated films accounted for 58% of all films CARA rated from 1968 to 2003 (Fig. 7.3). Interestingly from 1968 to 2003, the box office–rich PG-13 classification accounted for just 11% of CARA ratings. PG represented 22% of CARA ratings, G accounted for 7%, and NC-17 took the remaining 2%, according to the MPAA.

Of 2003's top 20 in box office, the highest grossing R-rated movie was *The Matrix Reloaded* in fourth place with $281.5 million in United States box office, according to the MPAA. R-rated films held only four

Figure 7.3 Top Grossing Films by Rating 1968–2003

Rating	%
R	58%
PG	22%
PG-13	11%
G	7%
NC-17/X	2%

Source: Motion Picture Association of America

slots in the top 20: the aforementioned *The Matrix Reloaded* from Warner Bros.; ninth-place *Terminator 3: Rise of the Machines* from Warner Bros.; tenth-place *Bad Boys II* from Columbia; and 11th place *The Matrix Revolutions* from Warner Bros.

Of the top grossers of 2003, Disney/Pixar's animated family film *Finding Nemo* was the only G-rated film in the top 20, but it was in first place and grossed a staggering $339.7 million, according to the MPAA. The remaining top 20 films included 12 releases that were rated PG-13, led by second-ranked *Pirates of the Caribbean: The Curse of the Black Pearl* from Disney with $305.4 million in box office, and three films rated PG led by seventh-ranked comedy *Elf* from New Line with $170.8 million.

Content that gets restrictive ratings includes violence, crude language, nudity, sensuality, drug abuse, and cruelty. CARA says it views a film in its entirety and does not focus excessively on individual scenes. Certainly, the standards for ratings change with the times. Acclaimed relationship drama *Midnight Cowboy* from United Artists got an X rating in 1969 (or NC-17 in today's scale) that was later revised to R, which gave it more marketability in the video release. The PG-13 category was added in 1984 when the public complained that the PG rating for *Indiana Jones and the Temple of Doom* was inadequate because of one scene in which a beating heart is pulled out of a man. The rest of the film was PG oriented.

In terms of rating restrictions, serious films seem to get more slack than low-brow fare. For example, Mel Gibson's *The Passion of the Christ* received an R rating and not the more restrictive NC-17, even though the film contains some of the cinema's most graphic torture scenes ever. Foreign films often face a tough time because imagery that doesn't raise eyebrows at home triggers a restrictive rating in the United States. For example, sensual Spanish art film *Sex and Lucia* from Palm Pictures was released to cinemas unrated in the United States. News reports indicate

Seattle newspapers balked at carrying advertising for *Sex and Lucia,* even though the film had won awards at the Seattle Film Festival.

In evaluating films, CARA does not ban films, unlike classification boards in other countries. Each rating is established by a majority vote of the anonymous CARA panel. Filmmakers have the right to ask why a rating was given and, with that feedback, to submit a revised version of a film that will be evaluated from scratch. Filmmakers can challenge a rating to a 14- to 18-person Appeal Board within CARA, getting the chance to formally rebut a decision. A two-thirds vote by the Appeals Board is required to overturn a rating. For example, in March 2004 the appeals panel supported an NC-17 cinema rating for *Young Adam,* a relationship drama with sexual content praised by critics, thus turning back a Sony Pictures Classics bid to lower the rating to an R. (Movies with NC-17 ratings for cinema may be edited for video release in order to receive an R rating because some video chains won't stock an NC-17 title.)

MPAA surveys indicate Americans find the CARA ratings system useful and effective. Of parents with children ages 13 or younger, 74% think the rating system is satisfactory. Indeed, the movie classification system gets surprisingly few knocks from the public considering the rating system's subjective nature. Independent film distributors sometimes complain that the CARA is more lenient with major studio films and tougher on independents. The allegation can be debated from either perspective. Independents tend to distribute more edgy and provocative films, so it's not surprising their films often get restrictive classifications.

Miramax, the Walt Disney subsidiary, is most famous for controversy over films and their ratings. Miramax co-chiefs and brothers Harvey and Bob Weinstein set up personal companies on occasion to distribute films bought by Miramax but which parent Disney later required Miramax to unload. When bleak social drama *Kids* seemed headed for an NC-17 rating for Miramax in 1995, the Weinsteins set up a separate entity called Shining Excalibur to acquire the film from Miramax and then distribute it on an unrated basis. Disney's corporate policy prohibited Miramax, which as a Disney unit is required to have every film classified by CARA, from releasing NC-17 rated films. The Weinstein's Spring 2004 tussle with Disney over *Fahrenheit 9/11* created a publicity sensation, although the high-profile flap was over Disney internal corporate policy and not film classification.

Because of difficulty in advertising films classified as NC-17, no major studio or studio affiliate released a film with such a restrictive rating for six years, until Fox Searchlight premiered Bernardo Bertolucci's *The Dreamers* in February 2004. An edited version of the movie received an R rating. Several other NC-17 releases from studio-owned specialty film distributors followed.

Group Screenings

Three distinctive types of private screenings, which are not open to the general public, typically are components of theatrical release for family, special interest, and up-market films. Some are revenue-generating affairs coming late in a film's theatrical run. Others are pre-release screenings aimed at drumming up word of mouth with a target audience.

One type of screening is private group sales designed to generate revenue. A youth organization screening a popular, mainstream family film is an example. For such screenings, a theater allocates an off-peak screening time or even a morning slot when a screening would not occur anyway. Paid private group screenings usually are scheduled a few weeks after theatrical release when box office is waning.

Groups for revenue-generating screenings typically pay theaters, which then make a film rental payment to distributors. Usually, a group must meet a minimum audience requirement to qualify for a private screening, such as 50 persons for morning screens when a theater would have to open early and perhaps 25 for an off-peak, early afternoon date. Prices—typically slightly discounted—usually are set by agreement among the film distributor, the distributor's group sales organizer (if it's an outside marketing consultant), and the theater.

Such special showings typically account for just 1% of revenue for a major studio release but can be one third of box office for low-grossing indie films. Film distributors usually book such special screenings because they control the distribution process. They also often hire outside marketing consultants that specialize in group screenings.

Another type of private screening is aimed not so much at generating revenue but rather positive word of mouth among an audience segment for which a film holds special interest. These screenings come prior to theatrical release for the purpose of building pre-release awareness, given that there's little point to mounting such an effort after a film is out. For example, a movie that has dancing as a focal point of the plot might use special screenings for dance music theaters, dance studios, and arts organizations. The prime purpose is to engage opinion leaders of the film's prime target audience; generating revenue is a secondary consideration. Admission may be at a reduced price or even free to entice opinion leaders to attend. A promotional tie-in partner, such as a dance clothing company, might pay for such screenings as part of a larger promotion tied to the movie.

"Specialty films and films that target a specific audience are ideal for group screenings," said film marketing executive Karen Gold, who booked group sales for *Schindler's List* and basketball documentary *Hoop Dreams.* "Targeted groups can include seniors; religious entities such as churches, Bible study groups, chabads, and choirs; youth groups such as YMCAs/YWCAs and community centers; book groups; party planners; fraternal, professional, social, and civic organizations; arts groups; schools, especially if the story in a film is part of the curriculum; and the like. Groups can also be 'broad' such as Irish or African-American ethnic groups." For *Hoop Dreams,* sports equipment outfit Nike and *Sports Illustrated* magazine helped pay for group screenings. As a sponsorship, they printed educational literature: 110,000 study guides dubbed play books that were given to teachers and students.

At major studios, the group screening plan usually originates in the marketing department, which focuses on consumer advertising and promotion. Control later shifts to distribution, which books films in theaters, for actual implementation. Ads for group screenings typically are modified from the mainstream release materials but use the same typeface, logo, and any other signature elements that the mainstream materials use.

Marketing efforts can include postcard mailings, poster mailings, and telephone solicitations. Typically, a toll-free number is available for groups to make contact and book theaters. The key to making group sales work is obtaining good mailing/contact lists for the target audience. Such lists are available for purchase or rental from direct marketing companies. Group sales marketers also hook up with organizations to gain access to their membership lists.

A final type of private screening is arranged by "cinephile clubs," which regularly book artistic films and are a staple for indie film releases. Again, this type of screening is designed to build a buzz in the marketplace and comes before regular theatrical release. Many clubs don't even let members know the name of the film showing and build a following with "surprise" screenings of provocative films.

Although distributors get low or no rental fees, cinephile clubs charge their members entry prices that typically are higher than a normal ticket. The clubs pay for the theater and for promotion to members. In some cases, the distributor provides a speaker to answer questions after the screening.

Overview for Booking Films

For their normal theatrical release, films typically are contracted for two- to four-week guaranteed runs and can be extended. Besides the length of the run, another negotiating point can be the length of time the big films are promised the largest auditoriums in multiscreen theaters. Seat counts range from 100 to 500 per auditorium in newer theaters. Films that are booked in the big rooms get the most marquee and promotion on-site in theaters.

If a big film that is promised a long run in a big auditorium is dead on arrival at the box office, distributors typically allow exhibitors to skirt the booking contract and quickly downgrade the film to smaller auditoriums in the same multiplex. It's in nobody's best interest for a distributor to demand a low-grossing film be held in a big auditorium, particularly if exhibitors have high-grossing films playing in small auditoriums that would do better if upgraded. Distributors and exhibitors have a year-round relationship spanning many films, so they need each other's good will and frequently cut each other slack in cases in which one party is stuck in an unfavorable situation because of unforeseen circumstances.

Each circuit has film buyers who preview films, making evaluations of their commercial prospects. The opinions of its buyers help a circuit decide how widely or narrowly to book a given film and what kind of financial terms to seek from distributors. Exhibitors say they also are keenly attuned to what a given film's classification will be in the evaluation process. Although films may not yet be rated when they are screened for theater buyers, distributors let exhibitors know what classification they are working to get. As described previously, films rated R and G have spotty box office records. Films with NC-17 classifications or films that are released unrated have poor track records in part because the media often rejects advertising for such movies.

Another part of the buyers' calculus is to estimate how long a given film will run, which is crucial in determining how clogged or uncrowded screens will be in the weeks and months ahead. The better a film's pre-release prospects are, the higher the film rental distributors typically can negotiate. Likewise, films with poor commercial prospects generally get lower than average deals from exhibitors. Thus, the booking strategy by exhibitors is an exercise in a kind of three-dimensional chess. It takes into account a given film's prospects, how crowded screens are expected to be when the film is scheduled to be released, and how long the film's run is expected to be.

Distributors are keenly interested in getting their film trailers in theaters to promote upcoming releases. The theaters control presentation of trailers that promote coming attractions, typically running five to an seven trailers at a time. As part of a booking negotiation, distributors often come to an unwritten agreement with exhibitors to receive specified trailer runs prior to a film's premiere. In a common scenario, the distributor receives greater trailer exposure for its films in exchange for granting an exhibitor more playdates for a desired film. Major studios issue 20,000–35,000 trailers for each big film. Some may not get used by cinemas. Others will be screened for one to three weeks.

Under agreement by industry trade groups, distributors attach no more than 2.5 minutes of promotional material to the front end of movies, which is a little longer than the running time of a typical trailer. On occasion, although not frequently, distributors agree to swap attached trailers so that a trailer runs before a film of a complementary genre. For example, a trailer for a kids film from one distributor is attached to the family film of another, in exchange for putting a trailer from an R-rated film on a violent action film of the other studio.

Most states have laws prohibiting "blind bidding"—booking films sight unseen—which requires distributors to hold trade screenings for films prior to licensing them to exhibitors. In addition, distributors cannot legally engage in "block booking"—making the sale of desired movies contingent on the buyer also purchasing unwanted films—under the so-called 1948 Paramount Consent Decree and other precedents. Competition regulations, while in place, are not a panacea for small theaters seeking access to big studio films. The big exhibitors have the financial muscle via higher-grossing theaters to outbid indie theaters.

Film Rentals

In exhibition parlance, the payment a theater makes to a film distributor for a movie is the film rental. The word *rental* is used because theaters contract for limited rights to the movies they screen. It is customary for the film rental to be based on dividing box office on a percentage basis. Nationally over the course of a year, the major studio distributors are thought to receive an average of 54% of the ticket price; thus, theaters keep the remaining 46%.

Independent film distributors, which lack the clout of majors, tend to get rentals of 40–50%. For arthouse theaters that shoulder relatively hefty marketing expenses, the film rental can be as low as 35–40%. The truly independent distributors—those not owned by major studios—normally account for around 6% of national box office, although Newmarket-distributed blockbuster *The Passion of the Christ* has ballooned the indie share for 2004.

Icon Distribution, which is part of actor/filmmaker Mel Gibson's company that made *The Passion of the Christ,* sued the top United States circuit Regal Entertainment in June 2004, alleging underpayment of film rentals. Icon alleges it was promised major "studio terms" for rentals, which it defines as 55% of box office. The lawsuit says Regal offered 34% at the end of the movie's run. Apparently, Regal made a low-ball offer, hoping to settle for some percentage in between.

There are two different types of film booking contracts. The long-standing industry custom is a two-part deal with a split of box office after the theater first takes a specified amount off the top. In this industry standard, the theater keeps all of the initial box office to a predetermined cap, called a house nut. After the house nut figure is reached, the distributor receives a percentage of box office. The box office split can change on a weekly basis and usually starts out favorable for distributors. For example, a booking contract might specify distributors get 70% of ticket revenue for the first two weeks of a film's run (after deducting the house nut), leaving 30% for theaters. For weeks three and onward, the ratio might shift in favor of exhibitors specifying, for example, that distributors get 40% of box office, leaving 60% for exhibitors.

If the house nut is $1,000, then the exhibitor pockets the initial $1,000 in box office before splitting additional box office in a given week under the sliding-scale formula. For a playdate that generates $5,000 in box office during a week with a $1,000 house nut and a 70/30 split thereafter, the exhibitor gets $2,200 and the distributor $2,800. For the exhibitor, that's the sum of the $1,000 nut and another $1,200 from a 30% slice of box office dollars from $1,001–$5,000. The distributor's take is entirely from the 70% of box office from $1,001–$5,000. To drum up sympathy, exhibitors often cite box office splits greater than 50% that seem highly favorable to film distributors without mentioning the house nut portion of the formula that is to their benefit.

Assuming the split moves to 40/60 in later weeks, then the exhibitor gets $3,400 and the distributor $1,600 for the same $5,000 gross. However, grosses tend to head downward in later weeks. Each week is treated as a separate event in booking contracts, partly because any film's length of run is not known in advance. The booking contract also may contain a floor, which is the minimum amount the distributor gets regardless of other contract points. The floor becomes important in the later weeks of a film's run when box office fades, and any house nut deductions off the top might leave distributors with little or no rentals without a floor clause.

An entirely different and more straightforward type of booking contract is the simple aggregate deal. All box office revenue is divided by a negotiated percentage formula, and there is no house nut. For example, if a screen grosses $5,000 with a 55/45 aggregate scale, the distributor gets $2,750 and the exhibitor $2,250. This is a small but growing type of agreement used to book films in cinemas.

The trend to opening films in more playdates than in the past—wider release—benefits film distributors because booking contracts tend to assign a higher percentage of box office to distributors in the early weeks of release. The thinking is that distributors are paying dearly for national advertising, for which they should be quickly compensated.

The final wrinkle to financial transactions in film bookings is the settlement. Traditionally, exhibitors and distributors round off figures at the end of a given film's run for the sake of simplification. Also, if a film performed above or below expectations, some kind of adjustment in the settlement process may be made to partly compensate the disappointed party, usually the exhibitor.

This give-and-take process is on the decline. One problem with the subjective nature of settlement adjustments is that royalty participants in films, such as actors with so-called profit participations, would be short changed if the distributor made concessions to exhibitors in settlements. Typically, such settlement give-and-take is customary and not mentioned in written booking contracts. In recent years, some distributors have insisted on firm terms that eliminate givebacks to theaters, thus streamlining the settlement process.

Distribution Economics

The consolidation of cinema circuits would seem to point to exhibitors being able to negotiate better terms in film bookings, essentially reducing the film rentals paid to film distributors. However, several factors have helped distributors retain the upper hand.

Despite growth of the biggest chains, no single circuit offers national bookings in the United States because all the circuits have gaps in their geographic coverage. For example, mega circuit Regal Cinemas is sizable, with 6,045 screens at 550 locations as of January 2004, but it does not have theaters in 11 states or Canada. No exhibitor has the coverage or clout to offer one-stop booking. Film distributors are accustomed to booking films via a patchwork of circuits to achieve national coverage. Another factor is that big megaplex theaters (see Chapter 8) have increased the overlap in coverage areas of individual theaters, so film distributors have more alternatives in selecting theaters to play a movie in a given city.

Finally, the booking clout of theaters has not risen commensurate with their growth in screens because the major studios have cut back the number of their wide-release films in the past decade. With fewer big films, the marketplace is less crowded, which offsets any leverage circuits gained from theater chain mergers. Looked at another way, booking films is something of an auction process. If fewer films are occupying screens, then the buyers—in this case theaters seeking future film bookings—can't be too choosy. The trend toward having more playdates for openings is not changing the equation significantly because ever-wider releases are offset by films not holding theaters as long as in the past.

From an exhibitor's perspective, a marketplace that is crowded with high-grossing films is two reasons for joy. Besides the obvious reason of a high revenue from films then playing, crowded screens give exhibitors negotiating clout in future bookings, as distributors find it difficult to secure playdates.

The average price for a United States cinema ticket was $6.03 in 2003 (Fig. 7.4). That figure is generated from 1.574 billion tickets sold in 2003, according to the MPAA. Assuming theaters in the United States keep 46% of ticket sales on average, exhibition retained $4.364 billion from the $9.488 billion. A 54% film rentals rate translates to $5.123 billion for film distributors in 2003 from the United States.

Figure 7.4 Average United States Ticket Price 1980–2003

Year	Ave. price $	% change prior year	% change 2003	% change CPI*
2003	$6.03	3.8%	–	1.9%
2002	$5.81	2.7%	3.8%	2.4%
2001	$5.66	4.9%	6.6%	1.6%
2000	$5.39	6.1%	11.8%	3.4%
1999	$5.08	16.8%	18.6%	2.7%
1995	$4.35	4.8%	38.5%	1.7%
1992	$4.15	−1.7%	45.2%	2.9%
1990	$4.23	19.0%	42.7%	3.3%
1985	$3.55	31.9%	69.8%	2.5%
1980	$2.69	–	124.0%	2.7%

*CPI is consumer price index, which is indicator of inflation for a given year
Source: Motion Picture Association of America, National Association of Theatre Owners

Historically, the split has been 50/50 nationally when averaging all types of films over long periods of time. However, in recent years, the majors have reduced output and films have played off faster, trends that shift negotiating clout to distributors.

The decline in major films so far this decade is pronounced. According to a *Marketing to Moviegoers* analysis, the number of "major" releases from studios hit a 13-year low in 2000 with 107 big releases. In the 1990s, big studio releases ranged from 135 to 153 films in a given year. The survey covers only Hollywood's seven major studios and startup DreamWorks.

Excluding the sharp low of 2000, in this decade the range is about a dozen titles fewer per year than in the 1990s. The cutbacks come primarily from Walt Disney, Warner Bros., and Sony/Columbia, which have trimmed output since the go-go 1990s. The big films from major studios that are geared for peak movie-going periods are referred to as tentpole releases because they are the high point of the majors' slates. The phrase evokes a vision of the major studios presenting a diverse circus under a big-top tent, with their big films as the pillars holding it up.

Box Office Trends

The major studios seem to come up with outsized blockbusters every year. Twentieth Century Fox's *Titanic* collected a staggering $601 million in domestic box office in 1997; Fox's *Star Wars: Episode 1—The Phantom Menace* generated $431 million in 1999; Sony Pictures' *Spider-Man* took in $404 million and New Line's *Lord of the Rings: The Two Towers* generated $342 million in 2002; and Disney's *Finding Nemo* finished at $340 million and *Lord of the Rings: The Return of the King* came in at $377 million in 2003. For films released at the end of one year, some box office came in the following year. The year 2004 got off to a promising start with Newmarket Films' out-of-the-blue February hit *The Passion of the Christ,* which posted $370 million in domestic box office. *Shrek 2* from DreamWorks later rolled up $437 million and Columbia's *Spider-Man 2* $373 million in 2004.

As for misfires in 2004, Disney's historical epic *The Alamo,* which reportedly cost $100 million to make, opened to a disastrous $9.1 million in April 2004 and finished its run with just over $22 million. Perhaps the biggest recent misfire is Sony Pictures' *Gigli,* the $55 million romantic comedy that generated just $6.1 million in domestic box office after an August 2003 premiere.

Traditionally, the peak summer season started in mid June, which coincided with the end of school when the prime youth audience starts vacation. In the 1980s, the summer film kickoff began to creep forward in front of the Memorial Day holiday in late May. A major shift occurred when *Rambo—First Blood Part II* pulled in a then-electrifying $32.5 million in its first six days after a May 22, 1985 premiere in what was an instant wide release, not building theater count gradually as was the custom at the time. The Columbia TriStar film became the year's second-highest grossing film, indicating late May was a suitable launch pad for blockbusters.

At that time, big studio films might have opened in small first waves in late May, as with *Star Wars* in 1977, and then added theaters for wide release in later weeks. The latter strategy is a platform release—starting small and then building incrementally over subsequent weeks. Today, the majors seldom use platform releases for their big summer event because the films open widely in their first week.

In the 1990s, big films in wide releases kept creeping earlier in May, each trying to take a lightly competitive weekend for a big opening. By 1996, the Warner Bros. tornado drama *Twister* established an even earlier start to the summer season, premiering May 10 and eventually grossing $242 million to rank second best for the full year.

The shift forward carries risks because the prime youth market is still in school and thus unavailable for moviegoing on weekdays. Another drawback to May premieres is the difficulty in holding screens because big films crowd into the marketplace relentlessly every week for two straight months.

The July 4 Independence Day weekend marks the traditional end of the cavalcade of the major studio tentpole releases. Any film released after the July 4 holiday faces a shortened summer run and relies on generating business in August, when many families take traveling vacations and tend not to patronize cinemas.

As a rule of thumb, the three-day weekend gross (Friday through Sunday) accounts for 75% of a week's box office in nonholiday periods. Monday through Thursday, which is a longer stretch of days, contributes the remaining 25%. For children's movies, the weekend share can go to 80% in nonholiday periods when school is in session. The difference between weekend and weekday narrows in the summer and during the Christmas–New Year week because kids are out of school and available to patronize weekday performances. During the peak summer vacation period, the three-day weekend's share of weekly box office falls to about 66%; the remaining third comes from the Monday–Thursday time frame.

Some pundits knock the major studios for going to ever-wider releases of 3000 playdates or more. Investment house Merrill Lynch estimated that opening week accounts for 45–50%, on average, of box office for a major studio film, versus just 20% in 1990.

There is, however, a method to the madness of front-loading box office. As described earlier in this chapter, film distributors take a bigger piece of box office in the first weeks of release, under the sliding-scale film rental contracts with theaters. The more box office that is earned initially, the bigger the slice that goes to film distributors.

Furthermore, a distributor that "buys" incremental domestic box office by sheer dint of heavy marketing expenses and wide releases receives a payoff in downstream video and television deals. A big opening and large box office prompt video retailers to increase orders once the film hits home video release. When major studios license films to pay television, the prices for films are set via a complex formula whose single most important component is a given film's box office. A common benchmark is to set a pay television license fee of $7 million for a film that generates $50 million in domestic box office and $10 million if the film hits $75 million in box office. Foreign pay and free television contracts for major studio films often also peg prices based on performance in domestic box office.

Finally, a boffo opening week presents a marketing tool, such as advertising that a film is "the number one comedy in America" even when the film is ranked third behind two dramas. Interestingly, a wide-release film's widest coverage typically comes in its second week, when extra playdates are added on top of the first-week release pattern.

A consequence of the sliding-scale formula is that exhibitors prefer unheralded hit films. These films build from a modest start to achieve long and steady runs, with a big part of their box office earned in the second half of the theatrical run when the box office take by exhibitors is highest. An example is the supernatural romantic drama *Ghost* starring Patrick Swayze, Demi Moore, and Whoopi Goldberg. The Paramount film premiered July 1990 with an okay $12.2 million three-day opening to rank second that week. The top film was holdover *Die Hard 2,* which had opened nine days earlier with a huge $35.5 million for the five-day Independence Day holiday.

However, *Ghost* held steady as the slow-to-materialize adult audience patronized the film in later weeks. The film finished the year number one at the box office (at $218 million including some box office carrying over into the next year). Its opening week—with a then-sizable 1,101 playdates—accounted for just 9% of its total box office, which is incredibly low when measured against today's era of front-loaded films. Meanwhile, *Die Hard 2* finished in seventh place for 1990.

Canada

Canadian box office, at US$636 million in 2003, is about 7% the size of box office for the United States (Fig 7.5). The Canadian movie business underperforms its neighbor on a per capita basis, partly because the Canadian dollar has less buying power. "After large increases following the construction of new multiplex theaters in recent years, we expect [Canadian] admissions growth to be modest through 2006, with somewhat faster increases to follow in 2007 and 2008," notes syndicated report *Global Entertainment and Media Outlook: 2004–2008* from consultancy PriceWaterhouseCoopers LLC.

The Hollywood majors all distribute their films in Canada themselves and films from the United States dominate box office. Independent distributors in the United States are required to sublicense their Canadian rights to local distributors. Canada's "proprietary rights" industrial policy, which dates back to the 1980s, mandates a film must be distributed by a Canadian company unless a non-Canadian distributor owns worldwide rights or contributes at least 50% to a film's production cost. In general, only the self-financed Hollywood majors meet the criteria.

Canada's big distributors include Alliance Atlantis Motion Picture Distribution (and its Viva Films and Odeon Films units), Lions Gate Films, Equinox, Mongrel Media, Seville Pictures, and TVA Films. Alliance Atlantis is the dominant distributor, with a market share on par

Figure 7.5 Canadian Cinema Data 1999–2004e

Year	Admission (mil.)	Box office (US $ mil.)	Ave. ticket (US$)
2004e	124.0	$663 mil.	$5.35
2003	123.0	$636 mil.	$5.17
2002	128.0	$635 mil.	$4.96
2001	123.0	$545 mil.	$4.43
2000	114.0	$485 mil.	$4.25
1999	111.5	$469 mil.	$4.21

Note: 2004 figures are estimates; all figures in United States dollars at average 2003 exchange rates
Source: Pricewaterhouse Coopers report *Global Entertainment and Media Outlook: 2004-2008*

with that of a Hollywood studio, because of the distributor's film supply deals for Canadian rights with top United States independent film suppliers, including New Line Cinema, Miramax, and Focus Features.

History of Distribution

Movie distribution enjoyed a spectacular upward trajectory for the first half of the twentieth century. The launch of television as mass medium in the late 1940s drained audiences and nearly killed cinema, especially because the Hollywood moguls were so ill advised in their response. Hollywood boldly invested big-budget spectacles to lure audiences away from television, initially with some success such as Paramount's $13.5 million production of *The Ten Commandments* in 1956, MGM's $15 million production of *Ben-Hur* in 1959, and Columbia's $15 million production of *Lawrence of Arabia* in 1962.

The moguls struggled in large part because they had little understanding of their audience, courting adults who increasingly were becoming glued to the tube. This strategy resulted in costly misfires, such as Twentieth Century Fox's *Cleopatra* in 1963 (reportedly made for an astronomical $44 million) and Fox's $20 million musical production of *Hello, Dolly* in 1969.

Salvation in the television era was obvious: cater to the youth audience, which is mobile and oriented to out-of-home entertainment. The major studios finally latched onto this formula starting in the late 1960s with Columbia's *Easy Riders* in 1969 (an added benefit was that the social drama presented via motorcycle cost just $375,000 to produce); Universal's coming-of-age youth comedy *American Graffiti* (just $775,000 for production) in 1973; Universal's *Jaws* in 1975; and Universal's college campus farce *Animal House* in 1978.

The apex in the movement of youth-films-as-Hollywood's-savior was *Star Wars*, the 1977 release from Twentieth Century Fox, which grossed an astronomical $461 million just in domestic box office and cost just $12 million to make. Reportedly, *Star Wars* generated film rentals pocketed by Fox of $1 billion from all media worldwide, including television and video. All these films were date flicks and were a far cry from moralistic Westerns, historical epics, musicals, and earnest family dramas that the majors were used to churning out.

In addition, the major studios—seeing edgy independent films break through—began releasing more controversial movies, such as *Bonnie and Clyde* in 1967 and *The Wild Bunch* in 1969. Both were

Warner Bros. films. Hollywood veered away from the avant-garde after the too-arty, $40 million-budgeted period Western *Heaven's Gate* bombed in 1980 for United Artists (now MGM). That stretch from the late 1960s through the 1970s set the tone for today's filmmaking, moving Hollywood away from sentimental, unrealistic films and installing a blockbuster mentality.

Smallish specialized film distributors popped up in the 1960s to 1980s and focused on family films that seemed underserved by Hollywood at the time. These family-film specialists included American National Enterprises, Sunn Classics (whose name is being revived as a distributor), and Pacific International. They were known for booking wholesome films on a four-wall basis, whereby the film distributor rented theaters for a flat fee and kept all the box office. This was a no-risk deal for exhibitors, who were uncertain that the small distributors would spend sufficient sums on advertising to promote films.

A famous four-wall episode involving a major studio occurred with PG-rated social drama *Billy Jack,* whose initial release via Warner Bros. in 1971 fizzled. After a court battle, filmmaker Tom Laughlin was able to re-release *Billy Jack* on a four-wall basis and generated substantial box office with regional saturation ad campaigns. In the aftermath, Hollywood distributors experimented with four-walling briefly, but today the practice is rare in exhibition.

Film classification underwent some upheaval as well because it marched in lockstep with changes in filmmaking. Within a week of taking the helm of the Hollywood studio trade group the MPAA in 1966, Jack Valenti recalls being thrust in the maelstrom of social change impacting film standards. The industry's highly restrictive Production Code Administration, which dated back to 1922 and was also known as the "Hays code" after creator Will Hays, was being challenged by filmmakers and audiences. "The first issue was the film *Who's Afraid of Virginia Woolf,* in which, for the first time on the screen, the word 'screw' and the phrase 'hump the hostess' were heard," Valenti recalled in a 2000 remembrance. "In company with the MPAA's general counsel, Louis Nizer, I met with Jack Warner, the legendary chieftain of Warner Bros., and his top aide, Ben Kalmenson. We talked for three hours, and the result was deletion of 'screw' and retention of 'hump the hostess.' But I was uneasy over the meeting."

By 1968, a four-point classification scale was set: G, M (mature), R and, X. The first three classifications were trademark protected, but not X, which was added at the last minute. Eventually, the erotic film industry misappropriated that final designation with such tantalizing come-ons as "triple-X" that had nothing to do with legitimate cinema classifications. As for the film classification system, the intent was not to prohibit some depictions, as the Hays code did, but simply to communicate to the public the nature of a film's content.

8 Exhibition

The play was a great success, but the audience was a disaster.

Oscar Wilde

The cinema business continues to hold its place in the movie distribution cycle, despite encroachment by DVDs, pay-per-view television in its numerous forms, subscription pay television, and film pirates.

Some prognosticators get attention with forecasts that theaters eventually will die, though in reality that's a highly unlikely scenario. Indeed, media merchant banker Veronis Suhler Stevenson forecasts that box office in the United States will achieve a compound annual growth rate of 5.6% from 2003 to 2008, which would be excellent for what is a mature business facing increased competition.

One reason to believe in medium's prospects is that film distributors like the economics of cinema. Cinema represents one of the few film platforms where distributors collect film rentals—their share of box office spending by moviegoers—on a per-person basis. One cinema ticket permits only one viewer, unlike television, video, and pay-per-view, where any number of persons may view.

Another factor is that no other movie platform captures the collective experience of a group huddled in a darkened auditorium sharing the laughs, the tears, and the wide-screen spectacle of cinema. Moviegoing is further entrenched by theaters investing in big screens, crystal-clear digital sound, plush seats, and stadium-style seat placement with unobstructed sight lines.

Overview

There are two halves to the cinema equation. One side of the equation consists of the distributors that control and market movies, such as Universal Pictures and independents such as Lions Gate Releasing. The other side of the equation is exhibition, which in cinema parlance means movie theaters.

Exhibitors can be viewed as retail store operators, and their cinema screens are shelf space. Their economics are driven by location, so exhibition is firmly rooted in the real estate business. About two thirds of operating profit at movie theaters comes from food/beverage sales (usually called concessions), which account for just one quarter of the theaters' overall revenue. Thus, ticket sales from the movie are a small piece of the profit picture for exhibitors. Yet, Shakespeare's axiom that "the play's the thing" is still operative because nobody would come to theaters to buy the high-priced popcorn and soda without a compelling feature film.

The United States, which had 35,786 screens at the end of 2003, and Canada, which had another 3,000 screens, are significant forces in global cinema. The United States and Canada account for approximately 28% of the world's 139,400 screens and only 20% of admissions (ticket sales in units), but roughly 50% of box office revenue in 2003, according to *Global Film: Exhibition and Distribution*, which is published by London-based Informa Media. The reason why the United States/Canada box office is disproportionately large is the far lower ticket prices in Asia and Latin America.

A few key phrases in describing the exhibition/distribution business are necessary to understand data, and these phrases often are misused. They are *screens, (release) prints*, and *playdates*. Screens refer to auditoriums. Release prints are the bulky and heavy film canisters with copies of the films. Because some modern multiplexes occasionally use one print for two screens via an interlock, prints and screen counts sometimes vary for the same movie. A playdate is a theater booked to show a film and is counted as one even when a film is shown on multiple screens at the same location. Another word for playdate is engagement.

In the multiplex era, the playdate count typically is much lower than screens and prints. A film that opens with more than 3,500 playdates can be on more than 8,000 screens because many theaters play the same film on multiple screens. At the end of 2003, there were 6,066 theater locations in the United States and another 725 theaters in Canada. The number of theaters has been shrinking as antiquated single-screen and other small theaters close. However, screen count grew as theaters averaged more auditoriums per location.

Audience Profile

The cinema industry is heavily dependent on a core audience of frequent moviegoers who go to at least one movie per month, or 12 movies per year. In 2003, frequent filmgoers represented 35% of the pool of people going to cinemas but 78% of all ticket sales, according to the Motion Picture Association of America (MPAA). The data come from the MPAA's *2003 U.S. Movie Attendance Study*, which dissects moviegoing in the population for people ages 12 and older.

Another strata are the occasional moviegoers, defined as persons who attend a cinema between 2 and 11 times per year. Persons in the occasional category accounted for 50% of the pool of the active moviegoer population in 2003 but just 20% of 2003 admissions. Finally, there are infrequent moviegoers who attend cinema about once per year. As a category, infrequent moviegoers account for 15% of the active pool of filmgoers but contribute just 2% to total admissions. The pool of active moviegoers consists of 72% of the population over age 12 that goes to movies at least once a year (embracing frequent, occasional, and infrequent).

Persons in the frequent, occasional, and infrequent classes come from all demographic groups. The most avid filmgoers are ages 18 to 20, of which 62% were frequent moviegoers in 2003, according to the MPAA. Looking at a broader demographic swath, ages 12 to 29 represent 30% of the population but an outsized 48% of admissions in 2003, according to the MPAA (Fig. 8.1).

Among the pool of active moviegoers, 44% of children/teenagers ages 12 to 17 are in the frequent category, according to the MPAA. Only 3% of this teenager demographic "never" attends movies versus never-goers who constitute 28% of the total population aged 12 and higher, according to the MPAA.

Although the youth/young adult demographic is the biggest, a trend today is for older persons not to lose the movie-going habit to the extent of previous generations. Active moviegoers between ages 40 and 59 increased by 7% in 2003, according to the MPAA. Moviegoing increased 2.1% for persons 50 years and older from 2001 to 2003.

The United States and Canada have very active moviegoers by world standards. In the United States, each person averaged 5.4 movie theater admissions in 2003. The per capita figure for Canada is around 4.0. In comparison, all of Europe musters just 1.6, or 2.5 when looking at just industrialized Western Europe, according to London-based researcher Informa Media. In Asia Pacific and Latin America, the per capita figures are even lower.

Figure 8.1 Percent of Yearly Admission by Age Group 1999–2003

Age group	1999	2000	2001	2002	2003	% civilian population
12-15	11%	10%	12%	10%	11% ⎤	7% ⎤
16-20	20%	17%	16%	17%	16%	9%
21-24	10%	11%	10%	12%	12% ⎬ 48%	6% ⎬ 30%
25-29	12%	12%	9%	11%	9% ⎦	8% ⎦
30-39	18%	18%	19%	17%	19%	18%
40-49	14%	14%	17%	15%	14%	19%
50-59	7%	10%	9%	8%	11%	14%
60+	8%	8%	8%	9%	8%	19%
12-17	17%	17%	19%	16%	18%	11%
18+	83%	83%	82%	85%	81%	89%

Source: Motion Picture Association of America

Economics

The movie theater business is coming off hard times. In the 1999 to 2001 time frame, 13 sizable United States theater chains landed in bankruptcy, a casualty of audience demand for state-of-the-art facilities and overexpansion of theater circuits. In this superheated period, exhibitors invaded the turf of rivals by expanding aggressively (see History of Exhibition at end of chapter).

Theater chains in court-supervised bankruptcies exercised rights to "reject" unwanted theater leases. They emerged stronger as they either shed unwanted theaters or renegotiated leases to lower payments by threatening to reject burdensome leases in court. Another fallout was a round of consolidation, particularly by Regal Entertainment, which grew to a whopping 6,045 screens in the United States at the start of 2004, accounting for 17% of the territory's total screens. Since 1995, the $2.2 billion-revenue Regal circuit gobbled up 14 other exhibitors of varying sizes as part of its growth spurt.

More theater circuit mergers are expected within the industry. With theaters downsizing because of bankruptcies, United States screen count peaked at an estimated 38,000 in summer 2000. From 2001 to 2002, the 1-year drop in screen count was a massive 14% before climbing slightly to 35,786 screens at the end of 2003 (Fig. 8.2).

Figure 8.2 United States Screen Count 1980–2003

Year	Total Screens	% change vs. 03	Indoor Screens	Drive-in Screens
2003	35,786	–	35,499	647
2002	35,280	1.4%	34,630	650
2001	36,764	–2.7%	36,110	654
2000	37,396	–4.3%	36,679	717
1999	37,185	–3.8	36,448	737
1995	27,805	28.7%	26,958	847
1990	23,689	51.1%	22,774	915
1985	21,147	69.2%	18,327	2,820
1980	17,590	103.4%	14,029	3,561

Source: Motion Picture Association of America

Some prognosticators forecast the United States screen count could bottom out at 30,000 screens in the next few years, although careful analysis indicates such a steep decline is unlikely. Newly built theaters still are going into service, offsetting closure of antiquated screens and unprofitable theaters. Not surprisingly, exhibitors who call for industry-wide reductions in screens typically want their competitors to do all the cutting.

One aspect of the cinema business that is extremely beneficial to exhibitors is their hold on cash. Typically, consumers pay for tickets in cash, which immediately goes to the coffers of theaters. However, the exhibitors don't pay out film rentals for 30 to 45 days after a film plays. Therefore, theaters can collect interest income on ticket sales cash before paying distributors, which is known as the float. Historically, exhibitors have been slowest to pay independent distributors, who complain about systemic slow payment and underpayment of film rentals, particularly from small-size cinema operators. Mel Gibson's Icon Distribution filed a lawsuit in June 2004, complaining that Regal Entertainment offered to pay 34% of box office from *The Passion of the Christ*, whereas Icon asserts a 55% film rental rate was promised.

Overall, distributor complaints about underpayment have diminished in recent years because today's top circuits are large publicly traded companies that are closely watched by regulators and investors. Also, the introduction of computer information technology makes underpayments more difficult to hide. Distributors sometimes use ticket counters to do secret spot checks of ticket sales of films, which are compared later against the final tallies provided by the theaters themselves. The Theater Entertainment Service unit of CMR/TNS Media Intelligence is one such verification service.

A centerpiece of exhibition economics is food/beverage sales, which account for roughly two thirds of exhibitor operating profit, as cited earlier. Those bags of popcorn and soft drinks each costing $3 generate gross profit margins of 80–85% (revenue minus direct cost, excluding overhead). A modern, top-grossing theater chain averaged around $2.40 in food/beverage sales per admission in 2003. The national average—when including low-grossing and antiquated theaters—works out to about $1.65 in food/beverage sales per ticket sold, or roughly $2.6 billion in aggregate. Exhibitors keep all the food/beverage sales, and a bloody riot certainly would ensue if distributors tried to get a piece of that revenue.

Movie theaters are becoming more aggressive in selling advertising to nonfilm companies, a trend that ultimately could cut into film marketing efforts inside theaters. Exhibitors note that the on-screen cinema advertising business is far larger in Europe, which they feel points to growth opportunities in the United States. On-screen advertising amounted to around $356 million in the United States and Canada in 2003, versus more than $700 million in Europe. However, Europeans see fewer ads on television. In the United States, consumers are barraged with more television advertising and may not be receptive to in-cinema ads. Researcher InsightExpress found high levels of moviegoer dissatisfaction with burgeoning on-screen advertising, in survey results released in November of 2004.

The most ambitious is Regal Entertainment, the biggest United States circuit, which is making a massive push to grow in-theater advertising. It seeks to expand a revenue stream by offering nonfilm marketers a chance to reach filmgoers via on-screen advertising and plasma-board displays visible in lobby areas. Regal Entertainment sold 265 million tickets in 2003. Most of its screens—though not all—are equipped for its advertising network, resulting in an estimated $74 million in 2003 ad sales, which is a revenue stream that barely existed a few years ago.

In the past, some major studio film distributors resisted on-screen advertising in auditoriums showing their movies, but the distributors mostly are silent now. Distributors backed off because theaters are coming off a tough economic stretch and because theaters pay high film rentals to distributors by historical standards. In any case, exhibition's best hopes for improving profits are in boosting returns from food/beverages, on-screen advertising, in-theater advertising, and facilities rentals to noncinema customers. In short, that's everything except from box office, because film distributors certainly would raise film rental rates at the first sign of improved profits from ticket revenue.

Another change in the exhibition landscape is that so-called dollar houses have shrunk to 1% of box office, down from 3% in the early 1990s. Dollar houses are theaters with low admission prices—typically $3 or less—that show movies that premiered at least 10 weeks earlier in other theaters charging higher ticket prices. Dollar houses tend to book well-known major-studio films, not indie titles.

The linchpin of a dollar house's economic return is food/beverage sales, because film rentals can eat up all the revenue generated by ticket sales. Such theaters sometimes book two or three films on the same screen, in a throwback to the double feature prior to the multiplex era. Older theaters with dwindling box office sometimes are reconfigured as dollar houses. These theaters often are in blighted city centers or small towns where theater leases are cheap.

The investment community is of two minds about whether the broad exhibition industry will thrive in the future. Some analysts suggest exhibition will be a low- or no-profit business because its infrastructure needs constant refurbishing, major studios hold the upper hand in negotiating film rentals paid by theaters, and—despite a modest reduction—plenty of screens still are available across North America.

A completely different thesis is that exhibition is something of a juicy money-making franchise for big, well-located theaters. Contributing to this rosy outlook is the industry structure in which theaters collect most of their revenue in immediate cash but pay expenses weeks later.

Megaplexes

The megaplex remade exhibition because of its ability to draw moviegoers from a wider geographic area than smaller multiplexes. These days, a megaplex is defined as a theater with a minimum of 14 screens at one location (some industry executives suggest 12 should be the minimum screen count).

In the boom of the late 1990s, the megaplex definition was a minimum of 20 screens. However, theater operators discovered that 20 screens were unprofitable in times of weak box office that periodically afflict the movie business, so the biggest new-build theaters today aren't as large as in the late 1990s. For example, Regal Entertainment says it now builds theaters with 10 to 18 screens, each with auditoriums ranging from 100 to 500 seats. A multiplex is a theater with at least six screens and up to 11 or 13 screens, depending on where one starts defining a megaplex.

Theaters with 14 or more screens tend to pull audiences from an 8- to 12-mile radius, depending on population density and geographic barriers in a given area. That number compares to the 3- to 5-mile radius for smaller theaters (13 screens or fewer). In very densely populated areas such as Manhattan, the zones can be smaller than 3 miles in radius.

Until the arrival of the megaplex in 1995, moviegoers almost always went to the nearest theater to see a movie. However, these days a moviegoer might drive past a nearby six-screen theater showing a desired film for the enhanced experience of seeing the same movie in a megaplex.

Megaplexes offer sheer size that makes going out a spectacle, particularly because they offer amenities such as extensive food/beverage service that can include cafes. More than that, megaplexes tend to have stadium-style seating where rows are sharply tiered, which provides better sight lines to the screen than the simple sloped floors at older theaters. The megaplexes also are apt to offer the latest digital sound, bright screens, and latest film projection equipment.

The megaplex revolution dramatically impacted film-booking strategies. Because megaplexes draw moviegoers from a bigger geographic swath than do smaller theaters, there is more overlap by theaters, which gives film distributors more choices in covering a city. This undercuts the negotiation leverage of exhibitors.

If there is more than one exhibitor in a zone, a distributor can literally auction films. Despite the availability of multiple exhibitors, film distributors tend to book movies with one exhibitor per zone because of the simplicity in dealing with just one buyer. If there are competitive theaters in a booking zone, it's advisable for distributors to maintain the appearance of being open to all comers so as not to leave themselves open to charges of anticompetitive practices. Zone exclusivity is referred to as *clearance*. Exhibitors can negotiate clearances in individual booking contracts that exclude nearby rivals from showing the same film at the same time.

Theater Chains

Due to consolidation, the top five circuits each operate thousands of screens that account for upwards of half of all United States screens. The top five circuits are Regal Entertainment, AMC Entertainment, Cinemark USA, Carmike Cinemas, and Loews Cineplex Entertainment (Fig. 8.3).

Figure 8.3 Top Theater Chains by Screens 1996 & 2003

Rank	Circuit	2003	1996	% change 1996-2003
		screens	screens	%
1	Regal Cinemas	6124	1018	501.6
2	AMC Entertainment	3280	1721	90.6
3	Cinemark USA	2265	1317	72.0
4	Carmike Cinemas	2251	2478	−9.2
5	Loews Cineplex	2143	831	157.9
6	National Amusements	1059	856	23.7
7	Century Theatres	856	408	109.8
8	Famous Players	838	475	76.4
9	Kerasotes Theatres	532	328	62.2
10	Marcus Theatres Corp.	488	227	115.0
11	Wallace Theatre Corp.	467	98	376.5
12	Pacific Theatres	403	350	15.1
13	Caribbean Cinemas	298		na
14	Goodrich Quality Theatres	279	124	125.0
15	Clearview Cinemas	272	47	478.7
16	George Kerasotes Corp.	266	256	3.9
17	Malco Theatres	266	159	67.3
18	Northeast Cinemas	261	618	−57.8
19	Georgia Theatre Co.	260	112	132.1
20	Harkins Theatres	259	118	119.5

Note: figures cover United States and Canada
Source: Dodona Research

The big-five circuits have slightly different profiles. The $1.9 billion-revenue AMC Entertainment concentrates on jumbo megaplexes. At the other end of the spectrum, the $500 million-revenue Carmike Cinemas operates smaller theaters in towns and suburbs. The $1 billion-revenue Loews Cineplex Entertainment is noted for theaters in big cities, having a mix of older (and in some cases historic) theaters and operating one of the two national Canadian circuits.

Regal Entertainment, AMC Entertainment, and the $950 million-revenue Cinemark USA are noted for modern infrastructure. For example, as of January 2004, Regal Entertainment said that 77% of its screens were equipped with costly steep-slope stadium seating and that it averages 11 screens per location.

Theaters face concentrated power on the other side of the bargaining table when booking movies. The top 10 film distributors—Hollywood's seven historic majors, startup major DreamWorks, New Line, and Miramax—generally account for approximately 94% of box office in a normal year. The 10 distributors are owned by eight companies, as New Line belongs to Warner Bros. and Miramax is owned by Walt Disney.

The trend toward wider theatrical releases has ended the segmentation between first-run theaters getting premieres and second-run theaters—often located in suburban or outlying areas—getting the same film print weeks later. City-center and outlying theaters play a film at the same time with today's wide-release patterns. Thus, all of today's national circuits operate theaters booking first-run movies.

Giant Screen

Large-screen theaters, once confined mostly to museums and institutions, are popping up as part of or adjacent to regular megaplex and multiplex theaters. Typically, one oversized auditorium is equipped as a giant-screen venue, whereas the other dozen or so screens at the same location are conventional. Giant screens can be 100 feet wide and 80 feet high, giving the viewer an immersion viewing experience unlike that of a smaller conventional cinema screen. Special effects-laden films, sci-fi, fantasy, historical epics, and action films are best suited for immersion treatment.

The sector leader is the publicly traded, $119 million-revenue IMAX, which is headquartered in suburban Toronto and was founded in 1967. Of the 240 IMAX theaters operating worldwide at the end of 2003, 115 are at institutional locations; the remaining 125 are in regular commercial locations. The United States had 120 IMAX screens (both institutional and commercial) and Canada another 23 screens at the end of 2003. Another giant-screen projection company in the field is MegaSystems, Inc.

With the march into multiplexes and megaplexes, IMAX seeks to book mainstream Hollywood blockbusters on the giant screen, diversifying from its roots with scientific and natural history documentaries. IMAX says that its run of Warner Bros.-distributed *The Matrix Reloaded* on 70 IMAX screens in June 2003 contributed 27% of the sci-fi yarn's domestic box office from just 7% of its screens. *The Matrix Reloaded* premiered in conventional theaters four weeks before its IMAX run. The November 2003 release of *The Matrix Revolutions* by Warner Bros. became the first Hollywood film to premiere on giant screens simultaneously with release on conventional screens. Still, most of the giant-screen all-time hits are science and documentary movies because Hollywood fare is a new wave.

There are two goals in putting mainstream films on giant screens. First, distributors seek film rental revenue because ticket prices are higher at giant-screen theaters. Ticket prices for the two *Matrix* movies ran 30% higher, on average, than in conventional screens. Also, films tend to run longer and can make effective re-releases on giant screens years after premiere. In 2002, IMAX screens offered a re-release of Universal's 1995 space disaster drama *Apollo 13*.

A drawback is that giant-screen prints are costly to make, and there's a separate one-time cost of $2 million for format conversion to adapt conventional 35-mm Hollywood films. Also, Hollywood films typically have running times that are twice as long as scientific/nature films, so giant-screen theaters don't squeeze in as many showings with mainstream films. As long as giant-screen theaters fill up with moviegoers, the economics work even with fewer runs.

IMAX release prints use 70-mm film in the so-called 15-perforation 15/70-format, which offers a superior picture and stability compared to conventional screens using 35-mm film with just four perforations per film frame. IMAX auditoriums in conventional multiplexes tend to seat around 350 persons, which make the auditoriums large capacity by multiplex/megaplex standards. IMAX also has a three-dimensional presentation in which moviegoers get a sense of depth when they wear special eyeglasses.

Canada

Canada generated Can$956.73 million in box office in 2003 (or about $636 million in United States dollars) from approximately 3,000 screens at about 725 locations. The territory has two languages: English and French (in the Quebec province). Canada's population is about 11% that of the United States, but its box office is generally 7–9% as large due to the impact of currency exchange on the weak Canadian dollar and lower per capita attendance.

Canada has two big national circuits. Cineplex Odeon is part of Loews Cineplex Entertainment, which is owned by Canadian financier Gerald Schwartz through his Onex Corp. The other national circuit is Famous Players that is part of Viacom, which also owns Paramount Pictures. Their decades-old duopoly was shattered when AMC Entertainment began building megaplexes in big Canadian metropolitan areas. The Kansas

City, Missouri-based AMC Entertainment entered Canada with high hopes in 1998, only to be blunted when Famous Players opened theaters wherever AMC built.

When the Cineplex Odeon–Famous Players duopoly reigned, film distributors booked one circuit for near-national coverage. Film rentals—the share of box office that goes to film distributors—were lower than in the United States at approximately 45% (theaters kept 55%), although distributors benefited from simplified film booking via just one theater chain.

As AMC and others fragmented the marketplace, an American style of booking by geographic zones (small areas) started to take hold. A distributor tends to place a film with just one exhibitor in a zone and covers Canada with a patchwork of exhibitors. Before AMC's entry, Famous Players booked on a national basis movies from Disney, MGM, Paramount, and Warner Bros. (and more recently DreamWorks). Cineplex Odeon was the circuit for Columbia/Sony, Twentieth Century Fox, and Universal Pictures.

For distribution purposes, Canada is combined with the United States in what is called the domestic market. The countries are combined because most of Canada's population lives along the southern border with the United States, where it gets American television broadcast channels (either over the air or via cable retransmission). Because Canadians see movie ads from the United States and there's no language barrier (except in French-speaking Quebec), films premiere simultaneously in both countries. For practical business reasons, the term "domestic market" is appropriate, although it irks some Canadians who feel the phrase makes Canada seem like part of the United States. However, such country combination designations exist elsewhere in the film business, such as the Benelux region in Europe (Belgium, Netherlands, and Luxembourg), without suggestion of undermining sovereignty.

Canada's contribution to domestic box office figures is a source of endless confusion and frequent misstatements. Weekend domestic box office grosses, which are issued in a rush, sometimes add Canadian grosses on a one-to-one basis with United States dollars. That practice results in an overstatement because the fluctuating currency exchange rate may call for Can$1.21 to equal US$1.00. In other frequent inadvertent misstatements, pundits often cite United States box office figures that also include Canada, or else they talk about "domestic box office" that in reality is only for the United States.

Canada has a more stringent regulatory regime than the United States. Six regional government entities operate a mandatory film rating system in Canada, whereas the United States film classification system is voluntary and industry run. Interestingly, in May 2004, a court in Ontario, which is the province that includes Toronto, barred the Ontario Film Review Board from banning films for a year while it rewrites legislation that was found to conflict with the federal constitution.

Marketing by Theaters

Exhibition is a business with little brand identification or loyalty. Consumers traditionally make a cinema decision primarily by choosing the nearest theater offering a desired movie or the nearest cinema equipped with sought-after amenities such as stadium seating for unobstructed sight lines to the screen.

In recent years, some United States exhibitors experimented with loyalty programs, offering discounts for frequent moviegoing in a bid to increase per capita attendance from their regular customers and to draw patrons from rivals. This ticket price cutting strategy borrows a concept used in Europe with mixed results. United States circuits mostly dropped such programs, partly because of conflicts with distributors over lower film rentals resulting from a drop in average ticket prices.

In another bid to foster consumer loyalty, theaters push gift cards and seek promotional tie-ins with distributors. For example, graphics from New Line Cinema's *The Lord of the Rings: The Return of the King* and Universal's *Dr. Seuss' The Cat in the Hat* were imprinted on Loews Cineplex cinema's Reel Dollars gift certificate in late 2003 to promote the films. Various images from the same film were offered in an effort to get moviegoers to collect the gift cards.

Independents

Independent films, which in the broadest definition are any movies not originating from the major studios, have grown in stature since the late 1960s. In that period, audiences gravitated toward edgy, realistic "new American cinema" films that stood in sharp contrast to tame studio fare. Due to that success, mainstream theaters started booking indie films, so theaters with a pure indie-film focus now face broader competition. The video revolution also cut into the indie theater business. Out-of-the-mainstream films became more accessible via DVD and VHS tape, putting less pressure on filmgoers to catch the films in cinemas.

The largest theater circuit devoted to independent films is Landmark Theatres, which has 204 screens at 57 locations in 11 states. Founded in

1974, the circuit has a footprint covering the top major United States cities, which enables Landmark to tap the bulk of the art film audience. Its theaters tend have diverse names such as the Nuart Theatre in West Los Angeles, Embarcadero Center Cinema in San Francisco, Kendall Square Cinema in Cambridge, Massachusetts, the Plaza Frontenac Cinema in St. Louis, and the Sunshine Cinema in New York City.

Dot-com billionaires Todd Wagner and Mark Cuban purchased Landmark in September 2003 for $80 million, with ambition to ride the digital technology wave now engulfing the movie business. Another company banking on digital technology to remake the indie sector, New York City-based Madstone, which was founded by a Wall Street executive, abruptly downsized its ambitions and pulled out of the art-house theater business in June 2004.

A fixture of independent exhibition are calendar houses, which screen out-of-the-mainstream films with short runs, sometimes as brief as a single day. The name comes from the promotional brochures, which show the theater's film schedule for one or two months with playdates presented in a calendar format. Calendar houses tend to be stand-alone theaters and not part of larger circuits.

Located in an outlying New York City suburb, the Jacob Burns Film Center is an example of a calendar theater that is set up as a not-for-profit. Established in 2001, the Burns Center proved to be a quick success, drawing 200,000 admissions in 2003 (including special group screenings) and booking 450 different film titles each year on its three screens. A salute to Italian cinema is an example, with thematic films making short runs (Fig. 8.4).

The Burns Center mails out 30,000–40,000 printed calendars per month, sends e-mail newsletters to 11,000 persons who request the messages, and uses the promotional muscle of sponsors. Its Web site and publicity-generating stories in outside media are other marketing mainstays. One employee devotes full time to publicity. "If it's the right kind of event, we can sell out a screening just using e-mails," said Steve Apkon, executive director of the theater, which is located in Pleasantville, New York.

The Burns Center has six corporate sponsors, including Pepsi, Fujifilm, and a local newspaper, which use the association to target their markets. To tap an audience interested in nutrition, a local health club chain that is a permanent sponsor and a health food store chain underwrote an event built around the screening of fast-food documentary *Super Size Me*. Given the segmented appeal of films, the Burns Center can deliver to audiences such as children, women, ethnic groups, and educators who otherwise are spread out geographically and difficult for corporate sponsors to reach.

Figure 8.4 Jacob Burns Film Center in suburban New York City uses its calendar schedule to promote a celebration of Italian cinema in 2004. Source: Reproduced by permission of the Jacob Burns Film Center

Indicating a consumer loyalty for edgy films, the Burns Center out-grossed a nearby multiplex by a ratio of 7:1 when both screened *Super Size Me*, according to Burns Center program director Brian Ackerman. However, Burns Center sometimes will not book indie films that are saturating mainstream theaters nearby because that strays from its mission to cater to underserved segments. One of the Burns Center's three screens turns over film on a daily basis or sometimes runs two different films on the same day. A second screen holds films for a half week to a week. The third screen has long runs, up to a maximum of five weeks.

Online Ticketing

Two big online ticketing services provide showtime information for films and sell tickets via the Internet. Some general entertainment Web sites also push cinema information and ticketing.

Among the big two services, Fandango positions itself as a ticketing service that encourages consumers to print tickets at home and make purchases of entertainment-related merchandise. The other big online player, MovieTickets.com, pursues a strategy of being a provider to handle online transaction services to third-party Web sites. For example, AOL Moviefone signed MovieTickets.com to handle its ticketing fulfillment in summer 2004.

The online ticketing providers generally add an extra $0.75–$1.50 per ticket as a service charge and sell tickets for screenings limited to 45 days in the future. The online services also offer tickets via toll-free telephone calls.

Volume for online ticket sales ranges from 2–8% of cinema ticket sales for various movies. The high end involves opening weekends of anticipated blockbusters with a possibility of sold-out performances. For example, Fandango says it sold $8.8 million of the $125 million five-day opening weekend box office for *The Passion of the Christ*, or about 7% of the tickets sold for the religious drama for February 26–29, 2004. The opening of *The Passion of the Christ* accounted for 98% of Fandango's sales for some dates. Online ticketing is more popular in other parts of the world where cinemas and seating capacity are in short supply, so how widespread usage will be in the United States and Canada where theaters are plentiful is unclear.

Reserved tickets can be picked up at the theater using a verification identification code. When tickets are printed at home, the printouts have individual bar codes for verification. The ticketing services are platforms for film distributors and their promotional partners to run sweepstakes and other promotions in connection with theatrical film premieres. For example, Paramount conducted a contest for the release of the remake *The Stepford Wives* in 2004. The grand prize was a trip to New York City, and the studio's partners—Marriott New York Marquis, travel agency Orbitz, and retailer Z-Gallerie—got plugs on a sweepstakes entry page of MovieTickets.com.

Los Angeles-based Fandango, which launched its service in 2000, claims its partner exhibition circuits account for 15,000 screens, of which approximately 70% are enabled for remote ticketing. Fandango's partner circuits are Carmike Cinemas, Century Theatres, Cinemark USA, Edwards Theatres, Loews Cineplex Entertainment, Regal Entertainment, and United Artists Theatres. Fandango entered the Toronto area in December 2003 in a deal with Cineplex Galaxy.

Elsewhere, MovieTickets.com is a joint venture with entertainment outfit Hollywood Media Corp., which is publicly traded, and several theater circuits. It books online theater tickets purchases for the following circuits: AMC Entertainment, National Amusements, Famous Players, Hoyts Cinemas, Marcus Theaters, Consolidated Theaters, Crown Theatres, Krikorian Premiere Theatres, Metropolitan Theatres, Rave Motion Pictures, Ritz Theatres, and Spotlight Theatres. Further, MSN Networks and Lycos use MovieTickets.com to handle transactions for their online ticket sales.

Film Piracy

Exhibitors find their venues are the front lines in the battle against film piracy. The MPAA estimates 90% of movies popping up unauthorized on the Internet originated from illicit camcorders making copies off cinema screens. Further, the trade group from Hollywood's major studios estimates total unauthorized duplication and sale of films from all sources cost its member companies $3.5 billion per year.

In a bid to thwart pirates, film distributors are moving up premiere dates in other countries closer to or, in some instances, simultaneous with North America release. That's because North America release spawns pirate DVD and Internet copies of films, including camcorder copies made surreptitiously in theaters. An illicit copy can be e-mailed within hours to other countries, where DVD bootlegs are immediately duplicated.

Close-to-United States releases dates in overseas territories have a drawback, however. Peak cinema periods and holidays in other countries are mostly out of synch with those in the United States and Canada. Still, the trend is for fast international release of films that are expected to be widely pirated, especially blockbusters and visual action/adventure films that don't face significant language barriers.

Since unauthorized camcorder copying off United States cinema screens became recognized as a major problem in 2003, exhibitors and their trade group the National Association of Theatre Owners (NATO) have mounted antipiracy efforts in theaters. Antipiracy trailers had screened in 5,000 theater locations by mid-2004 to educate the public that unauthorized copying of films is a violation of copyright law. Antipiracy signs are expected to pop up in theaters as well. Tens of thousands of brochures, developed jointly by NATO and the MPAA, have been distributed to theater employees to teach them how to identify and deal with in-theater pirates.

Electronic Projection Equipment

Digital electronic projectors, which replace mechanical film equipment using analog technology, are on the horizon. Digital cinema currently is a fringe part of exhibition because the technology faces technical and economic barriers in the short term.

At the end of 2003, there were only about 170 d-cinema screens worldwide out of 139,400 global screens. Most are simply test beds for theater chains that want to gain experience with the technology without taking the plunge of circuit-wide retrofitting. Exhibitors want to use digital projection as a vehicle to justify a higher-priced ticket, for example, charging $1–$2 more than screens showing the same film with conventional mechanical projectors. That ambition points to waiting—perhaps three or more years—for further quality improvements in digital projection equipment.

A big obstacle is economic in that theaters would have to buy digital projection equipment, whose utilization mainly benefits film distributors. Unless d-cinema screenings command higher ticket prices, the only benefit is freeing Hollywood distributors from shouldering the expense of supplying bulky analog film release prints and related shipping costs.

The equipment price tag is another economic issue. Mechanical projectors for conventional film projection cost about $30,000 each, whereas cinema-quality digital projection equipment for a cinema screen costs around $100,000 (including on-site digital storage equipment), although this expense is falling. On top of that, mechanical projectors are more durable and last longer. Less expensive digital projection systems are available, but they fall short of cinema quality and are used for noncinema image projection purposes.

A sporadic shift in technical standards for d-cinema is another deterrent to theater conversions. The first wave of digital projectors had 1.3K resolution and eight-bit color but were surpassed by 2K/10-bit color. In June 2004, Sony presented a 4K projector prototype that, if brought to commercial use, likely would make existing equipment obsolete. Experts say installing digital projection in all United States theaters would cost several billion dollars.

A final concern is that movies in d-cinema format will be easier for pirates to intercept. A digital copy can be used to make identical duplicates, which is not the case with analog technology in which copies made from film prints are of lesser quality than the original. Conventional film prints also are more difficult to intercept because of their bulk.

D-cinema electronic projection quality only became comparable to mechanical film projection for the naked eye in the late 1990s. D-cinema promoters obscured the inconvenient reality that the quality of digital projection was simply about the same as conventional film projection. Digital sound that is a fixture today in cinema represented a dramatic improvement, which causes some pundits to overestimate the impact of digital technology on image projection. The slow-to-materialize d-cinema revolution already claimed a casualty. Industrial giant Boeing quit its effort to lease transponders on satellites to the film industry and thus abandoned a plan to serve as a middleman.

Exhibitors look to digital projection as a way to book nonfilm attractions, such as sports events or concerts. If such alternative programming becomes pervasive, it likely will cut into screen time for films. The specter of alternative programming pushing movies off screens makes film distributors reluctant to help exhibitors pick up the cost of converting to d-cinema. In an example of alternative digital cinema fare clashing with movies, in March 2004 a concert from rock musician Prince's *Musicology* tour was offered at more than 40 d-cinema screens using electronic projection for an admission price of $15.

The consortium Digital Cinema Initiatives, formed by Hollywood's major studios, is evaluating equipment and trying to set industry standards without running afoul of antitrust laws. The film industry wants to avoid multiple standards, such as the DTS and SDDS audio standard war that fragments digital sound in theaters.

Eventually when the technology is more advanced and equipment costs fall, digital cinema certainly will sweep exhibition. Investment house CSFB estimated the United States film industry paid $800 million to make and ship film release prints in 2003. A single release print costs approximately $1,000 in a volume order. Shipping costs are substantial because film prints are bulky. If a theater destroys a print, distributors typically charge a $2,000 replacement fee to cover added shipping and to deter theaters from being careless with prints.

Whenever digital cinema arrives, it will level the playing field between major studios and independent film distributors. The Hollywood majors currently have an advantage because their large sizes enable them to pay for and manage thousands of cumbersome analog film release prints. D-cinema streamlines the delivery process by using satellite transmission, high-speed broadband connections, or inexpensive portable disks, which independents should be able to accomplish as easily as majors. As noted earlier, dot-com tycoons Todd Wagner and Mark Cuban bought the 204-screen Landmark

Theatre art-house circuit with the intention of pushing d-cinema as part of a broader foray into the movie business.

In one possible scenario, the United States trails the rest of the world in installing d-cinema because the United States infrastructure of mechanical film projectors is of top quality. Some pundits dismiss the standard 35-mm mechanical projector as obsolete, but that's not the case. The film projection platform experienced many improvements over decades, such as improved film stock, brighter light bulbs, and better screens.

As a result, d-cinema becomes established first in Third World countries with dilapidated theater equipment that is in dire need of replacement. The first-generation equipment for Third World countries would have lower quality than the film format, but later generations would improve. Thus, electronic film equipment would achieve economies of mass production scale with sales to other countries, which eventually drives down equipment prices worldwide.

A halfway measure is already creeping into the United States. Subcinema-grade digital equipment is making its way to theaters for projection of commercials and trailers, while mechanical projectors screen the main feature in the same auditorium.

In film production, Hollywood cinematographers and directors are expected to stick to using analog film for principal photography because of its soft "look." Many feel digital images are too sharp, bordering on being harsh to the human eye. However, postproduction editing is increasingly done electronically, and, of course, special effects are mostly digital creations.

History of Exhibition

The early days of film represent an industry that would be unfamiliar today, from the invention of motion picture to nickelodeons to silent films to the first talkies. The modern era was ushered in when a federal court in New York City concluded a consent decree in 1948, forcing a handful of Hollywood major studios to separate from their theater chains. The so-called Paramount Consent Decree broke up vertically integrated studios, whereby a film distributor owned the theaters playing its films. By the 1950s, Hollywood distributors and theaters were under separate ownership for the first time in decades.

For theaters in the United States and Canada, the multiplex era arrived in 1969 when what is now AMC Entertainment opened a brand new six-screen theater in Omaha, Nebraska. Until that time, the few multiscreen theaters were big auditoriums built in the pre-World War II Golden Era of cinema. They were later subdivided and thus not originally built with multiple screens. AMC, whose cinema roots date back to 1920, also is credited with introducing the megaplex theater to the United States when, in 1995, it opened the 24-screen Grand 24 in Dallas, Texas. The Belgium-based exhibitor Kinepolis originated the megaplex concept in Europe.

Another milestone for exhibition was the bankruptcy of 13 significant United States theater circuits between 1999 and 2001, following the boom in megaplex theaters from 1995-2000. Those events are intertwined because the megaplex building craze made theaters with smaller screen counts obsolete, including some six- or eight-screen theaters that were just a few years old.

In a sudden end to hard times, the Regal Entertainment circuit raised a whopping $342 million in its May 2002 initial public stock offering. The bonanza was due to good timing: the stock market was hot and box office was sizzling. Regal Entertainment also benefited from a decline in national screen count in the aftermath of the bankruptcies in 1999 through 2002. Telecom billionaire Philip F. Anschutz bought Regal Entertainment out of bankruptcy in partnership with distressed securities outfit Oaktree Capital Management shortly before the public stock offering. They also had acquired the United Artists and Edwards circuits and a chunk of the Hoyts circuit. Today, the Regal circuit encompasses a staggering 6,045 screens, or 17% of United States screens at the end of 2003.

Investment house Tejas Securities estimates that from 1996 to 1999, the then top-five exhibitors—AMC Entertainment, Carmike Cinemas, Cinemark USA, Loews Cineplex, and Regal—pumped a staggering $4 billion into capital expenditures, which mainly went to opening 5,325 screens. United States screen growth averaged 7.5% per year from 1995 to 2000, which was accelerated from an annual growth rate of 3.2% from 1990 to 1995. While screen count mushroomed, cinema attendance grew just 2.4% per year from 1990 to 1999, which meant ticket sales lagged behind the increase in screens in the late 1990s. Still, box office is on a growth track, having increased from $5.5 billion in 1995 to $9.5 billion by 2003 (Fig. 8.5).

A two-tier exhibition structure faded in recent years with the boom in theater building that erected modern theaters in outlaying areas. The building boom led to increasingly wide releases by film distributors that focused massive advertising on initial premiere. As a result, big films now open everywhere at the same time. In past years, the marketplace was segmented by first-run and second-run theaters. In the old system, release prints first went to city-center theaters, and then the same prints were used weeks later by outlying theaters.

Figure 8.5 United States Box Office 1983–2003

Year	Box Office ($ mil.)	% change prior year	% change vs. 2003
2003	$9.488.5	–0.3%	–
2002	$9,519.6	13.2	–
2001	$8,412.5	9.8%	13.2%
2000	$7,660.7	2.9%	23.9%
1999	$7,448.0	7.2%	27.4%
1998	$6,949.0	9.2%	36.5%
1997	$6,365.9	7.7%	49.1%
1996	$5,911.5	7.6%	60.5%
1995	$5,493.5	1.8%	72.7%
1994	$5,396.2	4.7%	75.8%
1993	$5,154.2	5.8%	84.1%
1992	$4,871.0	1.4%	94.8%
1991	$4,803.2	–4.4%	97.5%
1990	$5,021.8	–0.2%	88.9%
1989	$5,033.4	12.9%	88.5%
1988	$4,458.4	4.8%	112.8%
1987	$4,252.9	12.6%	123.1%
1986	$3,778.0	0.8%	151.2%
1985	$3,749.4	–0.7%	153.1%
1984	$4,030.6	7.0%	135.4%
1983	$3,766.0	–	152.0%

Source: Motion Picture Association of America

One fallout of the megaplex trend is that amenities such as digital sound, wide screens, and stadium seating increasingly are seen as mandatory for each screen. Until the mid-1990s, multiplexes tended to have two levels of luxury. A multiplex operator in this era might outfit two or four main auditoriums with top luxury at a location, while the remaining four or more screens would be sparsely appointed. Exhibitors complain that the audience demand for uniform luxury of digital sound, wide screens, raked stadium seating floor configuration, and plush seats with cup holders makes theaters at least twice as expensive to build than in the early 1990s, after adjusting for inflation.

The boom of the late 1990s and the following bust largely resulted from an invasion by investment from private equity firms, which pumped up exhibition with a flurry of investments. Private equity outfits buy existing businesses with the goal of increasing their value for resale in three to five years. Private equity outfits typically invest a relatively small amount of their capital to purchase companies and augment that capital with massive borrowing. The borrowing magnifies returns on their foundation capital when assets are sold.

Thus, theater chains acquired by private equity outfits carried hefty debt, which triggered some of the 13 exhibitor bankruptcies from 1999 to 2001. When the growth rate for box office revenue lagged behind the increase in screen count, the debt-heavy capital structure of exhibitors acquired by private equity outfits was untenable. Their cash flow could not service debt. The final nail in the coffin came when aggregate ticket sales fell in the period from 1999 to 2000.

9 Major Studios

Well, goodbye, Mr. Zanuck. And let me tell you that it certainly has been a pleasure working at Sixteenth Century Fox.

Director Jean Renoir

Hollywood's venerable seven major studios are criticized for being impersonal, stodgy, tight fisted, and unwilling to change with the times. The quote above, which plays off this viewpoint, is a farewell from the famous French director to the Hollywood mogul Darryl Zanuck.

However, the fact remains that the Hollywood majors are world beaters in business—nobody else comes even remotely close—so they must be doing something right. For all the knocks about inflexibility, the majors are changing with the times, as evidenced by their embrace of the DVD video format and entrance into the video-on-demand business.

The venerable seven are Walt Disney Studios, Columbia Pictures/TriStar Pictures (also known as Sony Pictures), Metro-Goldwyn-Mayer, Paramount Pictures, Twentieth Century Fox, Universal Pictures, and Warner Bros. Their worldwide revenues amounted to over $41 billion annually in 2003. These seven have been the eternal Hollywood giants since the 1920s. Today, an eighth giant is the emerging major DreamWorks, which is the studio startup.

Those eight—when including their affiliates—account for more than 97% of box office in the United States in a normal year (although less in 2004 because indies distributed blockbusters *The Passion of the Christ* and *Fahrenheit 9/11*). The remaining few percentage points of market share are highly fragmented among independents that are not affiliates of major studios, which illustrates an important characteristic of the United States movie business. There are no middle-size film companies, just eight giants on the one hand and a bunch of small players on the other. At one time, Orion Pictures (*Dances with Wolves* and *The Silence of the Lambs*) and A-picture producer Carolco Pictures (*Basic Instinct* and *Terminator 2: Judgment Day*) were hefty mid-sized players, but they landed in bankruptcy in 1991 and 1995, respectively.

It's not surprising that the middle ground is dangerous, because the movie business is capital intensive with unpredictable swings, both down and up. Large size is necessary to ride out financial and cyclical vagaries endemic to the business. Looking closer at the studios, Hollywood's top five majors each weighs in with revenue of over $5 billion per year (Fig. 9.1). Paramount is a step down, with estimated filmed entertainment revenue of $3.5 billion in 2003. MGM is the smallest, with about $1.7 billion in revenue. In contrast, the biggest independent, Lions Gate Entertainment, generates annual revenue of $650 million.

Overview

Although it's little understood, even within the film industry, the majors are essentially banks and distribution machines whose economic clout comes from their film libraries. The majors contract out for production talent with their piles of money, so production itself is not a core function (indeed, Metro-Goldwyn-Mayer and DreamWorks do not have production

Figure 9.1 Hollywood's Seven Major Studios Ranked by Revenue 2003–2004

Studio	Estimated revenue ($ bil.)
Warner/New Line	$11.0
Walt Disney Miramax	$7.4
Universal	$7.0
Sony/Columbia	$6.0
Twentieth Century Fox	$5.0
Paramount	$3.5
Metro-Goldwyn-Mayer	$1.7
Total	$41.6

Note: Revenue figures include television programming activities at studios
Source: *Marketing to Moviegoers*, based on company reports

lots). As banks, the majors have the financial resources to make or acquire films without presales. Thus, the majors are not forced to collect money in advance by selling off rights to third-party distributors to fund their current slates, as the independents are.

The distribution prowess of the majors results from their ability to sell films directly to theaters around the world (except for Metro-Goldwyn-Mayer, whose foreign theatrical distribution is contracted out to Twentieth Century Fox). Europe's big film companies don't have the ability to directly distribute films theatrically even to their next-door neighbor countries, much less to Asia or Latin America.

One consequence of their distribution muscle is that the major studios are perfectly suited to market big, glossy mainstream films but not specialized films, regardless of the film's artistic merit. Beverage giant Coca-Cola found this out the hard way in the 1980s when it owned Columbia Pictures (which was sold to Sony in 1989). Under the leadership of British filmmaker David Putnam, whose credits include *Chariots of Fire* and *Midnight Express,* the studio arranged to distribute quality films such as the Soviet-era Afghanistan war drama *The Beast* and Serbo-Croatian language *Time of the Gypsies.* However, Columbia's earnings suffered from the small streams of box office generated by such niche films, and the strategy was abandoned.

At any given moment, each major studio has about 150 films in active development, of which 12 to 25 typically are made each year. Their release schedules are augmented with acquisition of films from outside sources. For example, Walt Disney released *Around the World in 80 Days* to disappointing box office in 2004, although the adventure film remake starring Jackie Chan was actually produced by Walden Media, which put up its $120 million-plus production budget.

Another aspect of current film slates is that major studios sometimes pair up on films to make them joint ventures. In this arrangement, one studio handles domestic distribution and the other handles foreign distribution. After some deductions, net revenue goes into what is called a shared pot from which the two partners divvy up proceeds. The shared pot is an equalizer because there's always an imbalance between revenue streams from the foreign market and the domestic (United States and Canada) market.

The most noteworthy example of joint venturing is the $235 million production of *Titanic,* which Twentieth Century Fox originated. Fox enlisted Paramount as a financial partner in a complex deal, leaving Paramount to distribute the 1997 blockbuster domestically. The strategy of split rights represents a portfolio approach. Instead of owning whole films, studios divide some film investments into half ownership. This spreads their production investment over a broader slate—the portfolio—which tends to even out the ups and downs of the movie business. The majors also hedge their bets by producing a wide range of film types, with emphasis on genres that generate hits (Fig. 9.2).

Looking back in history, the major studios emerged in the 1920s and have dominated film distribution ever since. In those early days until the post–World War II period, there were two tiers of studios. The Big Five were Metro-Goldwyn-Mayer, Paramount, RKO, Twentieth Century Fox, and Warner Bros., although RKO eventually faded and was absorbed by Paramount. These studios were vertically integrated because they were distribution companies that also owned theater chains. The second-tier studios—known as the Little Three because they lacked theaters—were Columbia, United Artists, and Universal. Today, the United Artists library of films is owned by Metro-Goldwyn-Mayer.

Marketing by Majors

The major studios spend heavily on marketing—mostly paid ads—to launch their films, and their approach has grown in sophistication since the 1980s. The five biggest Hollywood majors spend somewhere between $350 and $600 million per year on advertising for domestic theatrical

Figure 9.2 Film Economics of Major Studio Releases Per Film by Genre 1996–2003

Genre	Number of films	Ave. domestic box office $ mil	Ave. worldwide revenue $ mil.	Ave. world costs $ mil.	Ave. gross profit $ mil.
Sci-fi/fantasy	62	$96.3	$300.0	$145.8	$154.1
Animation/ fantasy	103	$64.0	$236.1	$120.2	$115.9
Romance	68	$45.5	$121.1	$73.9	$47.2
Action	193	$61.5	$194.4	$121.9	$72.5
Horror	58	$38.4	$102.9	$66.3	$36.6
Comedy	291	$45.0	$123.0	$80.1	$42.9
Drama	202	$45.2	$127.4	$85.5	$41.8
Thriller	85	$43.4	$127.0	$89.2	$37.7
Western	5	$23.1	$70.2	$77.9	−$7.7
Total/ave.	1,067	$52.3	$156.8	$95.9	$60.8

Note: Dollar figures denote group performance on an average per film basis
Source: From Baseline/Film Tracker data published by Kagan Research in Motion Picture Investor #256, Apr 23, 2004. Used with permission.

releases. Thus, the job of studio marketing chief requires adroit management skills because ad expenditures are spread over a wide array of television, radio, print, and other media.

The complexion of the executive suites at the major studios began to change radically in the 1980s because of marketing considerations. For the first time, the top studio jobs went to executives with backgrounds in television, movie distribution (those who licensed films to theaters), and marketing. Television executives brought a sense of discipline from their spreadsheet mentality of weighing the cost of television programming versus the ad revenue potential of the program's intended time period.

Until the 1980s, studio bosses invariably came from inside the film business and had backgrounds in production, film development, and finance. The production and development executives displayed something of a riverboat gambler mentality by choosing films based on gut instinct and believing that their next blockbuster was always just around the corner. The executive suite makeover in the 1980s also reflected the importance of distribution expertise in management, as selling to television and video became important generators of revenue.

In examples of the new executive suite ladders at studios, former Warner Bros. co-chiefs Bob Daly and Terry Semel, who ran the studio for two decades in the 1980s and 1990s, climbed from careers in theatrical distribution and network television, respectively. Current Disney corporate chief Michael Eisner and Internet tycoon Barry Diller went from network television program jobs to jointly running Paramount Pictures in that era. The late Brandon Tartikoff, who briefly was chairman of Paramount from 1991 to 1992, began his career in local television station promotion and later segued to network programming.

Former Paramount and MGM chief Frank Mancuso and ex-Universal Pictures chairman Robert Rehme also climbed up the ranks from theatrical distribution jobs. Paramount motion picture group vice chairman Rob Friedman started his career in film publicity. The late Dawn Steel, who was head of production at Columbia, came from a promotions/merchandising background.

Two currently serving studio chiefs are part of the trend. Warner Bros. president Alan Horn broke into Hollywood via television programming and began his business career at packaged goods giant Procter & Gamble. Walt Disney Studios chairman Richard Cook spent much of his career in distribution and also worked in television.

The shakeup of the 1980s came after majors realized that the fickle youth audience was their salvation, with films such as Columbia's youth counterculture drama *Easy Rider* in 1969. Until that time, longtime movie publicity executives filled the key jobs in studio marketing divisions. Among the first wave of outsiders was Peter Sealey, who jumped from Coca-Cola to Columbia Pictures in 1983 shortly after the beverage marketer bought the studio. Other studios later recruited executives from cosmetics giant Revlon and from various Madison Avenue advertising agencies. In today's Hollywood, marketing executives wield real power to an extent that was unthinkable a few decades ago because they are asked for their opinions about revenue potential for films in development.

A marketing and distribution orientation became valuable as the velocity of film distribution quickened. Through the 1980s, movies spent months in theatrical release, but now they are often just a six-week business at cinemas. The time between a film's theatrical release and subsequent video rollout decreased from 5 months and 4 days in 2002 to 4 months and 23 days in 2003, and the time span continues to narrow.

Economics

The overriding objective of studios is to distribute films that are profitable. If the films are engaging, witty, thought provoking, and win awards, that's simply icing on the cake but not the first concern. From the studio viewpoint, studios want films that are as creative as possible without sacrificing marketability. Because the majors occasionally produce artistic masterpieces, such as Paramount's first two *The Godfather* movies, some pundits mistakenly believe art is an integral part of the equation.

Stating that the profit motive is the foremost concern may seem absurdly self-evident, but in reality it's frequently overlooked. Film talent may pursue lofty artistic visions while the studios don't want to stray too far from mainstream sensibilities. Critics then rap the major studios for picking safe subjects, for ordering movie endings to be re-shot after unfavorable audience response in test screenings, and for not catering to minority audiences. The premise that the majors are somehow faulty to pursue blockbusters is a silly notion because creating glossy, crowd-pleasing films that generate gobs of money is their primary business. What's overlooked is that majors attempt to balance their annual film release slate with the occasional thought-provoking, personal film, such as Warner's *The Green Mile* and Universal's *Schindler's List*.

The job of trying to consistently please critics goes to the studios' wholly owned indie-style subsidiaries, which are big winners of Oscars. This practice started in earnest with Disney's 1993 acquisition of Miramax, which went on to distribute Best Picture Oscar winners *Chicago* and *The English Patient*. Further, Warner owns New Line Cinema, which made the Oscar-winning *Lord of the Rings* trilogy. The studios dabbled with controversial films over the years but worried about triggering consumer backlash that could hurt other businesses of their parent companies. For example, in 1992 Paramount struggled with how to responsibly market urban drama *Juice*. The studio removed a handgun that was prominent in early advertising from later waves of ads, but that change watered down the film's impact in marketing to moviegoers.

The major studios created a layer of insulation by having their independent-style affiliates handle edgy movies. This method separated controversial films from the mainstream studio slate. The indie arms also represented an economic segmentation because they produce, acquire, and market films at far lower cost than their studio parents. Of course, some films are too controversial even for insulated indie subsidiaries, as evidenced by Disney forcing its Miramax unit to sell off Iraq anti-war documentary *Fahrenheit 9/11* in 2004.

Today is the best of times for major studios, as their revenue has soared since the early 1990s. In that decade, there was first a boom in overseas television sales and later in global video sales. Electrifying video, the cash-cow DVD format was introduced in North America in 1997. Revenue at the majors collectively increased about 7% per year from 1999–2003 and surpassed $41 billion by 2003, which is a stupendous rate of growth given that many other industries had little or no gains after the dot-com bust of 2000.

The high revenue growth rate is forecast to continue because of development of the embryonic video-on-demand business, streaming video, and an eventual replacement format for DVD. Media merchant bank Veronis Suhler Stevenson forecasts filmed entertainment spending in the United States will grow a healthy 8.2% annually at the retail level from 2003 to 2008. The only worry is that video and online piracy could significantly crimp legitimate sales.

While sales are robust, the majors struggle with sharply rising expenses, particularly salaries for star talent in movies and spiking marketing costs, largely due to broadcast network television advertising expenditures. "The core markets for end-point distribution are amazingly robust, which leads talent to ask for more dollars for their creative contribution," stated a report from investment house Harris Nesbitt Gerard. The most expensive studio films cost $125 to $200 million to make when royalty participations for talent are included, the investment firm added. Royalty participations are bonuses—sometimes called profit participations—that actors, directors, writers, producers, and others receive if films exceed contractually specified financial benchmarks.

The financial underpinnings of the majors are their film libraries of 800–4,000 major studio films, each stretching back to the silent era (and excluding nonstudio films acquired over the years). Each film library throws off more than $275 million in annual cash flow, which is a financial cushion that is critical whenever a studio's current releases suffer losses. The library films were long ago amortized, so the main expenses are minimal payments to talent for reruns, costs for physical manufacturing of DVDs, and overhead expenses of studio sales.

The film library assets would be a melting ice cube if new films are not constantly added, because fresh titles are locomotives that help sell older titles in video and television. A year's worth of new films at any of the big five major studios carries a price tag somewhere between $1 and $1.3 billion in production costs (excluding marketing expenses). However, each major tends to spend less than the full cost by allowing foreign rights to be sold off for some films, bringing in financial partners, and tapping subsidy funding overseas, particularly from Germany. A strategy of selectively parceling off some distribution rights weakens the clout of majors in licensing their slates to pay television and broadcast television outlets around the world, because films that are sold off in advance are excluded from studio inventory in certain territories.

A popular strategy of major studios is to acquire just domestic rights to independent films packaged outside the studio system. The majors pay 25–40% of the production costs of such films, yet those domestic rights can generate 55% or more of the films' economic benefit when video and television sales are factored in. Only the majors can extract that 55% value by virtue of their clout in theatrical distribution, high-volume sales of the video trade, and volume sales to television outlets.

History of the Majors

Columbia-TriStar-Sony Pictures

Sony Pictures, which is the parent of Columbia and TriStar, used to be the studio without any movie franchises, until its two *Spider-Man* blockbusters exploded at the box office. *Spider-Man 2,* which premiered in late June 2004, grossed over $373 million domestically.

Sony distributes about 25 studio films a year, after recently ratcheting down output. Revolution Studios, which is led by ex-studio chief Joe Roth, will supply about eight of those films in fiscal 2005, according to a

Sony regulatory filing. The studio is among Hollywood's most active in acquiring finished films, particularly to exploit their value in home video.

Brothers Harry and Jack Cohn incorporated Columbia Pictures in 1924, after entering the movie business in 1920. The studio was most associated with populist comedies of Frank Capra in its early days, such as the 1939 uplifting drama *Mr. Smith Goes to Washington* starring James Stewart. The studio thrived in the 1960s with films such as *Funny Girl, Lawrence of Arabia,* and *Easy Riders.* In 1989, Japanese electronics conglomerate Sony acquired the studio, which struggled from the early 1970s to the end of the century. In 1994, Sony took a staggering $3.2 billion write-down on the studio.

Walt Disney Studios

As its hallmark animation hit a rocky patch, the studio entertainment segment of Walt Disney increasingly relies on the financial performance of its live-action films. In early 2004, live-action films struggled with disappointments such as *The Alamo* and a new version of *Around the World in 80 Days.* The latter was financed outside Disney, which distributed domestically. In late 2004, *The Incredibles* and *National Treasure* became hits for Disney.

The studio plans to release about 21 films per year under the Disney and Touchstone banners, according to a Disney regulatory filing. The Disney studio entertainment business generates $7.4 billion in annual sales, when indie-style affiliate Miramax is included.

In animation, Disney's big hits came from outside supplier Pixar Animation Studios, which provided *Toy Story.* However, Pixar's supply contract runs out after *The Incredibles* and *Cars.* Disney's in-house animation has performed unevenly.

The Disney studio was nominally founded when brothers Walter and Roy Disney began producing cartoons in 1923. They achieved breakthrough with the 1937 hit *Snow White and the Seven Dwarfs,* which launched the modern company. The next decades were marked by up-and-down financial performance and memorable animated movies. Current management led by Michael Eisner arrived in 1984, which commenced a period of tremendous growth. The Disney film library contains 798 films, which is the smallest in terms of film count among the majors, but its full-length animated features are big revenue generators. Disney owns ABC Television.

DreamWorks

In 1994, ex-Disney executive Jeffrey Katzenberg, filmmaker Steven Spielberg, and entertainment entrepreneur David Geffen founded DreamWorks. Their goal was to create an artist-friendly studio.

Although not one of Hollywood's historic seven majors, today DreamWorks generally is viewed a major. DreamWorks' notable successes are the *Shrek* animation film franchise and Oscar winners *Gladiator* and *American Beauty*. To reduce overhead costs, DreamWorks distributes its movies in foreign theatrical and home video through Universal, under a contract extending to 2010.

Metro-Goldwyn-Mayer

The smallest of the seven historic Hollywood majors with $1.7 billion in annual revenue, Metro-Goldwyn-Mayer distributes just a few studio-caliber films per year. Its 22-title James Bond spy theatrical movie series is its most valuable property. The most recent Bond film *Die Another Day* accounted for 42% of the studio's domestic box office in 2002.

With its new films sputtering while the value of its film library was soaring because of the DVD boom, in September 2004 Metro-Goldwyn-Mayer agreed to sell itself to a consortium led by Sony Pictures. The purchase price was $3 billion plus assumption of $2 billion in debt. The seller was the publicly traded company, which is 74% owned by low-profile financier Kirk Kerkorian. Prior to being sold, Metro-Goldwyn-Mayer pursed a low-cost program to filmmaking. The studio's target was to distribute 7 to 10 studio films per year at an average cost of $23 to $27 million per film in 2004. This figure is far below the major studio average of $63.8 million per film in 2003.

Metro-Goldwyn-Mayer was founded in 1924, but its film library is the historic United Artists catalog. In its glory years, Metro-Goldwyn-Mayer boasted in promotions of having "More stars than there are in heaven." The original film library of Metro-Goldwyn-Mayer films was sold to Time Warner in 1986. United Artists was founded in 1919 by four creative figures, including Charlie Chaplin. After being hammered by the failure of 1980 arty Western drama *Heaven's Gate,* the studio experienced financial difficulties that continue to this day. In 1996, current controlling shareholder Kerkorian acquired the studio, added Orion Pictures in 1997, and took the studio public the same year in an initial public stock offering.

Paramount

Undergoing a big shift in strategy in 2004, Paramount deemphasized a longstanding practice of sticking to modest investment in films in order to minimize risk and now will mount occasional big-budget event films like the other majors.

Distributing about 15 studio films per year, Paramount is among the least prolific of the major studios in terms of number of film releases. Its parent Viacom is a significant operator of cable television networks, whose brand names and properties have been used in the marketing of the studio's films, such as MTV Films and Nickelodeon. Viacom owns movie pay television service Showtime as well as broadcaster CBS Television. Controlling shareholder Sumner Redstone separately owns National Amusements, one of the largest theater circuits in the United States.

Paramount was founded by New York furrier Adolph Zukor, who invested in nickelodeons in turn-of-the-century New York City with Marcus Loew, in a brief pairing of two eventual Hollywood moguls. In 1912, Zukor founded what became Paramount Pictures. Its roster of stars later included Gary Cooper, Mae West, Bob Hope, and Bing Crosby. The company was the first major studio to sign a deal with government antitrust authorities to separate theaters from film distribution, in what became known as the 1948 Paramount Consent Decree. In 1994, Paramount was acquired by media conglomerate Viacom.

Today Paramount ranks sixth among the seven majors by revenue, but in the 1970s and 1980s Paramount was a trendsetter. Its 1970s hits included *The Godfather, The Odd Couple,* and *Rosemary's Baby.* In the 1980s, its films captured the mood of the brash youth MTV generation with *Flashdance* and *Beverly Hills Cop.*

Twentieth Century Fox

Summer 2004 was particularly bright for Twentieth Century Fox as distributor of the blockbusters *The Day After Tomorrow,* sci-fi drama *I, Robot,* and comedy *Dodgeball: A True Underdog Story. Dodgeball* was the season's biggest sleeper hit; the film cost about $20 million to make and grossed over $114 million domestically. Twentieth Century Fox distributes about 15 studio films per year. In October 2004, the company told Wall Street it wanted to lift annual output of studio films to the 20 to 25 level.

The studio was transformed by its acquisition by Rupert Murdoch-led News Corp. in the 1980s, which aligned Twentieth Century Fox with a global media conglomerate that owns the Fox Broadcasting television network. Today, News Corp. owns 82.1% of the studio's parent Fox Entertainment. An earlier transforming event was the distribution of *Star Wars* in 1977, which turned around the studio's then precarious finances.

Twentieth Century Fox traces its roots to 1904 when young garment-factory owner William Fox opened a penny arcade in Brooklyn, New York, which eventually grew into a theater circuit. By the next decade, Fox Film Corp. was producing movies. The Great Depression vanquished the overextended, debt-heavy company. In 1935, it merged with small 20th Century Pictures led by Darryl F. Zanuck, who became the legendary movie mogul associated with the studio. The studio's stars of the past included Tyrone Power, Gregory Peck, and Marilyn Monroe.

Universal

Universal Pictures churns out hits but finds giant blockbusters elusive. The studio did well with *The Bourne Supremacy,* the glossy thriller that cost an economical $75 million to make and generated over $172 million in domestic box office in 2004. However, the studio has been less successful with bigger films, such as the $170 million production of horror yarn *Van Helsing* and the $110 million production *The Chronicles of Riddick* in 2004, and the $140 million production of *The Hulk* in 2003. The studio distributes 15 to 20 studio films per year.

Universal's founder is Carl Laemmle, a clothing store manager who opened a theater in Chicago in 1906. He soon moved into film distribution, creating the foundation for Universal Pictures. The studio struggled financially until after World War II, when its horror films and Alfred Hitchcock-directed thrillers were noteworthy.

A talent agency bought Universal in 1959, transforming it into a top-tier major studio with films such as *Spartacus* in 1960, *Jaws* in 1975, and *E.T. The Extra-Terrestrial* in 1982. In May 2004, General Electric's NBC broadcasting subsidiary purchased an 80% stake in the studio business from French conglomerate Vivendi Universal, in the first phase of a two-step sale.

Warner Bros.

Releasing about 25 studio films per year, Warner Bros. makes 4–6 especially large "event" movies such as the *Harry Potter* family films, according to a regulatory filing of its parent. For decades, Warner has been known as the sequels studio, with its *Lethal Weapon, Batman, The Matrix,* and *Harry Potter* series of movies. The studio is the long-time home for Clint Eastwood and is a leader among Hollywood's majors in distributing foreign language films overseas in their home countries.

To keep capital costs low on many of its fims, Warner Bros. takes on financial partners, including Alcon, Franchise Pictures, Gaylord/Pandora, and Village Roadshow. Parent Time Warner also owns Home Box Office and an array of cable channels, including Turner Classic Movies, which give the studio direct access to television outlets for its movies.

The studio traces its origins to 1903, when future Hollywood mogul Harry Warner opened an early movie theater. By 1913, he began producing and distributing in a company that became the Warner Bros. studio. Known for its gangster dramas in Hollywood's pre–World War II golden era, the studio was home for James Cagney, Errol Flynn, and Bette Davis. Its corporate parent began a long period of instability when high-flying video game division Atari crashed in the early 1980s.

10 Independent Distributors

I never knew why it took the majors at least 15 years to capitalize on summer releases geared for the youth market. . . . You (simply) made a film about something wild with a great deal of action, a little sex, and possibly some sort of strange gimmick.

Filmmaker Roger Corman

Independent distributors tend to fill market segments—meaning niches—not covered by the majors. They also focus on low-budget films. Roger Corman's book, *How I Made a Hundred Hollywood Movies and Never Lost a Dime,* from which the above quote is taken, recalls that the indies feasted on teen and youth summer movies in the 1950s to 1970s. The movies had provocative titles, such as *Sorority House Massacre* and *Piranha.* By the 1970s, the majors finally wised up by chasing the youth audience and dominated the summer seasons.

It's difficult to prosper in the hardscrabble independent sector today, yet scattered examples of films have achieved unbelievable riches, which keeps hope alive. The religious drama *The Passion of the Christ* generated a blockbuster $370 million in domestic (United States and Canada) box office via distributor Newmarket Films. Hollywood A-list actor Mel Gibson financed, directed, and cowrote the religious drama, which cost $30 million to make. That production budget is higher than most theatrical releases marketed by independent distributors, which typically cost $1 to $20 million to produce, versus an average $63.8 million production expense for a major studio film in 2003.

Besides *The Passion of the Christ,* the wacky comedy *My Big Fat Greek Wedding* cost about $5 million to make and took in $241 million in domestic box office in 2002 via IFC Films. *Crouching Tiger, Hidden Dragon,* the Chinese-language action drama that cost an estimated $15 million to make, rolled up $128 million in domestic box office for Sony Pictures Classics. *The Blair Witch Project,* the fictional documentary yarn that reportedly cost just tens of thousands of dollars to make, scared up $140.5 million in domestic box office in 1999 for what is now Lions Gate Films.

Reflecting the creeping impact of cost-saving digital technology, *Open Water,* a scripted drama about recreational scuba divers who encounter a school of sharks after being mistakenly abandoned by a resort boat, was made with digital cameras for a reported $130,000. The suspense drama received an estimated $15 million marketing campaign launch in August 2004 from distributor Lions Gate Films.

Indie companies can be divided into two camps. True independents do not have major studio backing; examples include Newmarket Films *(The Passion of the Christ),* Lions Gate Releasing *(Fahrenheit 9/11),* IDP Distribution *(Super Size Me),* and IFC Films *(My Big Fat Greek Wedding).* Then there are indie-film divisions owned by major studios such as Miramax (Disney) and New Line Cinema (Warner Bros.). The studio-owned indies dominate box office in the indie category (Fig. 10.1).

Overview

In pursuit of niches, indies look for openings in film release schedules. After the majors roll out big-budget, glossy youth films in the peak summer season, the indies counterprogram with up-market films aimed at underserved sophisticated audiences. Focus Features slipped *Lost in Translation* in an inauspicious September 2003 slot, yet the dry comedy rolled up awards and accumulated $44.6 million in domestic box office. *Lost in Translation* premiered at just 23 theaters and then mushroomed to 882 theaters at its peak, building on positive word of mouth. However, most indie films don't hit 600 theaters at any point in their run.

Although indie films seldom saturate the theater marketplace, some achieved sizable box office even though they never hit 1,000 playdates at any time during their theatrical runs (Fig. 10.2). Occasional indie films receive wide releases. Newmarket Films opened *The Passion of the Christ*

Figure 10.1 Top Independent Distributors 2003–2004

Rank	Name	Box Office ($ mil.)	Share %	Titles	Rank w/majors*
1	New Line Cinema	$870.8	9.273%	13	5
2	Miramax	$638.5	6.800%	29	7
3	Newmarket Films	$422.6	4.500%	4	10
4	Lions Gate Films	$147.9	1.575%	16	12
5	Fox Searchlight	$114.6	1.220%	15	13
6	Focus Features	$107.2	1.141%	7	14
7	Sony Classiics	$37.8	0.403%	31	15
8	Imax Film	$18.6	0.198%	6	16
9	IDP Distribution	$17.0	0.181%	15	17
10	Odeon Films	$14.4	0.154%	8	18
11	Artisan Ent.**	$14.0	0.149%	3	19
12	IFC Films	$8.8	0.094%	10	20
13	ThinkFilm	$8.6	0.092%	10	21
14	SK Films	$8.2	0.087%	1	22
15	Fine Line	$7.3	0.077%	2	23
16	RS Entertainment	$5.8	0.062%	2	24
17	Paramount Classics	$4.4	0.047%	9	25
18	New Yorker	$3.9	0.420%	10	26
19	Eros	$3.7	0.040%	8	27
20	Manhattan Pics.	$3.7	0.039%	1	28
21	Yash Raj Films	$3.4	0.037%	3	29
22	Magnolia Picutres	$3.3	0.035%	7	30
23	Televisa Cine	$3.2	0.034%	1	31
24	Film Foundry	$2.7	0.029%	1	32
	Total with majors	$9,390.9	100%	655	n/a

*Rank when including the eight major studio distributors
**Artisan merged into Lions Gate
Note: Covers 12-month period from July 4, 2003 to July 4, 2004 for the United States and Canada; the titles column includes both new films in the period and carryovers prior to July 4, 2003
Source: Nielsen EDI

at 3,043 theaters (translating to over 3,600 screens at those theaters) in its February 2004 premiere.

The indies find the cinema market increasingly crowded. "Ten years ago, you used to be able to find seams in the studio release schedules," said indie film marketer Richard Abramowitz. "There would be a lightly-contested weekend with maybe three or four new releases. Now it's 8–12 films. So it's harder to get screens, ad space is more costly, and there's less space available for the press to publicize any one film." Abramowitz

Figure 10.2 Top Grossing Films in Narrow Release 1982–2004

Rank	Title	Box Office ($ mil.)	Most theaters	Distributor	Premiere
1	*Everest*	$87.2	63	MacGillivray Freeman	Mar. 1998
2	*Space Station 3-D*	$52.3	65	IMAX	Apr. 2002
3	*Aamadeus*	$51.5	802	Orion	Sept. 1984
4	*T-Rex: Back to the Cretaceous*	$48.6	38	IMAX	Oct. 1998
5	*The Full Monty*	$45.9	783	Fox Searchlight	Aug. 1997
6	*Lost in Translation*	$44.6	882	Focus	Sept. 2003
7	*Gosford Park*	$41.3	918	Focus	Dec. 2001
8	*Mysteries of Egypt*	$40.6	27	Destination	Jun. 1998
9	*Hannah and Her Sisters*	$40.6	761	Orion	Feb. 1986
10	*Dead Man Walking*	$39.4	821	Gramercy	Dec. 1995
11	*The Sword and the Sorcerer*	$39.1	660	Group 1	Apr. 1982
12	*The Pianist*	$32.5	842	Focus	Dec. 2002
13	*Monster's Ball*	$31.3	714	Lions Gate	Dec. 2001
14	*Elizabeth*	$30.0	624	Gramercy	Nov. 1998
15	*Howards End*	$26.0	547	Sony Classics	Mar. 1992
16	*The Cotton Club*	$25.9	809	Orion	Dec. 1984
17	*Memento*	$25.5	531	Newmarket	Mar. 2001
18	*Beauty and the Beast: Special Edition*	$25.5	68	Disney	Jan. 2002
19	*Waking Ned Devine*	$24.8	540	Fox Searchlight	Nov. 1998
20	*Fargo*	$24.4	716	Gramercy	Feb. 1996

Note: Top grossing films never to exceed 999 theaters at anytime in their theatrical run; figures cover United States and Canada
Source: Nielsen EDI

operates Abramorama, a boutique theatrical distribution company. He also is a marketing and distribution consultant based in Armonk, New York.

The film business lives off income from video and television, which impacts the marketing push in the theatrical window. Buyers of video and pay television rights to independent films often specify in contracts that purchased films must have a minimum amount of marketing spending in theatrical release for the purpose of creating a marquee value.

A bare-bones expenditure is $1.5 million for prints and advertising (P&A), which is a sufficient amount to support a limited theatrical release in a few big cities. For a significant national release, the P&A spend needs to be much higher, starting at $5 million. An independent film distributor that pays $5 million to acquire United States rights to a film often really is making a $10 to $20 million investment. The distributor can easily spend another $5 to $15 million in theatrical marketing costs if it opts for a substantial national release. Thus, film buyers must evaluate if a given film has the screen power to earn back all expenses.

For decades, independents tapped the summer youth audiences with B films in the action and horror genres. These films were released in late July or August, when the big studio films had already premiered and were winding up their theatrical runs. Gradually, the studios began to release their own low-budget youth films in the late summer. For example, Paramount's *Friday the 13th Part 3: 3D* slasher film opened in mid August 1982, invading what had been exclusively indie film territory.

Indie distributors discovered they could counterprogram Hollywood's glossy summer blockbuster for the youth market with serious films when distributor Island Releasing enjoyed a successful box office run for *Kiss of the Spider Woman*. The prison drama film, which grossed a healthy $17 million, premiered in late July 1985. In later years, other up-market indie films also launched in mid to late summer.

Booking Theaters

Independents tend to select release dates three to five months in advance, with the idea that they might shift that date slightly if strong competition materializes later. Independent distributors move up release dates to take advantage of screen availabilities if one or more big films sputter and exit screens early. Likewise, if surprise hits occupy screens longer than expected, then indies push back release dates to let screen congestion diminish.

The ability to shift typically is restricted to one or a few weeks forward or back from the original date, because advertising and marketing promotions are difficult to move on short notice. If an 800-theater premiere is anticipated, usually 400–500 theaters are booked weeks and months in advance. The remaining 300–400 playdates are secured within the last 3 weeks on an opportunistic basis.

Prestige films aimed at sophisticated audiences premiere at art-house theaters in big cities. For New York City, opening in three Manhattan locations is common: East side, West side, and downtown. Within weeks, films expand to the suburbs of New York. Simultaneous with New York premiere, the film typically opens at a few screens in Los Angeles and

Chicago. Assuming press write-ups are favorable, a second wave of cities follows 1 week later, especially Boston, San Francisco, and college towns, which are art-house strongholds.

The relationship between exhibitors (theaters) and film distributors is characterized by a constant tug-of-war, with each side flexing its muscle in negotiating a booking agreement. A theater with few competitors in a geographic area has the upper hand, but the distributor wields the clout if a booking zone has many theater operators. Film bookings in mainstream theaters typically are for two to four weeks. If a film dies on arrival, exhibitors press distributors to end the run early, even if a four-week contract is in place.

Given that the flow of films from independents is less than the flow from major studios and independent films tend to gross less, independents generally negotiate film rentals of around 40–50%, which is about 10 percentage points lower than majors. Rentals are the distributors' share of the box office and typically are set by a complex, two-part contract (see Chapter 7). Art-house theaters sometimes negotiate rentals as low as 35–40% because they may shoulder more promotion/advertising expenses than mainstream theaters.

Reflecting the strain of indies collecting from theaters, Mel Gibson's Icon Productions filed a lawsuit in June 2004 against the giant Regal Cinemas circuit, alleging underpayment of film rentals on *The Passion of the Christ*. The suit alleges the 6,045-screen Regal circuit offered to pay just a 34% rental on the religious blockbuster, whereas Newmarket Films, which distributed the film for Icon, asserts it was promised "studio terms." Icon interpreted that as calling for a 55% rate. Elsewhere, in recent months, big theater circuits dropped contribution to cooperative advertising for certain independent films, ending a program of paying for ads jointly with distributors.

Independents are squeezed because of economic pressure to complete theatrical release quickly and on a national basis, whereas in past decades slow rollouts and regional bookings were feasible. Today, movie economics rely heavily on revenue from home video release—DVD and VHS—so films can no longer linger in the cinema market. A theater rarely books a movie when it is in video stores.

Before the video age arrived in the late 1980s, independent films usually were distributed in a patchwork of regional runs over a period of months or even a year, saturating one area for a time and then moving elsewhere. For example, the European drama *A Room with a View* went through a 14-month theatrical run starting in 1986. It grossed a then-spectacular $21 million-plus from just 151 theatrical prints moving around constantly and eventually played on many hundreds of screens. Today's imperative to collect revenue from a video release means theatrical runs must be of short duration.

The regional release still is used occasionally. Sunn Classic Pictures—a venerable name in indie distribution that is being revived—plans to theatrically distribute films regionally or in specific cities. Sunn president Lang Elliott believes a 15-theater opening in New York City supported by $200,000–$300,000 in advertising is feasible, using newspaper, radio, and local television commercials running 30, 15, and 10 seconds.

Self-Distribution

Independent filmmakers who are frustrated by an inability to place a film with an established independent distributor may opt to self-distribute their own films. In theory, this plan is feasible but has many drawbacks.

Filmmakers who go the self-distribution route usually are forced to quit making/developing new films because distributing is a full-time business. Another drawback is that even when self-distributors are able to book theaters, they find collecting film rentals can be difficult. Theaters can be slow to pay, or they may attempt to lower payments in negotiations after a film screened. Theaters that are geographically distant can be particularly difficult with regard to slow pay or underpay. Self-distributors do not have clout in collections because they do not provide a theater with an ongoing flow of films. National media outlets are not likely to cover self-distributed films because media editors know that their readers or viewers probably won't find the film at a nearby theater.

Still, there are occasional success stories for do-it-yourself distributors. One such out-of-the-mainstream filmmaker is Jay Craven, a movie studies teacher in Vermont who has created a string of movies devoted to regional themes that he self-distributes.

Craven's 1993 local period social drama *Where the Rivers Flow North* was reviewed by the *New York Times* and stars Oscar-nominated actor Rip Torn. It played at 212 theaters nationally using 23 theatrical release prints that moved around in clusters. The film's video distribution deal included a $200,000 fee earmarked for theatrical release, which generated around $1 million in box office from a series of regional bookings until the nation was covered. Theatrical marketing relied primarily on publicity and cosponsorships with media, such as radio stations.

Vermont has just 18 towns with movie theaters, so Craven books his films for screenings in nontheatrical venues such as town halls and church basements. This plan works in his home state and elsewhere in New England where Craven's films have particularly strong appeal because of their regional flavor.

To get the word out, Craven ties up with local groups, using their membership lists for e-mails and direct mail campaigns. Theatrical release "is the toughest, most costly and most labor intensive market" in the film distribution cycle spanning cinema to television, said Craven. Craven also made the 1999 social drama *A Stranger in the Kingdom,* which stars Ernie Hudson, David Lansbury, and Martin Sheen. The film sold over 92,000 videos after a regional theatrical run. *A Stranger in the Kingdom* is about the 1950s upheaval in a Vermont community that is surprised to find a local church's new minister is black.

In an interesting example of well-known talent carving out a market for a personal film, singer–songwriter Neil Young wrote, directed, and produced *Greendale,* which was booked in theaters in tandem with Young's music tour. The film, which is a social drama set to Young's music, grossed $290,000 in box office with less than $100,000 in marketing expenses. Its only paid media buys were print ads. Distributor Richard Abramowitz booked *Greendale* for 75 theatrical runs using 15 prints that followed the concert tour.

Young did press interviews via radio, television, and alternative press (arts and counterculture newspapers) to support *Greendale's* theatrical release. Promotions with radio stations offered CDs of Young's album, tickets to the film, and tickets to the concert. Young's personal Web site *(neilyoung.com)* promoted the movie with a cascade of positive reviews and information on playdates.

Theatrical distribution is a bottleneck because it is labor intensive and relies on release prints, which cost $1,000 to manufacture. On top of that, the bulky release prints are expensive to ship. The looming conversion to electronic digital cinema—replacing mechanical film projectors—will make distribution less costly because films can be delivered to theaters via satellite transmission, low-cost optical disks, or high-speed broadband connection (see Chapter 8).

Marketing Indie Films

Independent films don't fit in a standard profile, so generalizations are difficult. The more expensive indie films (costing $20 million and up to make) receive a marketing push that is similar to that of the major studios, given their heft. This process includes consumer market research, sizable purchase of television advertising, and wide releases of at least 800 theaters that cater to a general audience, all of which are described in depth in other chapters.

The bulk of indie films are released with smaller marketing budgets without benefit of formal test screenings before a recruited consumer audience and without broadcast network television advertising. Indie films with small budgets begin marketing via the Internet, which is a low-cost medium that can pull together a target audience that is widely dispersed on geographic basis.

The central strategy for indie film campaigns is to emphasize frequency over reach in buying advertising. The frequency strategy utilizes low-cost ads in media with small audiences that deliver the film's demographic target. Demographics are a slice of audience, such as the youth market, specific ethnic groups, age groups, etc. Piling those ads in a small media space saturates the core target audience, without which most indie films would be dead on arrival at theaters.

The indie strategy contrasts to that of the major studios, which place their ads on wide-reaching media—such as commercials televised during the Super Bowl football game—so there's substantial spillover to noncore audiences. With this reach approach, the goal is promoting to a broad audience, and achieving this goal requires hefty spending.

There's no uniform template for marketing low-budget films, which cost less than $5 million to make. Middle-range indie films, which cost $5–$15 million to make, can be released with shoestring marketing budgets or multimillion dollar campaigns, depending on the pocketbook and enthusiasm of their distributors. Much of the marketing for these films relies on publicity, where there's an element of serendipity. Audiences can discover indie films because of a critic's review or a buzz on the Internet. This is unlike launches for big-budget films by major studios. The majors spend tens of millions of dollars in advertising, which delivers a studio-manufactured message via a paid placement in media to a large audience.

For indies, titles are particularly important because a name alone should carry some weight to position a film in the mind of the audience. The title of the 1957 horror film *I Was a Teenage Werewolf* was a draw for the youth market. The 1983 youth comedy *Valley Girl* tapped into the trend of suburbia becoming hip. The audience knew just what to expect at a glance from the 2002 wacky comedy *My Big Fat Greek Wedding*. However, the up-market films in the indie sector tend not to use this philosophy, often because the films are adaptations of novels, such as the rather dry sounding *Howards End* from 1992.

Another frequent element of indie marketing is an effort to court controversy because controversy generates publicity, even if the attention is tinged with ill fame. The current wave of popular documentaries are particularly adept at bombast, and it's not just political firecracker *Fahrenheit 9/11*. Rock musician Anton Alfred Newcombe of The Brian Jonestown Massacre rock group posted a denunciation of his portrayal in the Palm Pictures-distributed music documentary *Dig!* "I was shocked and let down when I saw the end result," Newcombe wrote on the band's Web site. "I just feel ripped off by the 'lowest common denominator' culture machine [which is] something that I don't cater to." Although Newcombe felt obliged to present his view, his commentary does have the unintended ripple effect of raising the profile of the film.

For low-budget films, a fundamental strategy choice is whether to hold out for theatrical release as a first window or to try to create buzz with limited exposure in other media in order to create momentum for a theatrical release later. Certainly, theaters are loath to book films that have appeared in other media, but there are occasional breakthroughs. For example, after thriller *Red Rock West* gained acclaim from an HBO telecast, it received a theatrical release in 1992. It became the first of a string of titles that received theatrical runs after brief exposure on premium pay television.

Speakers at a panel discussion during the American Film Market in February 2004 were divided on which road to take. John Manulis, chief executive officer of Visionbox Pictures, believes it's a mistake to hold out for theatrical release initially. He said that few low-budget indie films are picked for theatrical release, and those that are selected tend not to receive much promotion. "Going after theaters is a losing game," he concluded.

In the same panel, Christopher Coppola, director of horror film *Bloodhead* (also known as *The Creature of the Sunny Side Up Trailer Park*), staked out a middle ground. He feels the best strategy is not to bypass cinema but to think of nontraditional venues for private screenings in order to first build a buzz for a theatrical release. "It's all about publicity—finding your core audience," said Coppola.

Internet Strategy

For indies, Internet publicity and promotion start months before theatrical release.

Some filmmakers launch into Internet marketing to connect with a potential audience while a film merely is in development and before the first frame of film has even been shot. The existence of an active fan base is used as a selling point to line up potential financial backers. George Romero, who directed the cult horror film *Night of the Living Dead,* landed a producer for his proposed movie *Diamond Dead,* a black comedy about musical zombies, after his movie's Web site generated heavy Internet traffic.

A centerpiece of the first stage of marketing for a grass roots campaign is a Web site. A full Web site can take up to 3 months to build and at the low end costs $8,000 to $20,000 to create. An early-stage Web site, which is cheap and can be set up quickly, can be simply a single page or poster—known as a splash page.

At the earliest stage, a core audience that will be most enthusiastic about a film needs to be identified as the target for low-cost Internet and other grass roots marketing, such as passing out handbills at events. For a film about dogs, circulating fliers at dog shows and e-mailing members of kennel clubs are examples of low-cost promotions that corral a tightly-defined target audience. For a movie about punk rock, rave parties—underground youth gatherings—can whip up interest, as when part of a film is screened at an evening gathering at a parking lot or warehouse.

A common complaint from film distributors that take over filmmakers' Web sites once they acquire distribution rights to films is that initial e-mail promotional materials sent to fan mailing lists did not include an opt-out—the ability for the subscriber to remove himself or herself from the mailing list. The lack of an opt-out makes use of those e-mail lists a sticky legal issue and is an impediment to a smooth transition in promotion.

Another early consideration is that filmmakers shoot lots of visual materials for use on Web sites and in other promotions. The material, which includes recording events promoting a film before it is even made, can be added to the official Web site. Systematically adding new content from a reservoir of material provides fans with a reason to keep coming back to the official Web site.

Marketing executives advise filmmakers to shoot scripted promotional vignettes for use on Internet sites when a film is in principal photography, because actors are assembled in costume and at movie backdrops. A growing trend is to present original content or big parts of the film in episodic television programming on the Internet in what are dubbed Webisodes. The segments are interconnected, which hopefully will prompt audiences to regularly seek out each new webisode.

A marketing milestone was the ground-up publicity campaign that used the Internet to promote *The Blair Witch Project* to a blockbuster $140.5 million in box office in 1999 for Artisan Entertainment, which later was absorbed by Lions Gate. The film—produced for a shoestring tens of thousands of dollars—is a faux documentary that is a disappearance mystery. The public eagerly pursued clips on the Internet while not knowing if the story about missing documentary makers was real or not. The strategy was held out as a model that other films could use, but in reality no other film since has generated the same heat as the original *Blair Witch*.

Still, film marketers expect Internet marketing will achieve innovative marketing breakthroughs in the future because a new Internet era is dawning, with high-speed connections enabling easy viewing of film clips that replace narrow-band dial up. "When it comes to pre-release marketing, I think you will see all kinds of new incarnations in the future," said Doug Hirsch, general manager of Yahoo Movies, which attracts 10 million unique Internet users each month. "And also, movies have stepped up activity on their own websites."

Festivals

The tried and true avenues for creating a favorable buzz are festival appearances and receiving acclaim in film reviews. Festival exposure is particularly vital for imported films (see Chapter 11), because festival awards influence art film aficionados. For films that run in festivals, excerpts from favorable reviews are used in later publicity and advertising for general theatrical release.

Festivals also are platforms for independently produced films to line up distribution deals. In buying finished films, distributors make an immediate cash payment, mount a general theatrical release at a later date, and—for films that are financial successes—make additional bonus payments to the producers. In some cases, distributors also finance partial reshoots or further polishing, such as improving music tracks for films they acquire.

In North America, the most important film festivals for unreleased films to reel in distribution deals are the Sundance Film Festival (Park City, Utah) in January and the Toronto International Film Festival in September. The United States and Canada have roughly 800 film festivals per year, meaning on average more than two fests start on any given day. The festival circuit is large because municipalities create them as part of arts/culture initiatives and to spur tourism. Some festivals have thematic slants, such as gay and lesbian film events in Philadelphia, Toronto, San Francisco, and Los Angeles.

In the United States, second-tier events, which also draw film buyers, include the AFI Los Angeles International Film Festival in Los Angeles (in tandem with the American Film Market), the Chicago International Film Festival, the Denver International Film Festival, the Florida Film Festival (Orlando), the Mill Valley Film Festival (California), the Palm Springs International Film Festival (California), the Santa Barbara International Film Festival (California), the Seattle International Film Festival, South by Southwest (Austin, Texas), and the Tribeca Film Festival (New York City). In Canada, the significant second-tier events are the Montreal World Film Festival and Vancouver International Film Festival.

Customarily filmmakers do not receive film rentals from screenings at the top two tiers of festivals. For the lesser festivals, however, filmmakers often negotiate a percentage of box office, given that the festival itself is subsidized by a municipality or business interests but at the same time the festival charges admissions to its screenings.

"In this era when there are fewer opportunities for theatrical distribution, festivals have become an alternative form of exhibition for independent and world cinema that don't find a place in the commercial distribution system," said Mitch Levine, partner in Los Angeles-based Festival Consulting Group. Producers always hope that a festival award or screening will be a catalyst for a distribution deal that results in commercial theatrical play for their films. Further, audience reactions can be used as *de facto* test screenings, so filmmakers and producers can re-edit to make a film more marketable.

Newspaper and magazine reviews are critical for the box office of up-market films aimed at sophisticated audiences. Television and radio reviews are influential to a lesser extent. Chicago-based Roger Ebert is the only film critic with a truly national following, and his film reviews have the clout to make or break an up-market film.

A favorable write-up in *The New York Times,* whose influence extends beyond its home city, typically propels box office for arty films, especially when they start with a low profile. However, films can survive unfavorable notices from *The New York Times.* Reviews in prestige print publications tend not to influence action–adventure, horror, and youth audiences, for which television reviews showing clips are influential.

Advertising and Trailers

The centerpiece of marketing campaigns for low-budget films consists of trailers and print ads. To create ad campaigns, independent distributors generally hire outside advertising boutiques to make their trailers and key art, which is the central graphic look for posters and print ads. At the low end of pricing, a trailer costs $25,000 from an outside shop. Besides being placed in theaters, trailers are put on Web sites and can be used to pitch theaters for bookings. The price tag for an outside agency to design the key art for the print ad campaign (which essentially is a one-sheet poster) usually starts at $5,000.

The major studios typically pay 10 times those fees for creative materials, receiving more services and consultation in shaping the creative message. The majors also tend to hire more than one shop for the same assignment, using two or three boutiques to make trailers for the same film even though only one trailer ultimately will be used. In contrast, independents tend to employ just one creative boutique per job in order to save money. For indies, the trailer house often makes any television commercials as well, which is another way to reduce costs and again is unlike the major studios.

Independent film distributors tend to provide a lot of direction to boutiques by identifying audience targets and elements of a film that should be highlighted. Creative approaches vary, of course, although for prestige films a centerpiece of advertising is quoting critics or citing festival honors. "We find trailer makers have different tastes and talent, which not necessarily encompass all types of films," said Michael Barker, co-president of Sony Pictures Classics, the specialty unit of major studio Sony/Columbia. "What's important is that the trailer maker understands and loves the film."

Advertising is purchased by outside specialists known as media buying agencies. Such media buying agencies don't offer the additional service of creating ads. In media buying, the essentials are print advertising (identifying theaters and showtimes) in daily newspapers and entertainment weeklies, starting days before premiere. A minimalist budget for such an ad campaign reaching some big cities is several hundred thousand dollars (Fig. 10.3). This price covers only print ads for playdates in newspapers, a Web site, some Internet ads, radio, and street posters.

A bigger campaign of $1.5 million enlarges media buys, adding spot television and magazine advertising (Fig. 10.4). Increases above the $1.5 million level expand from spot cable delivering audiences in local geographic areas to national cable network buys. Further enlarging ad spend-

Figure 10.3 Low-budget $220,000 Movie Ad Campaign

Category	Spending
Print/daily	$105,000
On-line/Web site	$15,000
Wild posting (labor)	$10,000
Radio	$10,000
Outdoor billboards	0
Print/Magazines	0
TV	0
Media subtotal	**$140,000**
Creating ads	$20,000
Duplicating posters & etc.	$15,000
Publicity & screenings	$35,000
Festival screening support	$10,000
Grand Total	**$220,000**

Note: The figures exclude cost of manufacturing and shipping release film prints
Source: *Marketing to Moviegoers*

Figure 10.4 Low-budget $1.5 Million Movie Ad Campaign

Category	Spending
Print/daily & weeklies	$780,000
On-line/Web site	$30,000
Wild posting (labor)	$10,000
Radio	$20,000
Outdoor billboards	0
Print/magazines	$70,000
Television	$450,000
Media subtotal	**$1.36 million**
Creating ads	$50,000
Duplicating posters & etc.	$10,000
Publicity & screenings	$50,000
Festival screening support	$30,000
Grand Total	**$1.5 million**

Note: The figures exclude cost of making and shipping release film prints
Source: *Marketing to Moviegoers*

ing extends buys to network broadcast television in off-peak periods and syndicated television programs.

A geographically wide but thin minimalist ad campaign for an indie film was $750,000 in the late 1990s but has climbed to $1.5 million these days. The higher price results from increased advertising rates and a greater willingness of distributors to spend because they figure to earn back the bigger ad expenditure from higher DVD sales of the film. The top end of indie film ad campaigns is around $15 million, which covers the initial 4 weeks of release.

The more expensive the television ad campaign, the more likely an independent distributor will hire a market research firm to test ads for their effectiveness (see Chapter 2). Usually, the ad campaign merits testing when the film is set for release in 800 or more theaters.

"Without question, television advertising is still the driving force in the marketing of a wide release film," said Tom Ortenberg, president of Lions Gate Films Releasing, which co-distributed *Fahrenheit 9/11*. "That's the one constant. The promotion and publicity are valuable to support the opening. But you cannot open a film on a wide basis [600–800 theaters] without a television campaign."

For network television, late-night entertainment and talk shows are relatively inexpensive ad buys, yet they deliver youth and young adult audiences that are heavy moviegoers. Another type of low-cost national ad is syndicated television programs, which are non-network programs televised via a lineup of broadcast stations. Daily magazine-formatted series *Entertainment Tonight* is an example of a syndicated television program. For movies not in national release, spot broadcast and cable ads are used. Spot television ads hit just individual metropolitan areas and thus minimize wasted coverage of geography where a film is not booked in theaters.

Ad buys always seek to reach a defined target audience, such as a youth audience. This strategy can mean aiming for children ages 8–14 with television commercials on cartoon and family channels or teenagers ages 13–19 with buys on rock music programs. Looking at a completely different target, adults ages 24–54 congregate at arts channels and news programs. The drawback of cable television ads is that cable/satellite penetration is just 84% of United States television households, meaning 17% of television homes have no chance of seeing a cable commercial. On top of that, cable networks have varying degrees of carriage within that 84% bloc.

Another way to slice the audience demographically is by ethnic group, such as blacks, Latinos, and Asians. For instance, African-Americans account for 13% of the population in the United States, or 36 million persons. Blacks are clustered in big-city metropolitan areas, representing 18% of the population in greater New York, Chicago, and Philadelphia.

Another audience segment is the college/university market, which is a prime target for film marketers when school is in session. Full-page ads in student newspapers can cost just $300. Other elements of college campaigns can include postering, street teams passing out handbills, closed-circuit television channels on campuses, and radio publicity via noncommercial stations that frequently are located at schools.

Indies occasionally release films not rated by the national film classification service, which is a voluntary service and was established by the trade group for Hollywood's major studios. A minority of media outlets, particularly daily newspapers, have policies against accepting paid ads for unrated films. However, most media run ads for unrated films as long as the ads don't present excessive sex or violence. The bigger problem is booking theaters, because films without ratings and films with the most restrictive classification of NC-17 (no children) have a poor track record in box office.

Publicity Strategies

After Internet and grass roots marketing start months before theatrical release, other waves of film marketing follow. Monthly magazines have a three-month lead time, so their press screenings are held four to six months in advance of theatrical release. The lead time for press screenings for weekly magazines is about eight weeks. Press screenings for dailies and electronic media come two to six weeks before theatrical premiere.

The objective is to interest editors and reporters in editorial coverage (excluding reviews), ranging from a capsule brief on a film to a cover story. Of course, meeting this sequence of deadlines depends on the film being finished months in advance of theatrical release. For the long lead press, presenting segments of the film may be sufficient if a movie is not completely finished.

Distributors usually set an embargo date for reviews so that they reach moviegoers just as a film premieres. Unfavorable reviews that are published far in advance risk undercutting theatrical release before the film even starts. Favorable reviews that appear far in advance of a film's premiere can be a problem as well because moviegoers may forget the reviews by the time the film hits theaters. Screenings for reviewers at daily newspapers with short lead times and electronic press might be as few as three days before theatrical release.

Screenings in film festivals generate reviews in print media, of course, but these reviews often are concentrated in trade press that is not read by moviegoers. They also may be so old by the time the film hits general theatrical release that the reviews are forgotten.

Documentaries

Feature-length documentaries are the hottest segment of the indie world as their numbers and their box office are on the rise. One catalyst is plunging production costs. With digital technology, shooting a full-length documentary with a sharp cinema presentation for about $200,000 is possible, and compact electronic cameras capture images that were beyond the reach of filmmakers using the bulky equipment of the past. Some popular documentaries are made for less, although they often suffer from uneven technical quality.

Many, but certainly not all, of the current generation of documentaries focus on promotable pop culture or political themes, turn on the Hollywood glitz in presentation and consumer marketing, and eagerly court controversy. A case in point for the new wave is *Super Size Me,* which generated a relatively strong $11.5 million in domestic box office for IDP Distribution. Its unsurprising message is that subsisting on a diet of McDonald's restaurant food is not particularly healthy.

Super Size Me, which filmmaker Morgan Spurlock reportedly made for just $65,000, has appeal because it deconstructs an American pop culture icon. The documentary uses McDonald's familiar images as props in the film and in promotion, even as the restaurant chain itself keeps a low profile and tries not to call attention to the film. At one juncture, IDP Distribution issued a press release claiming cable network MTV was balking at carrying commercials for *Super Size Me* (the ads show vomiting), although the ads eventually ran.

Of course, the big kahuna in the controversy department is the Iraq war critique *Fahrenheit 9/11,* whose step-by-step introduction to the marketplace represents a masterpiece in astute promotion. In May 2004, the headlines started when it was learned that Walt Disney would not let its Miramax Films distribute the film in what gave Disney bad press. The fact that Disney balked is no surprise, because major studios almost always steer clear of what would be perceived as inflammatory content for fear of suffering a consumer backlash on their other corporate interests.

Fahrenheit 9/11 premiered later that month at the prestigious Cannes Film Festival, which was a perfect launch pad given that Europe's cultural press corps is generally hostile to the Bush presidency. After the documentary got a rousing reception in Cannes, filmmaker Michael Moore asserted in press interviews that opponents were trying to block the film's release in the United States, even as distributors clamored to acquire the film. When the film was jointly released to theaters by Lions Gate Films Releasing and IFC Films in June, political groups such as the large MoveOn.com political action committee urged members to see the film immediately in an example of grass roots marketing that got the core audience into theaters during opening week.

Powered by a tsunami of publicity, *Fahrenheit 9/11*—which reportedly cost about $6 million to make—rolled up over $119 million in domestic box office. This total shattered the previous record for a documentary in mainstream theaters of $22 million held by United Artists-distributed *Bowling for Columbine,* which is another Moore film that won the Oscar for Best Documentary of 2002.

Both documentaries were award winners on the festival circuit, which bolstered their credibility and generated media coverage. *Super Size Me* received the Director's Prize at the Sundance Film Festival. *Fahrenheit 9/11* took the Golden Palm top prize at the Cannes Film Festival. Even the majors are jumping on pop culture documentaries, with Warner Bros. rolling up more than $19 million in box office for car-racing themed *NASCAR: The IMAX Experience* in mid-2004.

Old school serious documentaries are beneficiaries of the newfound popularity for the genre. The British-made insect documentary *Bugs!* generated more than $10 million for SK Films in a 2003–2004 release on big-screen theaters. Bird wildlife documentary *Winged Migration,* an import from France, posted $10.8 million in domestic box office in 2003 for Sony Pictures Classics. The scientific documentaries have an advantage of not being language specific because the narration voiceover can easily be changed to suit another country.

The documentary–reality film category has generated a number of hit theatrical films over the years (Fig. 10.5). The 1998 release of mountain exploration and disaster film *Everest* by MacGillivray Freeman Film generated $87.2 million in domestic box office in the big screen format.

Canadian audiences have long been receptive to documentaries, but until their recent popularity documentaries had been a hard sell in the United States. Audiences in the United States had preconceptions that documentaries were dull and simply educational, even though they usually were not. Smoothing the way for the current popularity of documentaries

Figure 10.5 Top Theatrical Documentaries 1982–June 2004

Rank	Title	Box Office ($ mil.)	Distributor	Maximum Theaters	Premiere
1	*Everest*	$87.2	MacGillivray Freeman	63	Mar. 1998
2	*Fahrenheit 9/11**	$80.1*	Lions Gate/IFC	n/a	Jun. 2004
3	*Space Station 3-D*	$52.3	IMAX	64	Apr. 2002
4	*Eddie Murphy Raw*	$50.5	Paramount	1,494	Dec. 1987
5	*Mysteries of Egypt*	$40.6	Destination	n/a	Jun. 1998
6	*The Original Kings of Comedy*	$38.2	Paramount	1,082	Aug. 2000
7	*Richard Prior Live on the Sunset Strip*	$36.3	Columbia	1,277	Mar. 1982
8	*Dolphins*	$27.4	MacGillivray Freeman	n/a	Mar. 2000
9	*Bowling for Columbine*	$21.6	United Artists	248	Oct. 2002
10	*Martin Lawrence Live: Runteldat*	$19.2	Paramount	752	Aug. 2002
11	*Thrill Ride*	$18.8	Sony Classics	23	Jul. 1997
12	*Michael Jordan to the Max*	$18.6	Giant Screen	56	May 2000
13	*Ghosts of the Abyss*	$16.3	Disney	97	Apr. 2003
14	*Richard Pryor Here and Now*	$16.1	Columbia	1,411	Oct. 1983
15	*Shackleton's Antarctic Adventure*	$15.5	WGBH	26	Feb. 2001

Note: Covers 1982–June 2004 box office in United States and Canada
*Fahrenheit 9/11 became top grossing documentary after survey period
Source: Nielson EDI

are reality television programs. Winnowing contest *Survivor,* intimate living romp *Big Brother,* and business-hustle *The Apprentice* are television programs that are true life, entertaining, and popular with audiences. Another boost for the current generation is that filmmakers increasingly think of presentation in cinema when framing projects and not just television as in the past.

A feature film typically is defined as having a minimum running time of 90 minutes (including opening sequence and all end credits); documentaries often are shorter. The documentaries shown in big-screen cinemas such as IMAX often run under 60 minutes, which benefits cinemas because they can squeeze in more screenings per day than they can with longer films. For Oscar classification purposes currently, the Academy of Motion Pictures Arts and Sciences classifies a documentary feature as running over 40 minutes. A documentary running under 40 minutes is classified as a short subject.

Studio-Affiliated Indies

It can be argued that the independent sector today has evolved into a wholly owned subsidiary of the major studios, as the majors operate 10 autonomous indie-style film arms. This trend started when Disney purchased Miramax *(Chicago, Cold Mountain)* in 1993 for a reported $80 million. As the major studio-owned players piled into the indie sector, competition intensified and marketing costs escalated. According to major studio trade group the Motion Picture Association of America (MPAA), the studio-owned indie distributors spent an average of $14.7 million in domestic marketing costs per film in 2003, up sharply from an average $6.5 million in 1999. Still, the 2003 figure is far lower than the $39.0 million average for marketing spend per major studio film.

Part of the increase may be attributable to counting a few major studio–caliber films that are on the slates of studio-owned indie divisions. Most conspicuously, Disney-owned Miramax distributed Civil War drama *Cold Mountain,* which reportedly cost $80 million to make, and Warner-owned New Line Cinema produced the three *Lord of the Rings* movies with an aggregate filming cost of around $330 million.

The studio indie divisions operate their own theatrical distribution business that covers the United States and are separate from the distribution divisions of their studio parents. The reason for this separation is that marketing low-cost films requires a smaller scale and different mentality than distributing big-budget extravaganzas. Foreign rights to the films of studio affiliates tend to be controlled by outside sales companies that sell to a patchwork of international buyers. In comparison, the majors market their big studio films worldwide through in-house distribution arms. In some cases, the studio-affiliated indies sell foreign rights to their films themselves to overseas buyers.

The studio-owned indie divisions occasionally nab distribution rights covering some foreign countries to films they handle domestically, and those additional rights are conveyed to their studio parents. For example,

Sony Pictures Classics co-financed and handled United States distribution to the Chinese-language blockbuster *Crouching Tiger, Hidden Dragon*. In addition, Sony Pictures Classics took the English-speaking international territories (such as the United Kingdom and Australia) and Latin America, where the film was distributed by Sony Pictures Classics sister company Sony Pictures Releasing International (formerly Columbia TriStar Film Distributors International).

Besides the previously cited Miramax, New Line, and Sony Pictures Classics, Hollywood's major studios operate other indie-like specialty distribution divisions. Sony Pictures Entertainment, the parent of Columbia, has a second specialty film distribution arm called Screen Gems. Metro-Goldwyn-Mayer has its United Artists unit. There's Paramount Classics. Twentieth Century Fox has Fox Searchlight. Universal Pictures owns Focus Features, whose predecessors were Good Machine, October Films, USA Films, and Gramercy. Warner Bros. has newly created Warner Independent Pictures. Emerging major DreamWorks formed the specialty film division Go Fish in 2003 to handle unusual films, such as Asian animation imports.

The economic rationale for studios to push into the indie business stems from the value they can extract for ancillary markets—home video and television sales. Theatrical release is the least of the economic motivations other than to build a marquee value that will propel a film in downstream windows.

In exchange for contributing 25–40% of the production cost for United States rights to films they distribute, the studio-owned indies capture over half the total economic benefit, when including video and television income. (Foreign buyers contribute the remaining production costs.) In video, the modest indie films that the majors handle are carried to stores on the coattails of studio blockbusters. In television, the majors can add the indie titles to film packages that they license to cable networks, local television stations, and, in some cases, broadcast networks.

Because studio affiliates can count on sales clout in the ancillary markets, the affiliates justify bigger spending in theatrical release than indies without studio ownership. This practice has led to escalation in movie production costs to an average $46.9 million in 2003 for studio-owned indies, up from just $18.4 million in 1999, according to the MPAA. The figures include the cost of making a film, studio overhead, and interest expense on capital. True indie distributors—those that are not owned by major studios—tend to struggle in sales to ancillary markets, which reduces the economic return of their films and crimps their ability to spend heavily for theatrical release.

Much has been made of the impact of Miramax, which was founded in 1979 by brothers Harvey and Bob Weinstein. Miramax, whose revenue is estimated at upward of $1 billion annually, is credited with getting mainstream movie theaters to play foreign imports and edgy independent fare made in the United States that previously only screened in art-house cinemas. Its breakthroughs came in the 1990s with the Irish terrorist hostage drama *The Crying Game,* slackers' lifestyle comedy *Clerks,* and surreal violent drama *Pulp Fiction.*

Miramax's starting point is acquiring from third parties or producing in-house inexpensive films that are edgy but still not too extreme for mainstream tastes. With films in hand, Miramax's large publicity department courts the press and is not shy about playing off the controversy of its films. Miramax usually distributes 30–35 films per year, which is about 15 more titles than a studio slate. In late 2004, Miramax engaged in cost cutting, which is expected to reduce its future film efforts.

Another favorite Miramax marketing technique is showing all or part of a film prior to release in private screenings to journalists, who often jump on a film because they want to be among the first to report on the next Miramax controversy. "If you say a film is great enough times and can back it up with some footage, the press will begin to believe it," notes one ex-Miramax marketing executive. Miramax also is known to be fond of conducting pre-release test screenings of its films to general audiences, whereas other indies test sparingly or not at all.

In advertising, Miramax scales its outlays to match anticipated box office, spending richly to push popular films. The flip side of its ad media formula, which is less obvious, is that Miramax is careful not to overspend for films that fall flat. This latter restraint also separates Miramax from major studios, which tend not to pull the plug quickly on costly advertising campaigns for failing films because of studio politics. At the majors, the marketing department is subject to second-guessing by studio brass and by powerful filmmakers of studio movies, who are quick to complain about stingy advertising support.

With its 30–35 film releases per year for the United States market, Miramax takes a portfolio approach to the independent business. A few Miramax hits each year are big profit makers—given the low cost of production and ad support—so passing $15 million in box office yields a big payback. The other releases that fizzle represent just a small deficit, especially because Miramax is willing to cut its losses early, so its downside is minimal.

Miramax's golden touch is its ability to distribute award-winning films that generate sizable box office. In 2002, Miramax was involved with three of the five films nominated for Best Picture: eventual winner *Chicago, Gangs of New York,* and *The Hours* (the latter jointly with Paramount Pictures).

Miramax also was a trendsetter in reviving the horror genre via its Dimension Films unit with *Scream,* which generated $103 million in domestic box office in 1996. *Scream* cost just $15 million to make. Led by Bob Weinstein, Dimension makes genre films that were staples of the indie business historically. The movies typically are unabashedly commercial films with no artistic pretenses aimed at the youth or some other narrow audience, such as Dimension's hit children's adventure *Spy Kids* movie series. The mass-market Dimension films are known to be Miramax's main profit engine, overshadowing returns from its higher-profile prestige films.

The Weinsteins have locked horns with parent Disney on occasion. Disney took a drubbing in the press for its edict that Miramax not distribute eventual documentary blockbuster *Fahrenheit 9/11* because of the film's political nature in an election period. That followed a familiar pattern of the Weinsteins buying back Miramax films such as the bleak youth drama *Kids,* which was distributed by a Weinstein-owned special purpose company in 1995.

Disney forcing Miramax to unload *Fahrenheit 9/11* generated unflattering publicity, but in other cases specialty divisions help their parent studios. For example, Sony Pictures Classics enables films from China and Hong Kong to crack the United States market, generating corporate good will for SPC parent Sony, which has extensive business ties with China. SPC co-produced *Crouching Tiger, Hidden Dragon* and distributed other Chinese-language films, including *House of Flying Daggers.*

Economics

Despite the occasional blockbuster such as *The Blair Witch Project* and *My Big Fat Greek Wedding,* in reality prosperity tends to be fleeting because the vast majority of independent films are unprofitable.

Vestron Inc. released the 1987 hit *Dirty Dancing,* which generated $63.4 million in domestic box office, and Michael Jackson's 1983 music video blockbuster *Thriller.* However, Vestron landed in bankruptcy by 1990, with its stock nearly worthless. Those same shares were valued at $486 million in Vestron's 1985 initial public offering. Among the prominent indie distributors that folded in recent years are Shooting Gallery (*Sling Blade* and *You Can Count on Me*) and Destination Films (*Thomas and the Magic Railroad*), both in 2001. Another promising indie film distributor, Savoy Pictures (*A Bronx Tale*), exited to concentrate on other media businesses with better profit potential.

The Achilles heel in the economic model is that most independent films either don't receive revenue from video and television sales that are commensurate with their box office or, even worse, net virtually nothing from these ancillary markets. In network broadcast television, the majors sell most of their films for $3–$15 million, whereas few indie films achieve network television sales. Non-English–language films are famous for doing poorly in video, even after generating decent box office. Also, rising media costs increase marketing expenses. Finally, the trend for consumers to wait for the DVD to catch up with non-blockbuster films hurts indie film performance at cinemas.

For all but the top-tier independent films, theatrical distribution in the United States is not a certainty. Many films never get any meaningful revenue out of what is the world's biggest film territory. Some producers are able to fully fund independent films based solely on international sales; thus, any revenue from the United States is gravy. A medium-budget indie film costing $10 million on occasion can snag a $4 million sale to a distributor in Japan and sizable but smaller prices from the major territories of Germany, the United Kingdom, Spain, and Italy.

The good news in the ancillary markets is United States pay television is highly competitive with three premium pay film channel groups: Home Box Office, Showtime, and Starz Encore. The bad news is that the groups increasingly spend program budget not already allocated to major studio movies on original programs, particularly television series. The pay television outlets are in search of the next hit original series, such as HBO's *Sopranos* or *Sex and the City,* which land high-value publicity such as cover shots of television listings publications. Theatrical films don't get such media placements because they've been widely exposed in cinema and video before hitting pay television. In the category of basic advertising supported television channels, it can be argued that independent film economics are improving given the growth of film channels IFC, Bravo, and the Sundance Channel.

An axiom of the indie business is that "there is death being in the middle" when looking at production budgets. Films that cost $5–$15 million to make are sizable financial risks and merit multimillion-dollar advertising campaigns. Yet that budget level typically doesn't provide star power, special effects, or screen spectacle, so the films lack elements for built-in promotion to mainstream audiences.

On the other hand, films produced on shoestring budgets of a few million or even hundreds of thousands dollars are relatively small financial risks with the potential of hitting it big, such as *The Blair Witch Project*. Looking above the middle range, big indie films with production costs of $16 to $50 million are less expensive than studio movies yet have production values and star talent that can hook an audience in theatrical release. The problem with big-budget indie films is that they compete with major studios for prime theatrical release slots, where the majors can out-muscle independent distributors.

The independent film sector, while never a cake walk, is coming off a period of easy money in the late 1990s. Unusual mechanisms, such as insurance-backed film loans and gap financing—lending against estimated values of unsold film rights—simplified financing of indie films. When the 2000 dot-com bust recession arrived, prices for indie films in the international market fell an estimated 20% in 3 years.

As a result, films did not generate anticipated revenue, resulting in a financing collapse. An estimated $3 billion in insurance-backed film loans were underwritten in the late 1990s, triggering $1 billion in claims for insurers that had collected just $400 million in underwriting fees. The financial savior for indies these days is "soft money," which are tax shelter financing and government subsidies that are most plentiful overseas.

History of Independents

The diverse independent sector defies easy categorization, other than to say it embraces films not distributed by the seven historical major studios (and emerging major DreamWorks). In the first 60 years of the motion picture business, various strands of specialty films rode waves of booms and busts for independents at the hands of marketplace economics.

Films made specifically for black audiences, going as far back as the silent film era, is one example of a strand. For instance, the Jacksonville, Florida-based Norman Studios made a string of polished films in the 1920s sporting "all-colored-cast," including *The Green Eyed Monster,* for which a poster promised "an $80,000 train wreck" scene. Drive-in movies, which emerged after World War II, supported frothy youth films such as *Teenage Cave Man* and good-old-boy action films set in the South, until the outdoor theaters died amid urban sprawl. Many of the youth films of this era were simply derivative of major studio hits, such as the 1965 James Bond spy spoof *Dr. Goldfoot and the Bikini Machine* from the era's notable indie distributor American International Pictures (AIP).

In the early post-World War II era, the majors indirectly helped the youth-focused indies by remaining stuck in a time warp. The majors served up mainstream conventional films catering to middle America, which was abandoning cinema in droves for the comforts of television. The major studios' idea of a youth film in this era was the wholesome *The Sound of Music,* which did not connect to the youth culture or satisfy restless teenagers.

Meanwhile, independents jumped on the youth audience, which at the time was viewed by the movie industry as simply a limited segment and not recognized as the dominant force for movies that it is today. A famous indie distributor of this period was AIP, which was founded in 1954 by Samuel Z. Akoff. Its provocatively titled films included *She-Creature* and *Dragstrip Girl.* Films from AIP, the Woolner brothers' Dimension Pictures (*Super Dude*), Roger Corman's New World (*Women in Cages*), and others catered to undemanding youth audiences at drive-in theaters that flourished in the 1940s to 1970s.

The emergence of television in the 1960s reduced the cinema-going public in general and undercut the fragile economics of independents. In the ashes rose the New American Cinema of the late 1960s, which stressed realism and serious subjects. This opened a new direction for independents by targeting sophisticated audiences, representing a break from the prior emphasis on frothy youth and adventure films. In the 1960s and 1970s, serious independent films made a statement with Avco Embassy's *The Graduate* starring Dustin Hoffman in 1967 and the battle of the sexes drama *Carnal Knowledge* in 1971. Martin Scorsese directed social drama *Boxcar Bertha* from AIP in 1972. Up-market distributors of this era included Aquarius Releasing, Audubon Films, First Run Features, New Yorker Films, and New Front Films.

In response, the majors co-opted the trend. Breaking from their orientation of middle-of-the-road movies, the majors cranked out big-budget versions of edgy cinema concepts. Two examples from 1969 were antisocial road drama *Easy Rider* from Columbia Pictures and gunfest *The Wild Bunch* from Warner Bros.

Another boom came in the 1980s when Wall Street showered money on indies, expecting small-fry distributors to flourish in the then budding home video revolution. Investors pumped into independent film companies a staggering $3.5 billion raised in public securities offerings from 1987–1989. However, most of the investment went sour, mainly because independent companies that suddenly were flush with capital unwisely tried to battle the majors head-on. Cannon Group—led by the go-go boys Menahem Golan and Yoram Globus—churned out films at a dizzying rate using Wall Street money until an accounting scandal deflated their balloon.

With the sector in disarray by the early 1990s, independents staged another comeback with a new wave of edgy films coupled with clever film marketing. The studios helped clear the way when they veered back to the middle market with glossy entertainment fare such as *Superman* and *Batman,* which aimed right at the youth audience. But the majors again co-opted the indies, this time by buying them, starting with Disney's 1993 purchase of Miramax for $80 million. The majors let their indie affiliates operate autonomously to keep talent and marketing costs from spurting up to major studio levels.

11 Foreign Language Films

I like a film to have a beginning, a middle and an end, but not necessarily in that order.

Filmmaker Jean Luc Godard

When discussing foreign movies, what is generally top of mind is art house, which is esoteric cinema most closely associated with Western Europe. Such thought may have been the case in past decades, but in today's reality, several diverse strands of foreign films have penetrated the domestic market (United States and Canada).

Nobody can overlook the Hong Kong school of glossy martial arts action films—dubbed chopsocky by *Variety* years ago—whose signature is highly choreographed and exaggerated fight sequences. These films are popular across Southeast Asia and *Crouching Tiger, Hidden Dragon* rolled up an astronomical $128 million in domestic box office. Sony Pictures Classics distributed the film in the United States.

A following is growing for Japanese animation known as anime, whose signature look includes characters with big eyes and hair. Anime often targets adult audiences, unlike most Hollywood animation, which aims at kids and families. Odd-ball animated fantasy *Spirited Away,* which grossed over $200 million in Japanese box office, collected a respectable $10 million domestically via a Disney release in 2003. India's signature song-and-dance Bollywood films are also a force outside their home country, in part playing to large expatriate Indian communities. Films using both English and Spanish languages that tell stories about the Latino population in the United States are another strand aiming at a mainstream audience.

Even continental Europe is diversifying from its historic emphasis on art house, which remains a staple. A new generation of European film-makers is embracing the mass market with broadly accessible films, in sharp contrast to high-brow arty fare. Examples are comedies such as the whimsical French hit *Amelie,* which posted $33.2 million in United States/Canada box office in 2002. Miramax handled the import in the United States. The wry comedy set in Paris presents a lonely lead charac-ter portrayed by the engrossing pasty-face actress Audrey Tautou, who is on a mission to do good in the world. Whereas Germany used to take pride in its serious dramas, its recent blockbusters at home have been the unpre-tentious comedies *The Shoe of Manitu,* which is a parody of American Westerns that grossed more than $55 million in Germany, and the post-communism black comedy *Good Bye, Lenin!* that grossed over $41 mil-lion in Germany.

It could be argued that highly localized films from English-speaking territories, such as South Africa, Ireland, New Zealand, Australia, and even the United Kingdom, fit into the foreign film category when dialog is heavily accented and the subject matter is decidedly exotic. *Waking Ned Devine,* a quirky Irish comedy that grossed hit-caliber $24.8 million domestically for Fox Searchlight in its 1998 release, is a slice of the Emerald Isle with thick accents that are a chip off the old Blarney Stone. English-workingman comedy *The Full Monty* rolled up $45.9 million in domestic box office for Fox Searchlight in 1997, despite Yorkshire-tinged dialog. Thus, another description for this category might be non–United States films, although this chapter uses the streamline phrase "foreign language."

The highest-grossing foreign language film in the domestic market is *The Passion of the Christ,* which had a staggering $370 million in box office via Newmarket Films, although the film is a special case given its religious orientation. The period epic from Mel Gibson uses subtitles because the dialog is in the ancient Aramaic language.

The audience for foreign language films in the United States and Canada can be subdivided into three segments. Two of the categories are poles apart—art house and ethnic. Art house is cinema geared toward sophisticated tastes and is a staple of film festivals. Ethnic films are pop-ular-culture films from other countries that are not high brow and appeal mostly to an immigrant population. The third category is a middle strand from a new generation of mainstream foreign films that is neither par-ticularly arty nor so country specific that only ethnic audiences embrace them.

Despite occasional hits, foreign language films are a small slice of domestic box office; just $1.5 million in domestic box office is considered a hit. A small number of foreign language films have achieved a larger, sizable box office (Fig. 11.1). Foreign language films often face a tough going at the voluntary ratings service in the United States, because imagery that doesn't raise eyebrows at home can trigger a restrictive audience classification in the United States. Canada's patchwork of ratings authorities also can impose stringent classifications. One option is to release films unrated in the United States, although ratings are mandatory in Canada.

Figure 11.1 Top Grossing Foreign Language Films

Title	U. S. Distributor	Box Office ($ mil.)	Year	Origin
The Passion of the Christ	Newmarket	$370.0	2004	n/a
Crouching Tiger, Hidden Dragon	Sony Classics	$128.1	2000	Hong Kong
Life is Beautiful	Miramax	$57.6	1998	Italy
Amelie	Miramax	$33.2	2001	France
The Postman	Miramax	$21.8	1995	Italy
Like Water for Chocolate	Miramax	$21.7	1993	Mexico
La Dolce Vita	n/a	$19.5	1960	Italy
And Your Mother Too	IFC	$13.6	2002	Mexico
Cinema Paradiso	Miramax	$12.0	1990	Italy
Winged Migration*	Sony Classics	$10.8	2003	France
Shall We Dance?	Miramax	$9.5	1997	Japan
All About My Mother	Sony Classics	$8.3	1999	Spain
Eat Drink Man Woman	Goldwyn	$7.3	1994	Taiwan
The Wedding Banquet	Goldwyn	$6.9	1993	Taiwan
Nowhere in Africa	Zeitgeist	$6.2	2003	Germany
Good Bye, Lenin!	Sony Classics	$6.1	2004	Germany
Cyrano de Bergerac	Orion Classics	$5.8	1990	France
Kolya	Miramax	$5.8	1997	Czech
The Crime of Father Amaro	Goldwyn/IDP	$5.7	2002	Mexico
Central Station	Sony Classics	$5.6	1998	Brazil
Indochine	Sony Classics	$5.6	1992	France
Europa Europa	Orion Classics	$5.6	1991	Germany
Belle Epoque	Sony Classics	$5.4	1994	Spain

Note: Box office figures cover United States and Canada through June 2004; *Winged Migration* is a French wildlife documentary with narration in French-accented English language; listing excludes animated films; many films are co-productions involving multiple countries
Source: *Marketing to Moviegoers, Variety*

Art-House Overview

The art-house crowd tends to be college educated (or in college) and oriented to high culture. This group gravitates toward esoteric and personal auteur films that are popular on the festival front but which mainstream audiences find stuffy and too talky.

Auteur is the French word for author. Auteur films are associated with a cinema philosophy that originated in France in the early 1950s. The auteur theory asserts that the director should be the dominant creative force. In this philosophy, a film should bear the personal imprint of the director, with producers, writers, and actors of secondary importance.

The high-brow art-house audience has one important characteristic in common with the youth audience, whose taste is markedly different. Both audiences consist of heavy moviegoers, and the frequency of their cinema attendance varies depending on whether films in theaters are compelling. "The size of the pie for foreign language films will expand if there are a lot of good movies," said one art-house film marketer. "The moviegoers in this category will go two or three times a week if the films are really good."

Hard-core art-house filmgoers insist on subtitles, which contrasts with mainstream American audiences that historically have shied away from films in foreign languages unless the films have dubbed English soundtracks. The art-house crowd wants to experience the voice inflections of native actors. Although mainstream audiences as a rule are adverse to foreign languages, an exception is *Crouching Tiger, Hidden Dragon,* which was a blockbuster film with subtitling of its Chinese-language dialog.

Attempts to dub foreign language films into English voices have a spotty record. Such dubbing attempts usually are made for films aimed at a children's audience, which would struggle with reading subtitles. Miramax's 2002 release of *Pinocchio,* a live-action Italian film starring Roberto Benigni that reportedly cost a hefty for $45 million to make, was a box office disappointment with just $3.7 million in domestic box office. Hong Kong martial arts/sports yarn *Shaolin Soccer,* another 2002 Miramax film, mustered less than half a million dollars in domestic box office, again presented with dubbed voices.

Art-House Marketing

Foreign language films aimed at the art-house market usually open on an exclusive basis—one theater per city—hoping to ride a wave of positive reviews in media and audience word of mouth to wider release. The goal is to expand to 50–100 theaters. The flip side of this strategy is that if critical kudos and audiences don't materialize in the early, narrow release, then the wider release is scaled back or even abandoned.

The opening may be just two to six theaters in total in New York City, Los Angeles, and possibly some other big cities. Opening a film in one theater in New York costs $10,000 to $40,000 for a print ad campaign. Los Angeles requires about the same. Given the low box office potential from a small theater base, the initial advertising usually is limited to just daily newspapers and weekly print publications.

A small preopening ad typically appears the Sunday before a Friday premiere. Listing print ads appear two days before the Friday opening. The print vehicles are daily newspapers with upscale audiences, local entertainment weekly publications, and alternative weeklies, which tend to be read by art-house aficionados.

The publicity routine follows the template of English-language films but on a smaller scale because publicity budgets for foreign films tend to be much less. Journalists from mainstream media are less inclined to jump on foreign language films because they don't sell their print publications or boost their television ratings. At a minimum, a publicity campaign hopes to generate "opening this week" items in print publications, which are the small stories, sometimes with photos.

Occasionally, a foreign language film makes a surprisingly big publicity splash. In 2002, Gael Garcia Bernal—a lead in the Spanish-language coming-of-age film *Y Tu Mamá También* (And Your Mother Too)—made a guest appearance on David Letterman's late night CBS Television talk show. *Esquire* magazine, which is a prized outlet given its circulation surpasses 700,000, published an upbeat 700-word write-up of the off-beat French animated chase film *The Triplets of Belleville* in November 2003. Several weeks later, the film received two Oscar nominations.

Many publicity challenges are unique to foreign films. Creative talent may not speak English well or at all, which eliminates interviews with English-language press. Talent from outside the region may not be able to travel to North America to participate personally in publicity efforts because of expense. Personal schedules can be an obstacle because directors, actors, and others who typically participate in publicity for home-country release have moved on to their next films by the time the United States and Canada premieres come around.

The key marketing material is the trailer, where again foreign language films represent a challenge because of language. Film distributors for domestic release tend not to present dialog or subtitling; instead, they emphasize music and mood, and they usually include narration in trailers. One reason for this practice is the lack of time needed to insert subtitles, so dialog isn't presented. Another reason put forth by film marketers is that some filmgoers who have no experience with foreign films might find the trailer intriguing, so there's no need to call attention to the language barrier. Even without dialog, film marketers say they're not fooling anyone because a language difference usually is obvious from the scenes and atmosphere.

Awards

In the chase for awards, the obvious outlets are film festivals—which number 800 in the United States and Canada—and various film industry organizations. The Cannes Film Festival in France may be world renowned, but its top award the Golden Palm is not a catalyst for big box office in the United States because winners over the years were of uneven quality, which is a result of film industry politics in Europe.

Hands down the most prestigious award is the Oscar for Best Foreign Language Film because of the consistently high quality of past winners and the stature of its originator, the Academy of Motion Pictures Arts and Sciences (AMPAS). Winning the Best Foreign Language Film Oscar—in fact, just being one of the five finalist nominees—ensures relatively wide theatrical distribution in the United States and Canada. The 2002 Best Foreign Film winner *Nowhere in Africa* rode the coattails of Oscar glory to a gross of $6.2 million domestically, which is around four times the box office expected for a high-quality German drama without the award.

The domestic marketing campaign for *Nowhere in Africa*—a drama that centers on a Jewish family that flees Nazi Germany—resulted in placement at approximately 20 festivals, including the 10th Hamptons International Film Festival in suburban New York City during October 2002. The film won the Audience Award at the Hamptons, which raised its profile in nearby New York City. Its United States distributor, Zeitgeist Films, pushed hard for prestigious opening or closing screenings, which the film mostly received.

"We had a feeling it might not necessarily be a critics film but we felt it would be an audience film," said Nancy Gerstman, co-president of New York City-based Zeitgeist Films. "At the Toronto festival, after we screened it for critics we heard reactions such as, 'Oh it's conventional and it's long.' But the film got a standing ovation at one of the public screenings at Toronto. The public went crazy."

Zeitgeist had already acquired the United States rights to *Nowhere in Africa* when cinema promotional organization Export-Union des Deutschen Films selected the film as Germany's official Oscar entry in October 2002. *Nowhere in Africa* made its United States premiere in March 7, 2003, at two theaters, coming after its nomination on February 11 as one of five finalists for the Best Foreign Language Film Oscar. Zeitgeist's bet that the film would get a nomination paid off, making it easier to book theaters and promote the film to audiences in the United States (Fig. 11.2). *Nowhere in Africa* then won the Oscar on March 23, which gave the German film even more cachet. Through its entire run, the film played at about 300 theaters in the United States, and its highest number of theaters screening the film simultaneously was 78.

In a wrinkle for the ad campaign, Zeitgeist bought print advertising in specialty newspapers read by both the Jewish and German populations, in addition to customary mainstream print media. Finally, because Zeitgeist viewed *Nowhere in Africa* as an audience film, the movie was given to 10 cinema clubs—private aficionado organizations that screen movies for an adult membership with sophisticated tastes. The screenings came prior to commercial theatrical release to build word of mouth.

An example of a highly specialized festival providing a theatrical platform for foreign films is the Spirit of Sarajevo Arts Project held in Los Angeles in January 2004. More than 2,000 moviegoers screened 11 films from the Balkan region of South Eastern Europe.

Figure 11.2 *Nowhere in Africa* **theatrical rollout 2003**

Date	Theaters	Cities/Comments
Mar 7, 2003	2	New York, Los Angeles
Mar 14, 2003	11	No change
Mar 21, 2003	16	Chicago
Mar 23, 2003		Wins Oscar for Best Foreign Film
Mar 28, 2003	33	Philadelphia, Seattle, Boston, Florida
Apr 4, 2003	42	San Francisco, San Diego, St. Louis, Atlanta, Minneapolis
Apr 11, 2003	61	Cleveland, Baltimore, Palm Springs, wider Florida, Columbus, Ohic.
Apr 18, 2003	65	Cracks top 25 for first time with $352,746 three-day weekend gross to rank 24th nationally

Source: Zeitgeist Films

Besides marketing to local ethnic audiences, the organizer solicited movie aficionados via ads in Hollywood movie trades and by extensive e-mailings to fellow international arts communities and organizations, diplomatic corps at local consulates, and film school students at local universities. "If you hitch yourself to only one demographic, you exhaust the possibilities rather quickly," said Vera Mijojlic, a marketing consultant and head of the Los Angeles-based Spirit of Sarajevo–International Arts Exchange, which organized the Balkan film program. The American Cinema Foundation sponsored the event.

For the 2004 Best Foreign Film Oscar, AMPAS—which has conferred Oscars for 77 years—invited 89 countries to submit a single national film. A film organization in each country selects the national entry submission. For the Oscar to be conferred in the 2005 awards ceremony, the deadline for submitting entry forms was October 1, 2004. "In the Foreign Language Film category, additional documentation, including a synopsis of the film in English, a biography and photograph of the director and a copy of public notification of exhibition, such as an advertisement, is [also] due by October 1," the AMPAS stated in an announcement. Film prints for submitted films were due October 15, 2004. The announcement of the five finalists came January 25, 2005. The five finalists are required to submit a second print, which eventually is returned.

The five nominees are selected by secret voting of the Foreign Language Film Award Committee of AMPAS. Several hundred academy members are on this committee, which is divided into three blocs. Each bloc screens one third of the more than 50 films submitted each year. The five nominated finalists are selected by weighed average when results from the three groups are combined. Because the committee members have a demanding screening schedule, the committee is believed to rely heavily on semiretired academy members. Once the five finalists are chosen, the winner is selected by a vote of the full academy of those members who screened all five nominees (the academy has just over 5,800 voting members).

The five Best Foreign Language Film nominees also may receive nominations in other categories if they conduct a specified commercial screening for qualifying in the Los Angeles area. Such double dipping is rare, although the Italian-language *Life Is Beautiful* milked that rule in 1998. The World War II tragicomedy won Oscars for Best Foreign Film, Best Actor (Roberto Benigni), and Best Original Musical Score. It also was Oscar nominated for director (Benigni again), editing, screenplay written directly for the screen, and best picture. *Life Is Beautiful* generated a blockbuster $57 million in domestic box office for Miramax.

To be eligible, a film submitted for Best Foreign Language Film of 2004 must have had its first public showing in a commercial theater in its country of origin for a minimum of seven consecutive days between October 1, 2003, and September 30, 2004. Projection must be 35 or 70 mm, which eliminates video projection of subcinema quality. The film print submitted for Oscar consideration must be identical to the version presented in the home country (except for the addition of English-language subtitles).

The film's sound track must be mainly non-English dialogue track and in an official language of the submitting country. If a film contains languages that are not English and are not official country languages, the film still can qualify as long as the languages are germane to the submitting country (for example, dialog of Turkish immigrants in a German film). Nominated films need not have received a commercial theatrical release in the United States, although any of the five nominated films without theatrical release quickly receives offers.

The rules for Best Foreign Language Film may sound simple, but they do eliminate some high-profile films from non-English language countries. In an era of co-productions where a film can have numerous producers from multiple countries, the language requirements knock out some foreign films, particularly bigger-budget productions made for the global market. For example, *Enemy at the Gates,* the 2001 World War II drama about the battle of Stalingrad, was a European co-production (Germany–United Kingdom–Ireland) that was shot in English by French director Jean-Jacques Annaud. The war drama cost $70 million to make.

Rules also disqualify co-productions that erase any central nationality for the foreign film category, such as Spanish-language *The Motorcycle Diaries.* The historical drama's producers came from Argentina, Peru, Chile, and United States, and the film was directed by a Brazilian. In another example, the academy revoked the eligibility of 1992 foreign film *A Place in the World,* which was Uruguay's entry, after the film was selected as one of the five nominee finalists. The academy disqualified the movie upon learning it had been filmed in Argentina and made with "insufficient Uruguayan artistic control" to be considered a national film.

Ethnic Audience

Ethnic audiences are a far cry from the diverse art-house crowd. They are demographically homogeneous, encompassing immigrants and export workers from foreign countries. The ethnic groups also include offspring that may have been born in the United States or Canada but are imbued with the heritage of the parents' homelands and are bilingual. The immigrant and expatriate worker groups have tastes for films that are more broadly focused, including slapstick comedy imports and foreign pop culture movies, which are not favorites of the festival circuit.

A huge Latino population in the United States accounts for 13% of the total population or 37 million persons, with a strong moviegoing culture despite the Latino population's weak economic profile. The Latino market (sometimes referred to as Hispanic, although technically that excludes Brazilians) is a youth-skewing group with a median age of 26 years, which is 10 years below the United States average. The ethnic Latino market itself is somewhat segmented, with 60% of Latinos in the United States having roots in Mexico, making this bloc the most significant cultural force from Latin America.

"If you want to make it with this population in the United States, you need Mexican films," said Louis Balaguer, president of Latin World Entertainment, a talent management, consumer marketing, publishing, and production outfit operating in the United States. "Anything with a Spanish or Argentine accent doesn't fly."

Despite being a large population segment, the Latino audience is only slowly being harnessed by mainstream Hollywood. In recent years, the only major studio films with a heavy Latino theme to cross over with ethnic audiences in a big way was the 1997 English-language biography drama *Selena,* which provided Jennifer Lopez with her first starring role in a big film and generated $35.3 million in box office. In 1987, Columbia Pictures achieved success releasing the Latino-themed rock music period drama *La Bamba,* another English-language film. Little else followed in a similar vein from the major studios.

Three sizable film distributors and various smaller players specialize in marketing Latino films in the United States. The big three are Arenas Entertainment, Televisa Cine, and Venevision International, which operate out of offices in Los Angeles and Miami. Each has significant corporate backing.

- Arenas released the 2002 hit *Empire,* an action drama starring John Leguizamo about a Latino drug dealer trying to go straight. Although primarily English-language, the film deals with a Latino subject. *Empire* grossed a sizable $17.6 million domestically, and Arenas said it paid just a $650,000 minimum guarantee for United States rights. The big Spanish private equity firm Marco Polo Investments is a shareholder of Arenas.

- Televisa Cine is owned by giant Mexican broadcaster Televisa, which is a $2.1 billion-revenue company whose stock trades on the New York Stock Exchange. It distributed the dry comedy *A Day Without a Mexican,* which grossed $4.2 million after a May 2004 release and was launched with a big ad campaign. Televisa Cine is the newest player and hopes to release six to eight films per year. Latin World Entertainment handles Televisa's consumer marketing.
- Venevision International has distributed a trickle of films since 2000. It is part of the Venezuelan conglomerate Cisneros Group, which has large interests in television media and Coca Cola bottling.

A few of the mainstream Spanish-language films achieved modest hit status in domestic theatrical release in recent years. Films include the 2002 romantic drama *The Crime of Father Amaro* ($5.7 million in box office), the 2001 romantic comedy *Tortilla Soup* ($4.5 million), and the 2003 family drama set in New York City *Raising Victor Vargas* ($2.2 million). All three were distributed in the United States by Samuel Goldwyn Films that, along with Miramax, occasionally releases films that connect with ethnic and art-house audiences. HBO Films actively produces films with Latino themes, including *Maria Full of Grace,* a 2004 drug world drama distributed by Fine Line Features, and *Real Women Have Curves,* which Newmarket Films distributed in 2002.

Another large ethnic audience in the United States is the Asian-American demographic, which has a moviegoing culture and a higher income and education standard than most other ethnic groups. In the 2000 census for the United States, 10.2 million persons, or 4% of the total population, put themselves into this ethnic category. While having attributes attractive to film marketers, the Asian-American audience is highly fragmented. Its dozen main ethnic groups can be grouped into three broad regional categories: Northeast Asians (China, Taiwan, Japan, Korea, Vietnam), Southeast Asians (Philippines, Malaysia, Indonesia, Cambodia), and South Asians (India, Pakistan, Bangladesh).

Ethnic Marketing

Ethnic audiences tend to be clustered geographically, prompting film marketers to emphasize local media in advertising buys. For example, the Latino population is concentrated in the Southwest, Florida, and New

York City. Asian-Americans are most clustered in Los Angeles; New York City; San Francisco; Honolulu; Vancouver, British Columbia; Sacramento; Chicago; San Diego; Toronto; Seattle; Washington, DC; and Houston. Audiences can be even more localized. For example, Filipinos tend to cluster near hospitals and military bases, which are sources of employment.

Latinos make up 13% of the total population but by some estimates constitute approximately 20% of United States box office. For ad spending, the main buys are broadcast television and cable networks with a mix of national and spot buys. The spot buys tend to be for Los Angeles, cities in Texas, Chicago, and New York, which have active Latino moviegoing populations and therefore are worthy of extra media weight. Miami's big Latino population is a weak moviegoing group. For broadcast network, the United States has two national Spanish language broadcasters: Univision (the dominant player) and Telemundo.

Latino marketers also emphasize Spanish-language radio, newspapers, and magazines in the United States. Univision.com is a leading Latino Web site.

A key decision for film distributors is whether to utilize English-language media in marketing efforts or to stick to low-cost, narrowly focused ethnic media. Nationally, 62% of Latino adults have lived in the United States for fewer than 15 years, which points to an immigrant orientation and exclusive focus on Spanish-language media. Latino films aimed at ethnic audiences sometimes are co-productions in which English is an integral language, which points to marketing to an English-speaking audience.

Films with both English and foreign language campaigns tend to use two separate publicity teams because the targeted media are segmented. An extensive national publicity campaign for a foreign language film costs $30,000 to $80,000.

Among the films that used advertising in both English-language and Spanish-language media are *Y Tu Mamá También* (And Your Mother Too) and *A Day Without a Mexican*. The former is a Mexican import that was released unrated in the United States because of sexual content. The film grossed $13.6 million in 2002 for IFC Films playing to both Anglo and Latino audiences.

A Day Without a Mexican is the fable about the chaos that would ensue if Latinos suddenly disappeared from California. The film's advertising mix included outdoor billboards, bus shelter billboards, television, and radio. The film was primarily in English language, although it is a Mexico/United States co-production dealing with a Latino theme.

A stark English-language billboard in Hollywood simply saying "On May 14, There Will Be No Mexicans in California" triggered an outcry, generating publicity. Two such billboards for *A Day Without a Mexican* were taken down because of public complaints that the message was derogatory, although the film is a satire. Meanwhile, a Spanish-language billboard in Los Angeles that read, "On May 14th, the Gringos Are Going to Cry" did not elicit protest. "We knew that the title of our film and our ad campaign would be bold and risky," wrote moviemakers Sergio Arau and Yarelli Arizmendi in a letter to *Variety,* saying they wanted to raise awareness of Latino contributions to prosperity in the United States.

In 2000, startup distributor Latin Universe bought ads only in Spanish media for the drama *Santitos,* which grossed just $400,000 domestically after being a modest hit in its home territory of Mexico. The distributor later disbanded.

An example of a highly concentrated ethnic audience is the Filipino population in Cerritos, a suburb of Los Angeles. Specialty film distributor Richard Abramowitz has distributed several Filipino films in the Cerritos area that are supported by advertising strictly in Filipino-language media. The ads are placed on local cable television, radio, and newspapers. The local cable systems import a Philippine television channel for which local commercials are offered. The cable television ads for the Filipino movie include a text crawl citing specific theaters and starting times at Cerritos-area theaters. The television commercials are simply carry-over ads from the Philippines release of a given film.

In general, the Internet and e-mail are viable platforms for Asian films because Asian-Americans are affluent. Half have college degrees, versus the 25% average for the United States. In addition, Asian-Americans have a personal income growth that is about 50 percentage points higher than the national rate.

In deals with theaters, foreign language films tend to get film rentals of 35–45%, which is the distributor slice of box office. That's about 15 percentage points less than major studio films in mainstream theaters. Over the years, the big theater circuits in the United States have dabbled with booking ethnic films, for example, allocating one screen in a theater having eight or more screens. However, mainstream cinemas generally found the payoff was not worth the extra work.

As a result, ethnic film distributors tend to book small theaters and not the new multiplexes. Ethnic audience films can generate high per screen averages. A popular Filipino film can easily bring in $15,000 per week in a Southern California screen, which is double the box office of a mainstream film. However, ethnic films play on one or just a few screens, so marketing costs are high on a per screen basis, unlike mainstream English-language films, which are shown on far more screens.

History of Foreign Language Film Imports

At the birth of the feature film business a century ago, Europe was ahead of the United States and Canada. France, Britain, and Germany each had sizable domestic industries that exported movies globally. In the earliest period, films traveled easily because silent films did not face language barriers. Domestic audiences initially were not demanding and accepted, for example, that Indians had mustaches in European-made films about the American Wild West.

An early foreign blockbuster in the silent era was the 1913 Italian historical epic *Quo Vadis,* which at nine reels running two hours (including two intermissions) was twice as long as feature-length American films. *Quo Vadis* commanded a $1 ticket price that was 10 times the average. A contemporary *Variety* review praised its epic scenes of "the burning of Rome, the rushing to and fro of the inhabitants, the general confusion, followed by violence, robbery, lust, etc."

European films lost their grip on the international market as a result of business isolation stemming from World War I and, it can be argued, have never really recovered. Hollywood flourished from the neutrality of the United States in the first half of World War I and also because Americans viewed film as a business, while Europeans took an artistic orientation that was not a draw for a mass market.

After World War II, foreign language films made larger inroads in the domestic market. In one catalyst, AMPAS began conferring a special Oscar to a foreign film annually starting in 1947. The formal foreign film category was established in 1956, thus placing five nominees into the spotlight.

Europe's orientation to high brow intensified as the French wing of cinema propagated the auteur theory in the early 1950s. The auteur philosophy asserts that a movie's signature should come solely from its director. One consequence of this philosophy is that Western Europe, except for the United Kingdom, extends significant legal protections and controls to creative figures. In contrast, Hollywood producers—most conspicuously in the form of the major studios—wield the power over creative affairs. Furthermore, mainstream Hollywood aims films at the mass market, and the major studios do not view movies as high-brow art.

Europe's new wave of provocative and mainstream films in the 1960s grabbed audiences worldwide but then petered out. In their era, films such as life-in-the-fast-lane Italian drama *La Dolce Vita* (The Sweet Life) from 1960 were able to skirt United States censorship restrictions that hamstrung studios at the time. Another landmark film was the French art-house drama *Breathless,* whose rebellion against society was influential cinema.

Asian films began making a mark in the domestic market in the 1980s. For decades a backwater, Asia now cranks out hits such as martial arts blockbuster *Crouching Tiger, Hidden Dragon,* Japanese animation success *Spirited Away,* and a stream of Bollywood song-and-dance fests from India.

These days, international filmmakers display flashes of mainstream appeal with big hits such as the Italian-made World War II comedy–drama *Life Is Beautiful* and sophisticated French comedy *Amelie.* The grip of the auteur loosened in Europe and elsewhere as filmmakers embraced comedy and popular cultures, which represent sharp breaks from the dreary social dramas of traditional European art house.

Another factor in broadening the appeal of foreign language films is that foreign television outlets, which are purveyors of popular culture, increasingly are financiers of movies at home. They tend to fund projects aimed at mainstream audiences. The rise of privately owned commercial broadcast television and pay television in Europe during the late 1980s spurred this trend.

12 Prints and Advertising Funds

A horse, a horse, my kingdom for a horse!
William Shakespeare, Richard III

Hollywood knows how King Richard felt while he was stranded on foot in the thick of battle and with victory within his grasp, but lacking a trusty steed. The movie business has its own version of this plight of not being able to go a short way to achieve a glorious finish. Because filmmaking is capital intensive, the money spigot can run dry when it's time to pay for marketing expenses. An independent producer who lined up enough financing for production or even has finished a film can't gallop into the theatrical market because of a lack of funds.

The independent film sector buzzes about the availability of prints and advertising (P&A) funds, which are investment vehicles focused narrowly on covering marketing costs for theatrical releases. In reality, such financing vehicles are frequently talked about but seldom materialize. For example, an off-shore fund promising hundreds of millions of dollars in money for movie release expenses—a mind-boggling sum—made a splash in the film business in 2003, but more than a year later no films received the money.

In the jargon P&A, "P" refers to the prints, the bulky reels used by theaters to project films. The reels cost about $1,000 per movie to manufacture. "A" is the advertising expense for newspaper, television, and other media to support theatrical release. Ad expenses can range from a couple of hundred thousand to millions of dollars for a film.

Recipients of Funding

P&A funding can be channeled to individual producers, who can use the funding as a bargaining chip to line up a film distributor, or to distribution companies themselves that want outside financing. A producer can negotiate a better deal with a distribution company if the producer has already financed production and can also cover marketing costs. When domestic theatrical distributors acquire independent films, they usually cover the P&A expenses of theatrical releases but are more inclined to acquire and offer better financial terms if a third party puts up money for marketing.

One active P&A fund is Palisades Pictures, a New York City-based entity. "Because of the big growth of content, we will do 48 films [in 2005] for over $21 million [invested]," forecasts Palisades Pictures chairman Vincent Roberti. Palisades's funding comes from McGinn, Smith & Company, Inc., an investment banking and brokerage firm founded 24 years ago in Albany, New York. Elsewhere, Los Angeles film distributor First Look Media tapped $7 million dollars in P&A funding from Seven Hills Pictures.

Palisades is providing between $200,000 and $750,000 in P&A funding per film. One beneficiary is *The Agronomist,* a documentary about a Haitian freedom advocate from Hollywood filmmaker Jonathan Demme. The ThinkFilm release generated only $226,000 in box office, although Palisades is confident it will recoup from sales to television and video. "We never make a loan based just on box office [revenue expectations]," said Roberti.

Marketing expenditures in the hundreds of thousands of dollars support theatrical releases in big cities but are short of a national release. At about the $5 million threshold, a national release is possible and should noticeably lift a film's sales later in home video.

Much of the huffing and puffing for theatrical release aims to improve the film's prospects in home video, the film business's cash cow that typically accounts for half of total film revenue. P&A spending in theatrical release helps establish values in subsequent windows, thus building consumer awareness even if box office is poor.

Drawbacks

P&A funding usually comes with some onerous strings attached. One drawback is that P&A financing usually is structured as the last money in and first money out. Entities such as banks, which provided earlier funding for production and thus enabled the film to be made in the first place, balk at standing in line behind any later investors. P&A funds usually insist on getting a cut of a film's revenue stream beyond theatrical, such as home video, which is another stumbling block to making deals. The major studios find traditional P&A funds too expensive given the studios' ability to raise capital at low rates.

However, hardscrabble indies, which have few other financing options, will consider daunting financial terms. "There are probably 500 movies a year that get made with average budgets of $500,000–$1 million," notes Dave Davis, a Los Angeles-based film finance consultant. "They pretty much don't get a theatrical release and don't make money. They're all self financed. Collectively, they're losing maybe $200 million a year. Of course, that doesn't mean you don't strike oil with one of them occasionally."

In a final stumbling block, the independent sector's most promising movies are snapped up by indie distributors in conventional acquisition deals, leaving slim pickings from which P&A funds can choose. "This doesn't mean just a few executives at a studio passed on a film," said Rob Aft, who is partner in Los Angeles-based Compliance Consulting. "All the buyers from the majors and the independent companies look at every single movie that's available. Sure, every once in a while some good films slip through the cracks and don't get picked up. It's maybe a movie a year but that's nothing to base a business plan on."

Confirming that assertion, no shortage of suitors was seen when Miramax was forced to offload the Iraq war critic *Fahrenheit 9/11;* two distributors ultimately shared the film. Lions Gate Films and IFC Films reportedly each put up $5 million toward marketing as part of their distribution deal for the film, which grossed $119 million domestically.

Mel Gibson's religious-themed blockbuster *The Passion of the Christ* got a berth at Newmarket Films, although Gibson reportedly paid the P&A expense himself in order to get a lion's share of film rentals. Film distributors typically charge a 35–40% distribution fee for films financed by third parties but only 8–15% when they don't have to cover marketing expenses. The lower fee essentially is to rent their distribution organization, because the distributors do not put up any cash.

Home video giant Blockbuster stepped up to acquire distribution rights to 40 films per year via its DEJ Productions. About one fifth of the films get theatrical release, including gripping serial murder drama *Monster,* whose star Charlize Theron won the Oscar for best actress in a leading role in 2003.

Several companies have tried to enter theatrical distribution with a business plan calling for no production and just acquisitions, meaning they essentially fulfill the role of a P&A fund. Theatrical distribution veteran Mitch Goldman assembled startup Premiere Marketing & Distribution in the 2001–2003 period to distribute films worthy of wide release. Its business plan called for only handling films that merit release to 2,000 theaters at minimum, which statistics show is a safe bet to generate some box office return (Fig. 12.1). The producers received no guaranteed minimum payment, but the theatrical release would help sell the film in foreign markets. However, no films were ever distributed. "The obstacle was at the end of the day, we couldn't generate enough interest for financing," said Goldman.

When the $58 million production of *Lolita,* a remake starring Jeremy Irons, could not secure a regular theatrical distribution deal, premium pay cabler Showtime picked up the film in 1998, reportedly for $4 million. Showtime arranged for the film to get a small theatrical release via Samuel Goldwyn Co., and the film generated $1.1 million in box office.

Profitability is a big stumbling block for P&A financing. "If you are going to spend $16–$20 million to market a film, and have to pay another $6–$10 million to producers to acquire a film, that hole is too deep," said entertainment media analyst Doug Lowell. "You can't recoup that money domestically unless you end up doing $50–$60 million in box office," which is a sizable hurdle. Films costing less than $30 million potentially can be profit gushers, although there's also the risk that they'll flop at the box office (Fig 12.2).

Figure 12.1 Relationship of High Box Office to Wide Theater Release 1998–2002

Box Office ($ mil.)	All Films in 2000+ Theaters
$100+	68
$75-99.9	27
$50-74.9	66
$30-49.9	79
$25-29.9	15
$20-24.9	16
$10-19.9	48
under $10	7

Note: Figures cover July 1998-March 2002
Source: Nielsen EDI, IMDB

Figure 12.2 High & Low Grossing Films At 2,000+ Theaters 1998–2002

Title	Box Office ($ mil.)	Maximum Theaters	Distributors	Estimated Production Cost ($ mil.)
Top Five Box Office/Under $30 mil. Productions				
There's Something About Mary	$176.5	2,186	Fox	$23
The Waterboy	$161.5	2,664	Disney	$23
Scary Movie	$157.0	2,912	Miramax	$19
Big Momma's House	$117.6	2,802	Fox	$30
Analyze This	$106.7	2,518	Warners	$30
Bottom Five Box Office/Under $30 mil. Productions				
Three to Tango	$10.6	2,334	Warners	$20
Head Over Heels	$10.4	2,338	Universal	$14
Bats	$10.1	2,540	Destination	$6.5
Ghost of Mars	$8.7	2,048	Sony	$28
Lost & Found	$6.5	2,469	Warners	$13

Note: Figures cover films released July 1998–March 2002; tracks films distributed to over 2,000 theaters in theatrical run that cost $30 mil. or less to make; full list of films is 80 titles
Source: Nielsen EDI, IMDB

From 2002–2004, the Hollywood major studios went shopping in Europe for more than $1 billion in P&A funding tax shelters, although tax authorities appear to have slammed the door on them. The majors sought European funding because European financial terms are relatively easy. Since European investors receive generous tax breaks, less emphasis is placed on receiving back in excess of what they put in.

The majors already tap European tax shelter funds for a steady $1 billion per year in film financing that goes to Hollywood production. Applying such funding to P&A marketing would be a new wrinkle.

The major studios don't comment on their financing, although other sources say that all their European P&A deals fell through. Walt Disney, Metro-Goldwyn-Mayer, Sony Pictures, Twentieth Century Fox, Universal, and Warner Bros. went as far as to commit to specific fund brokers when some adverse tax rulings from authorities in early 2004 spooked investors. Hollywood's use of tax shelter funding is sensitive in Europe, with local filmmakers complaining they—and not foreigners—should be the biggest recipients.

Glossary

Acculturated Describes an ethnic audience that is bilingual and displays traits from more than one culture

Admission Ticket sale; refers to each person admitted to a theater

Aggregate Deal (or **Contract**) Simplest type of film booking deal, which specifies the film distributor gets a percentage of cinema box office without first deducting a House Nut

Ancillary Market Film media after theatrical release, such as video and television

Answer Print First complete version of a film, but of rough technical quality and perhaps lacking some special effects and music

Art House Esoteric films, geared for sophisticated tastes, that are out of the mainstream, often with the creative drive provided by the director

Artbuster Small-budget film, tailored for sophisticated audiences, that is a hit; the phrase combines art house with blockbuster

Avail (from **Availability**) In television and radio advertising buys, a commercial slot that can be purchased

Banner Ad In Internet advertising, a graphical web unit measuring 468 pixels wide and 60 pixels high that usually is presented like a billboard

Billboard In media, a large outdoor sign with advertising; also, a short audio or visual announcement preceding or following a program that identifies a sponsor

Blind Bidding Licensing movies to theaters on a sight-unseen basis, which is illegal in most states

Block Booking Illegal practice of bundling unwanted titles in a sale with desired titles

Blockbuster Mentality Eternal hit-orientation in Hollywood that every few years some pundits lament is something "new"

Boost In advertising, purchasing additional advertising after the pre-release advertising campaign ends; goes beyond basic newspaper listings

Boutique Specialized ad agency that usually creates ad campaigns

Box Office Theater ticket sales at the consumer-spend level

Buena Vista Spanish phrase used by Walt Disney as the name for most of its film and television program distribution divisions

Calendar House Art-house movie theater that uses monthly mailings (presented as calendars with film titles and playdates) to promote its schedule; most films run just a few days each, not the customary full week

Calling Tree In marketing, an organized network in which recruited persons agree to systemically pass on a message to others to create a mushroom effect, typically via telephone and/or e-mail

Clearance In exhibition, theaters receiving exclusivity to a film in a geographic area, typically limited to several weeks; in television, coverage of the country as a percentage of households for a television program, particularly in syndication

Comp (from **Comprehensive**) Designed movie advertising poster made for internal review and possible further modification

Co-op Advertising (from **Cooperative**) Paid advertising whose expense is shared between distributor and exhibitor

Cost per Thousand (or **CPM**) In advertising buys, cost per thousand viewers reached to measure efficiency

Creative Boutique Independent ad agency that specializes in developing posters, television commercials, trailers, and other source materials for movie advertising

Cross-collateralize In finance, offsetting gains from one sector with losses in another sector, such as lowering profits from video release of a film by subtracting losses from theatrical release

Cross-over Film (or **Audience**) Attracting an additional audience segment that was not the prime target; this often occurs later in a film's theatrical run, indicating a film has broad appeal

Cume (*see* **Reach**)

Day-and-Date Simultaneous release

Demographics (or **Demos**) Segmenting a human population by some metric, such as age, wealth, education, hobbies, religion, or geography

Distribution Process of licensing films to consumer media outlets such as as theaters and television channels

Distributor Film company that markets films to theaters, video stores, and television

Documentary Cinema genre recording actual events to tell a true story or using interviews after the fact

Domestic Market The United States and Canada that, for purposes of theatrical distribution, are serviced as a single territory by major studios because most films open in both countries simultaneously

Engagement (*see* **Playdate**)

Exclusive Run (or **Screening**) In theatrical distribution, booking just one theater per city

Executive Summary Several-sentence description of a movie's plot and nuisances; often used by marketing executives to fashion the early advertising/promotion campaign

Exhibition Movie theater business; a theater operator is an Exhibitor

Exit Survey (or **Study**) In consumer research, quizzing moviegoers with a list of questions about the film they've just seen immediately after they leave the theaters

Firm Terms In theatrical distribution, insisting that financial obligations be met as stated in the theater booking contract with no post-run adjustments

Floor In film booking contracts, the minimum amount of box office that distributors receive; the amount is particularly oriented to later weeks of any film's run when box office revenue is low

Focus Group In research, recruiting 5–10 moviegoers to discuss content that is presented by a moderator in a closed room for the purpose of learning consumer attitudes

Four Walling Booking arrangement where a distributor or filmmaker rents a theater for a flat fee and keeps all box office revenue; this method of distribution is rare

Frequency Number of times each viewer in a target group, on average, sees an advertisement; the higher the number, the more a target audience is saturated

Genre Film Movie with highly focused subject matter (such as horror, children, karate action, blood-and-guts, crime) that itself is promotable; in the indie business, it suggests subject matter that is down-market and highly marketable

Grass Roots Campaign (or **Marketing**) Localized publicity and promotions

Grosses (see also **Box Office**) Revenue from ticket sales at the consumer-spend level

Guerrilla Marketing Unconventional marketing typically done at the local level that aims for maximum results from a miniscule budget

House Nut (also called **House Allowance** or **Expense**) In film booking contracts, a negotiated amount of box office revenue that theaters keep and thus is not shared, after which movie distributors begin to take a percentage

High Concept Movie idea that is so unconventional that it alone is a promotable element

Hit In the Internet world, the request for a file from a server

Impressions In media buying, the number of persons reached via an advertising placement, including duplications

Indie (from **Independent**) Literally any film company that is not one of Hollywood's seven major studios

Inventory In advertising, available commercial slots on television and radio outlets

Junket In film publicity, a mass press event at a single location that brings together journalists and film talent for interviews; in some cases, multiple films are publicized at a single junket

Key Art Basic poster design used as a consistent graphic for all print advertising; key art also is incorporated into trailers and television commercials

Key Copy Line Frequently repeated advertising slogan that summarizes the selling message for a movie

Legs Ability of a movie to hold screens and build audience in theatrical release

Licensing Renting a movie to a theater or other media outlets such as television channels; in merchandising, conveying the right to use elements of a movie property in movie-themed products

Live Action Film footage with real actors, as opposed to animation or computer-generated images

Limited Release (or **Run**) In theatrical distribution, a booking pattern of a few theaters per city or theater zone

Lobby Card In movie promotion, an 11 × 14-inch miniposter printed on heavy stock paper for use in theaters; decades ago these were made in sets of eight with seven different scenes from the film plus a title card with film credits

Lobby Stand (or **Standee**) Large cardboard displays in lobbies of theaters that promote films

Major Studios Columbia Pictures/TriStar (part of Sony Pictures Entertainment), Walt Disney Studios (and its Buena Vista distribution divisions), Metro-Goldwyn-Mayer, Paramount Pictures, Twentieth Century Fox, Universal Pictures, and Warner Bros.; startup DreamWorks is an emerging major

Make Good In media buys, free ads to cover any shortfall in promised audience delivery or to compensate for spoiled ads

Marketing Promoting a product or service to a target audience

Marketing Cost Expenses for creating advertising; buying media to place ads and consumer research; publicity for generating editorial coverage; and manufacture and shipping costs of theater release prints

Media Buy Purchasing advertising on television, newspapers, magazines, etc.; excludes costs of creating the ads themselves and consumer research

Media Stunt In advertising, purchasing a highly concentrated burst of advertising 2–4 weeks before a movie premieres

Megaplex In exhibition, a theater with 14 or more screens

Merchandising (see also **Licensing**) Contracting with third parties to sell movie-themed products

Monadic Test In research, allowing a respondent to see only one element under consideration, such as a single movie title, and not any alternative choices

Money Shot Most gripping scene in a trailer or television spot that, in terms of pacing, is the climax or payoff

MPAA Motion Picture Association of America, the trade group of the seven major studios

Multichannel Television Any television service delivered to homes outside of regular broadcast signals; includes cable, satellite, microwave, etc.

Multiplex Theater In exhibition, a theater with 6–13 screens

New Hollywood Realistic films with edgy stories and mass market potential that emerged in the United States in the 1970s, in a sharp break from the middle-of-the-road movies churned out for decades by the studio system

NATO National Association of Theatre Owners, the trade group for movie theaters

Negative Cost As in film negative, the expense of making a movie to the point where a master copy is ready for duplication

Niche Film Movie with strong appeal to a narrow audience segment

Norms (from **Normative**) In research, expected patterns based on past data covering similar films

One-sheet (or Poster) Used in theaters, a standard-size movie poster typically measuring 14 × 22 inches and printed on thin paper

Outside Agencies Marketing consultancies hired to handle marketing functions in full or in part

Platform Release Theatrical release strategy of opening a film in a relatively small number of theaters initially, intending to build on positive critic reviews and word-of-mouth buzz; a high-risk strategy because wide release won't materialize if initial reaction is unfavorable

Playdate In theatrical distribution, booking a film at a theater that is counted as one even when the same film is shown on multiple screens at a single location

Positioning Study In research, developing a detailed movie marketing plan at a very early stage based on a script and casting

Press Kit Distributor-supplied packets containing press releases and photos for use by journalists

Preview Screening (also **Test Screening**) Private showing of a film prior to theatrical release to a recruited audience for the purpose of gauging moviegoer reaction

Principal Photography Main film production period, typically 7–16 weeks for a feature film

Prints (or **Release Prints**) Bulky reels of a movie used by theaters for projection; a single print can service more than one screen in modern multiplexes

Prints and Advertising (or **P&A**) Sum of theatrical release marketing expenses for both the bulky reels that theaters use to project films and for paid advertising

Print Media Newspapers and magazines, usually in the context of advertising buys

Product Placement Arranging for brand name items to receive exposure in films, television programs, and other media

Promotion Special one-off marketing efforts such as contests and display stands, often mounted in concert with third parties

Publicity Editorial exposure such as film reviews, talent interviews on talk shows, stories in newspapers, etc.

Quads (from **Quadrants**) In movie research, a standard presentation of results dividing the audience into four groups: male, female, over age 25, and under age 25

Qualitative Research Relatively unstructured research where feedback from small focus groups is open to subjective interpretations; tends to be exploratory; findings from its tiny samples shouldn't be statistically projected to a larger audience

Quantitative Research Findings that are acquired systematically in a uniform way from all respondents and can be boiled to numeric values and projected to a larger population

Rating (or **Rating Point**) Audience in broadcasting and cable television expressed as a percentage of the total target; in United States national television, a 1 rating equals 1.09 million households, or 1% of the total 109 million television households

Reach (also **Cume**) In advertising buying, unduplicated audience expressed as a percentage and thus excludes double counting; expresses breadth of coverage of a target audience

Red Band Trailer Movie trailer for age-restricted audiences, such as R-rated films

Rent a Distributor Theatrical distribution method where a film's producers or related party agrees to cover all out-of-pocket expenses, such as prints and advertising, incurred by a distribution company in exchange for a low distribution fee; this arrangement is rare because distributors typically want lucrative video and television rights as well

Rentals (or **Film Rentals**) Payment that film distributors receive from a movie theater for rights to a movie

Road Block Advertising Placing the same television commercial on multiple television channels at the same time

Rough In creating advertising, a crude mockup

Rough Television Spot In creating advertising, a first draft version of a commercial

Royalty Payment for the right to use intellectual property or for personal services; in movie merchandising, this fee usually is a percentage of wholesale revenue

Run of the Book Ads that are not promised any specific placement in print media

Run of Schedule (or **ROS**) Commercial time that can appear at any time at the discretion of the broadcaster; such time is cheaper than purchasing specific time slots

Rushes Production footage straight from the laboratory viewed by filmmakers, studio executives, and marketing executives

Saturation Release In theatrical distribution, a film playing at 2,000–2,999 theaters

Scatter Market In media buying, television advertising purchased close to airdate when the television season is already underway

Screen Theater auditorium with a movie screen

Screener Questionnaire Form soliciting demographic and other personal information from a respondent

Settlement Financial adjustments by an exhibitor and distributor after a film finishes its run in a theater; such adjustments are not necessarily specified in the written contract

Showings In advertising buys, the audience exposed to an outdoor billboard expressed as rating points

Sneak Preview Limited commercial release of a film to build word of mouth in advance of a broader regular theatrical release

Splash Page Internet Web site with only a simple introductory page and offering no capability to click through to additional content

Spot Television (and Spot Radio) Local commercials purchased by a national advertiser, such as a film distributor, to increase the advertising spending in selected cities

Story Board Series of still photos or graphics that are key scenes of a film trailer or television commercial used when developing ideas

Story Point Product Placement Branded item referred to in dialog, handled by a character, or in some way integral to the movie's plot

Street Team Marketing foot soldiers who, on an organized basis, fan out in neighborhoods and spread commercial messages by posting handbills, passing out promotional items at events, wearing branded clothing, and chatting up strangers

Stunt (see **Media Stunt**)

Target Rating Points (TRP) In buying television and radio advertising, the number of times each person in a defined demographic group is exposed to a commercial; a TRP of 300 means each person in the audience target is hit three times on average

Teaser Campaign Short burst of advertising, promotion, and/or publicity weeks or months before a movie opens, designed to raise simple awareness

Teaser Trailer Shorter than normal promotional film for theaters meant to be played in theaters weeks or months before the regular trailer

Television Syndication Programming seen nationally on a patchwork lineup of television stations in various time slots

Tentpoles Biggest films on a distributor's slate that are released in peak moviegoing periods; given that Hollywood is like a carnival, the phrase evokes the idea of a circus tent with big films as its center pillars

Test Screening (see **Preview Screening**)

Tie-in Promotions Joint marketing efforts in which a film distributor partners with a consumer goods company to promote movies

Title Treatment Signature typeface and graphic look of a movie's name in advertising

Tracking Survey (or **Study**) In research, measuring comparative audience awareness of films prior to or at their premiere

Trailer Short promotion film, typically two to two-and-a-half minutes long, that touts upcoming films and is screened in theaters prior to the main feature

Trailer Derby In creative advertising, showing outside creative shops that are working on an assignment the materials made by rival shops working on the *same* assignment

Unit Photographer Photographer on the set of a movie who takes still pictures for use in publicity

Unit Publicist Marketing executive assigned to prepare foundation publicity materials during production and possibly arrange selective press access of talent for interviews during production

Universe In research, the entire potential audience in a target market; the target can be groups defined by gender, race, age, household income, etc.

Upfront Market In media buying, television advertising purchased long in advance before the television season starts

Urban Audience Populations of inner cities

Vendor Outside consultant, such as a shop, specializing in creating advertising or providing research services

Viral Marketing Communications that encourage recipients to pass on the message or materials to peers in order to achieve a snowball effect

Webisodes Episodic content on the Internet that is a publicity vehicle for films

Wide Release In theatrical distribution, a film playing at 600–1,999 theaters

Word of Mouth Moviegoers praising or knocking a film in conversations with peers

Bibliography

Beaupre, L. *American Film Distribution: A Survey*, Coppola Cinema Seven, 1974

Edmunds, H. *The Focus Group Research Handbook*, NTC Business Books, 1999

Goldberg, F. *Motion Picture Marketing and Distribution: Getting Movies into a Theatre Near You*, Focal Press, 1991

Surmanek, J. *Media Planning: A Practical Guide*, NTC Business Books, 1996

Warshawski, M. *Distributing Independent Films & Videos*, Foundation for Independent Video and Film Inc., 1989

Index